BLACK LIFE AND CHRISTIAN SPIRITUALITY

Andrew Prevot

ORBIS BOOKS
Maryknoll, New York 10545

Founded in 1970, Orbis Books endeavors to publish works that enlighten the mind, nourish the spirit, and challenge the conscience. The publishing arm of the Maryknoll Fathers and Brothers, Orbis seeks to explore the global dimensions of the Christian faith and mission, to invite dialogue with diverse cultures and religious traditions, and to serve the cause of reconciliation and peace. The books published reflect the views of their authors and do not represent the official position of the Maryknoll Society. To learn more about Maryknoll and Orbis Books, please visit our website at www.orbisbooks.com.

Published by Orbis Books, Box 302, Maryknoll, NY 10545-0302.

All Vatican documents mentioned in this text are available at Vatican.va.

Manufactured in the United States of America

Library of Congress Cataloging-in-Publication Data

Names: Prevot, Andrew L. author
Title: Black life and Christian spirituality / Andrew Prevot.
Description: Maryknoll, NY : Orbis Books, [2026] | Includes bibliographical references. | Summary: "Essays on the relation between Black Life and spirituality, drawing on both African American spirituality and other classic sources of Christian mysticism and spirituality"—Provided by publisher.
Identifiers: LCCN 2026007760 (print) | LCCN 2026007761 (ebook) | ISBN 9781626986800 trade paperback | ISBN 9798888661543 epub
Subjects: LCSH: African Americans—Religion—History | Black theology | Race—Religious aspects—Christianity | God (Christianity)—Love | Spirituality—Christianity—History
Classification: LCC BR563.B53 P74 2026 (print) | LCC BR563.B53 (ebook)
LC record available at https://lccn.loc.gov/2026007760
LC ebook record available at https://lccn.loc.gov/2026007761

Contents

Part 3
Let Us Flee the Wickedness of This World

Introduction

This book is a work of love for Black people, including myself. I have written it for members of my racially labeled community: past, present, and future. We need a very particular and focused love to overcome all the scorn that has been heaped upon us. God created us for love, not apathy, abuse, or derision. We proclaim this truth with our songs, sermons, prayers, and protests. We know it intuitively, but sometimes we need a gentle word to remind us of it or a consoling touch to make us feel it again. There are too many stories and statistics shouting the opposite sentiment: you are nothing, worthless, scary, insignificant, pitiable, the lowest of the low, and lucky to be alive. Our bodies and souls suffer these blows daily, taking hit after hit. Breath, memory, art, activism, community, and spirituality help us bounce back.

The visible darkness of Black bodies should remind everyone of the invisible darkness of God, in whose image all human beings are lovingly made (Genesis 1:27). It should inspire reverence for the Creator who fashioned everything out of an abyssal darkness too deep for words; who formed the dark soil from which green grasses and many-colored flowers grow; and who graces darkly colored bodies with warm shades of ebony, umber, chocolate, bronze, and oak. Christians should know by now that their savior likely had light-brown or olive skin, curly hair, and dark eyes typical of the ancient Mediterranean and Near Eastern world and could not have been racially White by modern standards. But his outward appearance is ultimately of little significance. What matters is the human-and-divine, Spirit-powered, outcast-embracing, empire-defying, rising-again love that he embodied.

Christian spirituality is the attempt to participate in this great mystery and make it one's own. Black Christians seek and find God's love for them in their daily interactions with the Holy Spirit. They sense the Father's luminous darkness in their unbowed consciences and renew their strength through friendship with Jesus. For many, this trinitarian faith has been a lifeline that has kept them from sinking down. It has been their rock of shelter in a violent storm. It has taken charge of their feet, hands, and voices and moved them to act.

The following study of Black life and Christian spirituality highlights such Black Christian experiences and efforts but is not limited to them. Taking a wider scope, it argues that Christians of any given racial identity should respond lovingly to Black persons of whatever religious background, because the social vision of Jesus and the precarious circumstances of Black life demand it. It interprets a wide range of Christian texts, practices, and traditions that are not typically considered Black through a lens shaped by the conditions and aspirations of Black life. It affirms that all persons are precious in God's eyes, whatever their color, language, or culture, and it discovers this universal message precisely in Black sources. The love that Black persons receive from God overflows by its very nature and cannot be confined to a single group. It spreads widely through the many pores, mixtures, and intimacies that make up human existence, and it is but one stream from an infinite source. The divine Spirit who breathes life into mortal flesh moves wherever it wills, irrespective of racial constructs.

Nevertheless, there are good reasons that the Movement for Black Lives has concentrated on Black people in particular. When virulent fear and hatred target a specific racial community, a loving antidote must be directed specifically toward them. This book incorporates ideas I have formulated for the last decade or more, in a period marked by this decentralized, grassroots social movement and its various forms of rebellion, creativity, and vitality. This text represents my attempt as a Catholic theologian and scholar of Christian spirituality to understand how the love that is the mysterious heart of the eternal God breaks into history, into our own time and place, in order to comfort, uplift, and embolden those who have been forsaken and left for dead.

What does it mean to pray for and through such Black life-affirming love? What mystical awareness results from contemplating it? What freedom of mind and body is unleashed when it becomes incarnate in action? This book shares my reflections on such questions, arranged in the form of a spiritual–theological triptych. Its three parts illustrate the liberative meanings of prayer, mysticism, and asceticism, in that order, though with significant points of overlap. Alternatively, the structure of this book can be likened to a novena, a nine-step spiritual exercise motivated by a specific intention. My intention is that the world learn to love Black people in the boundless, immoderate ways that God loves us. One method of engaging this text, then, would be to read one chapter per day for nine straight days, while keeping this or some similar intention in mind. Although each chapter can be studied by itself, they do speak to each other, and reading them together reveals additional layers of meaning.

The first part of the book, "O, Give Me Little Time to Pray," takes its name from a line in one of my favorite Negro spirituals: "I've Been in the Storm So Long." The three chapters composing this part are inspired by the cries of pain and hope through which Black persons have stretched their hearts toward God. To pray is to attest that the world can be better than it is, and to entrust this desired reality to a power that is capable of achieving it. To pray is to denude one's soul, stripping it of any pretense of mastery or concealment, and to accept the truth that one is a humble creature radically exposed to the violent forces of the world and the almighty torrent of God's healing grace. To pray is to know that one is not alone, however isolated or abandoned one may feel. It is to rest one's life in another's hands.

The first chapter, "Christian Prayer in Black and Blue," largely focuses on various ways in which Black Christian communities have prayed throughout modern history, from slavery to the present. However, it begins by confronting White supremacist practices that distort the promise of prayer. As examples, it considers the ambiguous tears of the Portuguese chronicler Zurara, as analyzed by Willie James Jennings, and the dubious acts of self-surrender advocated by the Rev. Mr. Pike from Harriet Jacobs's *Incidents in the Life of a Slave Girl*. It contrasts these ill-fated cases with the prayers of the enslaved persons themselves, including those voiced by Jacobs and others at a Methodist prayer meeting and those preserved in the musical tradition that W. E. B. Du Bois calls "Sorrow Songs." Turning to the twentieth century, the chapter discusses the dynamic integrations of prayer and social action manifest in Martin Luther King Jr.'s struggle for racial equality and Ida B. Wells-Barnett's campaigns against lynching and unjust incarceration. It concludes with a section that was painful to write and may be painful to read, which describes the prayers that occurred before, during, and after the 2015 massacre at Mother Emanuel AME Church and reflects on what they may have meant to those who uttered and experienced them.

The dark mystery of prayer envelops the next chapter as well. Thomas Aquinas, a towering figure in the history of Catholic theology who both defended slavery and thought deeply about the nature and purpose of prayer, finds his work confronted in this chapter by the songs of Black persons who endured slavery and laid their souls bare before God. Called "Interpreting Desire: Prayer in Thomas Aquinas and the Slave Spirituals," this chapter stages a dialogue between these two spiritual traditions. Although it unequivocally condemns Aquinas's permissive attitudes toward slavery, which are unacceptable even when understood in their historical context, it does not dismiss his theology altogether. Instead, it retrieves helpful insights, such as his idea that prayer is an act of a rational creature; that it has great value in both silent and spoken (including musical) forms; that it is distinct from but closely related to devotion; that it ought to seek lasting goods such as eternal life and virtue, along with temporal goods that help one reach these ends; and that, as part of God's providential order, it ought to be practiced with confidence and hope. By demonstrating that these characteristics of prayer which Aquinas elaborates also figure prominently in the spirituals, this chapter suggests that he may help us better appreciate the theological significance of these songs. At the same time, it shows that he—or, more accurately, current scholars following his lead—have things to learn from this Black spiritual tradition, particularly about the urgency of seeking deliverance from evil and the emotional force of prayers that arise from the depths of suffering.

The final chapter in this first part of the triptych, which bears the name "Spiritual Resistance to Race-Related Sexual Violence: Black and Native Perspectives," expresses my anguished prayer that all forms of racial and sexual violence may cease. As its title indicates, this chapter emphasizes the need for solidarity between Black and Native communities who have faced distinct forms of sexual oppression in the midst of White supremacy and who have fought back in spiritual ways that are simultaneously political. Although this chapter supports liberative interpretations of Christian spiritual practices, it also follows the lead of Native authors by acknowledging that the historical institution of Christianity has often functioned as a murderous system of racial, patriarchal, and colonial domination that must be opposed. By conceiving authentic spirituality in pluralistic, as opposed to exclusivist, terms, this chapter opens the way toward honoring Indigenous traditions that affirm the sacredness of all life and that are vital to the holistic well-being of Native persons and nations. In its effort to tell the unvarnished truth about racialized sexual violence, this chapter gives particular attention to the sexual abuse of children by Catholic clergy in both Black and Native contexts, which has been an egregious stain on the moral credibility of the Catholic Church. The graphic content of this chapter may be especially difficult for some readers.

Among its Black sources, this chapter considers James Cone's account of Black Christian resistance to the eroticized spectacle of lynching, M. Shawn Copeland's interpretation of Henriette Delille's celibacy as a refusal of sexual objectification, Alice Walker's depiction of Celie's triumph over domestic violence in *The Color Purple*, Tia Noell Pratt's indictment of clergy sexual abuse targeting Black children, and Emilie Townes's womanist theological vision of sexual freedom and wholeness. It puts these arguments into conversation with various Native counterparts, including

Sarah Deer's scholarship on the rape of Indigenous women and spiritual and legal means of resisting it, Marius and Tanya Tungilik's testimonies about the devastating effects of sexual abuse on Inuit children in Catholic residential schools, Inés Talamantez's defense of Apache spiritual practices in the face of Christian-supported cultural genocide, and Marie Therese Archambault's association of the crucified Christ with the crucified peoples of Native America. The prayer that this chapter articulates is both a supplication and a lament: How long, O Lord, will such desecrations of Black and Native lives continue?

The second part of the book, "In the Brilliant Darkness of a Hidden Silence," borrows its name from a line in Dionysius's *The Mystical Theology*. His paradoxical image of a darkness that is aglow with light points to the unknown God who is the exalted source of his contemplation. This image can also symbolize Black life, insofar as it, too, intermingles the obscure with the radiant and hides in a silence that defies straightforward exposition. The first chapter in this part, "Divine Opacity: Mystical Theology, Black Theology, and the Problem of Light–Dark Aesthetics," clarifies the promise of such a connection, building on the precedent of Howard Thurman's blending of mystical and Black traditions.

However, this chapter also warns that both darkness and Blackness have negative associations in theological literature that could undermine the potential of such a synthesis. Passages in Dionysius, Bonaventure, John of the Cross, and Angela of Foligno that intriguingly characterize peak mystical experiences as dark also treat darkness as a metaphor for ignorance and suffering. Even Cone may not fully avoid this sort of danger, insofar as his pursuit of Black liberation relies on an account of Blackness as a condition of oppression. To mitigate these problems and to seek a better answer to racially pernicious biases in theological aesthetics, this chapter proposes two spiritual paths forward: a *via positiva* that celebrates the phenomenal beauty of divine and creaturely darkness, including Black life, and a *via negativa* that seeks the mysterious presence of God even within the suffering, ignorance, and oppression that have troubled Black life. In addition to Thurman, Cone, and the aforementioned classic mystical theologians, this argument draws on theorists such as James Noel, Sarah Coakley, Victor Anderson, Jean-Louis Chrétien, Linda Martin Alcoff, W. E. B. Du Bois, Charles Long, and Édouard Glissant.

The fifth chapter, "Love for the Annihilated: A Black Theological Reading of Angela of Foligno's *Memorial*," continues the previous chapter's work of integrating mystical theology with Black theology but does so in a different way. It contends that medieval mystical accounts of divine love, like that provided by Angela, may have important insights to offer Black persons who dwell in a world that regularly denies their worth and discards them as nonbeings. What this chapter retrieves from Angela's text is not so much her imagery of darkness, which, as the previous chapter indicated, remains questionable. Instead, it concentrates on the ups and downs of her subjectivity, particularly her struggle with self-deprecation and the ways she is buoyed by God's words of loving affirmation. These mystical locutions are the kinds of uplifting spiritual messages that Black persons, perhaps especially young ones who are tempted toward nihilistic despair, need to hear.

This chapter's extension of Black theology's area of interpretive activity into the European Middle Ages is inspired by Frantz Fanon's choice to claim the fullness of humanity's cultural heritage and not limit himself to materials specifically designated as Black. It is also prompted by Copeland's engagement with another medieval mystic, namely Catherine of Siena, in her treatment of African American religious experience. In certain respects, it resembles chapter 2's reckoning with Aquinas and chapter 8's consideration of Ignatius of Loyola (to be discussed further below). By focusing on self-empowering words of divine love, this Black theological interpretation of Angela deviates from postmodern readings of her by Georges Bataille and Amy Hollywood, which emphasize the dissolution of the self. It likewise resists Afro-pessimist theories, which downplay the possibilities of Black selfhood by defining Black life in terms of the structural position of nothingness to which Western culture, politics, and philosophy assign it. Without denying the seriousness of such an annihilative situation, this chapter grounds the meaning of Black life in a divine love that outstrips any possible anti-Black ontology. With Fred Moten, it takes Black study into a mystical region beyond being, but what it locates there is not Blackness per se but a divine love that shelters Black life and guides it down humanizing paths.

The final chapter in this middle "panel" of the triptych, called "Race, Gender, and Christian Mysticism: The Life of Zilpha Elaw," rounds out this book's exploration of the nexus between mystical theology and Black theology. It tells the story of a nineteenth-century Black Christian mystic, the titular Elaw, and assesses how the racial and gender politics of her context and spirituality may challenge us today. Her Methodist formation and mystical experiences of justification and sanctification during the Second Great Awakening set her on a path to becoming a vessel of God's Word: a traveling preacher in both free and slaveholding states who risked her life to proclaim the gospel.

Following the lead of Joy Bostic, this chapter defends Elaw's inclusion in an expanded canon of mystics, defying Eurocentric and Orientalist restrictions. It regards Elaw as an ordinary person transformed by grace, not a depersonalized figure of "dark continent" otherness, as certain post-Freudian accounts of the mystical constitution of Blackness and femaleness would lead one to do. It argues that Christian theologians need not avoid the category of "mysticism," despite its associations with modern subjectivity and doctrinal indeterminacy, but can instead use it, like the older term "mystical theology," to name the grace of divine union that shapes the lives of holy persons such as Elaw. That a socially marginalized Black woman experienced a profound intimacy with God that empowered her to transgress the racial and gender norms of her day is a sign of hope for those battling similar forces now. However, we must acknowledge that her politics of transgression was not absolute. In certain respects, she remained caught in demeaning racial and gender hierarchies and even partly condoned them. That her soul was susceptible to such pressures reveals her fragile humanity and holds a mirror to ours as well.

The third part of the book, "Let Us Flee the Wickedness of This World," takes its name from a line in Saint Ambrose's ascetical classic, *De fuga saeculi (Flight from the World)*. It clarifies the spiritual significance of Black persons' efforts to escape, resist, and overcome the evils of anti-Black racism and other intersecting structures of sin. It gives examples that reveal how important it is to claim one's own moral agency and strive for holiness, regardless of one's racial background. If prayer is the meeting of divine and human desires and mysticism is the grace of God in human life, asceticism is the human community's attempt to take responsibility for its actions and align them more closely with God's will. Unfortunately, Black life is seldom recognized for its ascetical prowess. It is often misrepresented as a quintessential site of the unchecked lust, hostility, and irrationality that asceticism seeks to subdue.

The seventh chapter, "Black Asceticism," traces this problem back to early Christian monasticism and its tendency to associate Ethiopians with hypersexuality and demonic evil. This elision is evident in Athanasius's *Life of St. Antony* and other monastic texts influenced by the imperial aesthetics and politics of fourth-century Egypt. Although this vilification of Black life could seem to estrange it permanently from Christian asceticism, such a one-sided account overlooks the many important and lasting ties that bind them together. There is a venerable tradition of Black asceticism, exemplified by the extraordinary story of Abba Moses the Black: an emancipated slave, reformed robber, desert hermit, and martyr of peace. This tradition continues in modernity, hidden in Black practices of fugitivity, nonviolence, power, and eros. While bringing this clandestine ascetical tradition to light, this chapter reveals surprising resonances between Ambrose and Sojourner Truth, Evagrius and Thurman, Plato and Cone, Saint Mary of Egypt and Audre Lorde, among other sources.

The next chapter, "Training the Soul: A Black Catholic Journey Through the Spiritual Exercises," has a more personal touch. It shares my story of participating in the unique ascetical program called the "Spiritual Exercises," which Saint Ignatius of Loyola devised as a method for confronting sin, following Christ, and making sound decisions in one's life. This chapter describes the feelings and thoughts that I experienced as a Black person while doing this retreat during the early days of the Movement for Black Lives. It also presents my ideas about how Ignatian spirituality can become a helpful tool in the fight against racism, insofar as this struggle is not only about protecting vulnerable bodies but also about strengthening and transforming souls. As in other chapters, so too in this one, the argument proceeds by making unexpected connections. It links Ignatian *indiferençia* with the moral fortitude of Black activists in the Civil Rights movement, the First Week's "Meditation on Hell" with the real-world hells of slavery and Jim Crow, the "consolation without preceding cause" with Jarena Lee's ecstatic experience of sanctification, the Third Week's immersive experience of the cross with Billie Holiday's haunting performance of "Strange Fruit" (an insight I owe to Christopher Pramuk), and "The Contemplation to Attain Love" with the encouraging idea that God generously bestows everything we need to prevail over oppression. The only question is whether we will receive these gifts and use them as God intends.

The final chapter, "People of Action: Black Catholics on the Path to Sainthood," completes the ascetical part of the triptych by telling the stories of seven saintly African Americans who are presently being considered for canonization in the Catholic Church. Each of these persons strove for holiness by engaging in courageous actions that benefited others in the Black community and the larger multiracial society. The Haitian-born Pierre Toussaint used the financial resources he gained from styling wealthy women's hair in New York City to care for orphans and emancipate enslaved persons, including himself. The free woman of color Mary Elizabeth Lange founded the Oblate Sisters of Providence in Baltimore, Maryland. This first-of-its-kind congregation of Black Catholic nuns gave Black girls life-saving educational opportunities they were otherwise denied. Another free woman of color, Henriette Delille, founded a similar religious order in New Orleans: the Sisters of the Holy Family. The formerly enslaved Julia Greeley did odd domestic jobs in Denver, Colorado, while gathering donations and giving what little she had to serve the needy. Augustus Tolton also began his life in slavery. Once freed, he overcame racial barriers to become the first (non-passing) African American priest, ministering to poor Black communities in Quincy and Chicago, Illinois. Following Tolton's lead, Martin de Porres

Maria Ward answered a call to the priesthood and became the first Black person in his religious order, the Conventual Franciscans. His work sent him far from his hometowns of Boston and Washington, DC, to the missionary field of Andrelândia, Brazil. Raised in Canton, Mississippi at the height of Jim Crow, Thea Bowman became the first Black woman to join the Franciscan Sisters of Perpetual Adoration. She was a leading voice in the development of an inculturated form of Black Catholicism in the postconciliar U.S. church.

While providing further details about each of these virtuous persons, this chapter discusses differences and similarities in their ways of uniting Black life and Christian spirituality, emphasizing in each case their highly active character. It reveals that they not only prayed but endeavored to let God use them to answer prayers. It suggests that whatever mystical graces they received did not lead them to plunge deeper into themselves, forgetting the wider world, but to go out into the streets, wherever there were people who needed a helping hand, and to become a benevolent presence in their lives. Finally, it shows that their asceticism—their commitment to practices of chastity, simplicity, and humble self-sacrifice—was not an end in itself but a gift to others. They took the freedom they had, however limited it was by their daunting political circumstances, and used it to bring greater freedom to those around them. Like the first apostles, they sought to follow Jesus's example of energetic compassion. As a Black Catholic Christian, I am particularly moved by their stories and can think of no better point on which to bring this volume to a close.

Together, these chapters clarify that, although Black life and Christian spirituality are not identical, they do converge in numerous obvious and not-so-obvious ways. At their best, they are mutually illuminating and strengthening. For Black Christians, of course, they are inseparable. Every morning after I wake, the racial determinations of my existence and the divine whispers in my conscience are immediately present in my embodied thoughts, feelings, and actions, and there is no way to pull them apart. However, this intermingling also happens in the wider culture, as artifacts of anti-Black racism and movements of resistance to it interact with an ambient Christianity that is both complicit in and antagonistic toward worldly powers of domination. In the midst of such a potentially confusing swirl of associations, I hope that this book will provide some clarity. If any of its arguments remain obscure (and I grant that some chapters veer toward dense, technical discussions), a safe bet is to return to the central thesis, which is that Black people are made to be loved. This is God's unambiguous will, and anything that contravenes it is incompatible with true Christian spirituality.

Part 1

O, Give Me Little Time to Pray

1

Christian Prayer in Black and Blue

The story of Christian prayer in modernity cannot be told without remembering the lives and deaths of those millions of God's darkly colored children whose existence was torn from West Africa and "remade" through resistance against the body- and soul-crushing instruments of the slave ship, the auction block, the plantation field, the lynching tree, the segregated church, the impoverished ghetto, the underfunded school, and the prison cell. This refashioned existence may be called "black," and in the same breath it may be called "blue." These colors express deep wounds from centuries of horrific mistreatment and a human beauty difficult to describe, consisting of rich hues, textures, rhythms, strengths, loves, sorrows, victories, and untold possibilities. They define a sense of peoplehood without necessarily implying any racial essence or narrow Black nationalism. These colors are not meant to be accurate representations of any human body, however dark it may be. Rather, they are symbols of a phenotypically diverse people united by a particular set of traumas, strivings, and modes of creative endurance. Louis Armstrong gives voice to the

---

A version of this chapter appears in *T&T Clark Handbook of Christian Prayer*, ed. Ashley Cocksworth and John C. McDowell (Bloomsbury, 2022), 667–84.

spirit of this people when he croons, "My only sin is in my skin. / What did I do to be so black and blue?"[1]

For many of these "black and blue" children of God, survival (even today) depends on carving out spaces of refuge within, or apart from, dominant structures of racialized terror. Black people seek safe havens for love and sadness, for music and food, for the healing presence of family and friends, and for that most intimate experience of all: dialogue with God. Such dialogue, such prayer, means knowing that whatever hateful things the world says about you and does to you because of your supposed racial identity, God has created and redeemed you, God loves you and will vindicate you. A living communal memory of African ancestors preserves some traces of their (often) non-Christian spiritualities and habits of devotion even in the midst of explicitly Christian forms of worship. The shouts, songs, silences, and ecstasies of the ancestors live on in their "New World" Christian descendants. Embodied connections with both such Indigenous roots and with the mysteries of Jesus and his Spirit bring solace and power. In countless life-giving ways, Africa prays in the Americas.[2]

This prayer of the black and blue becomes recognizably Christian in those cases where it addresses itself to the triune God of Christian faith attested in scripture. Some have lamented this Christianization of Afrodiasporic prayer because it seems to draw it uncomfortably close to the deadly prayer of White supremacists who for centuries have treated darkly colored peoples like animals, commodities, or worse—with a Bible in one hand and a whip or rope or gun in the other. Despite this unsettling connection, the concrete political, psychological, moral, and theological significance of these two traditions of (at least ostensibly) Christian

[1] Louis Armstrong, "Black and Blue," *The Essential Louis Armstrong*, BMG Music/Sony, 2004.

[2] Albert J. Raboteau, *Slave Religion: The "Invisible Institution" in the Antebellum South* (Oxford University Press, 2004); M. Shawn Copeland, *Knowing Christ Crucified: The Witness of African American Religious Experience* (Orbis Books, 2018), 37–58; and Dwight N. Hopkins, *Down, Up, and Over: Slave Religion and Black Theology* (Fortress Press, 2000), 107–54.

prayer could hardly be more dissimilar. If modern Christians were asked to decide which of these two traditions best represents the essential meaning and promise of Christian prayer in the present age, the correct choice would be obvious. A study of Christian prayer in black and blue allows one to glimpse the healing and liberating power that Christian prayer should, but sometimes tragically does not, bring into this violent world. From the prayer remembered in slave spirituals and narratives (section 1), to the prayer of the Black freedom struggle (section 2), to the prayer of the victims and survivors of the 2015 massacre at Charleston's Mother Emanuel (section 3), this black and blue tradition is revelatory of what Christian prayer must remain and become if it is to render true worship to the living God of infinite justice and mercy revealed in Christ and the Holy Spirit.

Christian Prayer in the Midst of Slavery

Slaveholders prayed and did so while supposing themselves to be good Christians. This is a disturbing fact we must not forget. We cannot even say (as if to reassure ourselves) that their prayers generally took the tearful, self-interrogating, and somewhat empathic form that Willie James Jennings finds in the records of Gomes Eanes de Azurara (Zurara), the chronicler who told the story of the arrival of 235 African slaves in Portugal on August 8, 1444. Such morally conflicted prayer seems to have been a rarity. This is how Zurara prayed that day:

> O, Thou heavenly Father—who with thy powerful hand, without alteration of thy divine essence, governest all the infinite company of thy Holy City, and controllest all the revolutions of higher worlds, divided into nine spheres, making the duration of ages long or short according as it pleaseth Thee—I pray Thee that my tears may not wrong my conscience; for it is not their religion but their humanity that maketh mine to weep in pity for their sufferings. And if the brute animals, with their bestial feelings, by a natural instinct understand the suffering of their own kind,

> what wouldst Thou have my human nature to do on seeing before my eyes that miserable company, and remembering that they too are of the generation of the sons of Adam?[3]

Zurara's praise of God is followed quickly by his confession that he recognizes the humanity of the Africans being imported as slaves. Their suffering causes him to "weep in pity." His request of God is not for their liberation, however, but rather that his weeping "not wrong [his] conscience." Why would it? He indicates the reason when he notes that it is not "their religion" that moves him to cry, but rather "their humanity." His Christian judgment against their non-Christian religion provides such a strong rationale in his mind for their enslaved condition that he is pressed to find an acceptable justification, not for their slavery, but for his emotional response. He feels the need to defend his tears before God. He does so by appealing to the common humanity he shares with the slaves, and certainly this aspect of his prayer is commendable as far as it goes, but strictly speaking the aim of his prayer is only that God understand his reasons for weeping. Although Zurara's prayer displays some surprising empathy (surprising because he is an agent of a slaveholding state), this empathy inspires no meaningful resistance on his part to the violence being perpetrated against the hundreds of Africans before him.

Other examples of Christian prayer among slaveholders prove more callous still. Consider the case of the Episcopalian priest, "Rev. Mr. Pike," described in Harriet Jacobs's 1861 *Incidents in the Life of a Slave Girl*. Jacobs, writing under the pseudonym Linda Brent, recounts the following episode:

> After the alarm caused by Nat Turner's insurrection had subsided, the slaveholders came to the conclusion that it would be well to give the slaves enough of religious instruction to keep them from murdering their masters. . . . When the Rev. Mr. Pike came, there were some twenty persons present. The

[3]Quoted in Willie James Jennings, *The Christian Imagination: Theology and the Origins of Race* (Yale University Press, 2010), 17.

> reverend gentleman knelt in prayer, then seated himself, and requested all present, who could read, to open their books, while he gave out the portions he wished them to repeat or respond to. His text was, "Servants be obedient to them that are your masters according to the flesh, with fear and trembling, in singleness of your heart, as unto Christ."[4]

Perhaps Pike's kneeling in prayer was supposed to symbolize the sort of submission to earthly masters that he instructed his enslaved congregants to practice, "as unto Christ." If so, he may have experienced only the highest coherence in his sermon about obedience and his own practice of Christian prayer, unable (or unwilling) to perceive any grave moral contradiction between them. But the contradiction was real and terrible. Pike was in effect asking his Christian brothers and sisters to give themselves over to cruel, life-destroying powers whose interests he represented. Compared to Zurara's prayer, Pike's is more hardened and orchestrated. There is not the slightest trace of cognitive dissonance in it and thus, evidently, a more thorough forgetting of shared humanity. Pike's is the more typical example of Christian prayer among slaveholders: untroubled, self-righteous, and coldly indifferent to the misery that surrounds it.

Slavery was hell. It was rape, torture, and murder. It was physical, psychological, sexual, and every other kind of abuse. One slaveholder "shot a woman through the head, who had run away and been brought back to him. No one called him to account for it. If a slave resisted being whipped, the bloodhounds were unpacked, and set upon him, to tear his flesh from his bones." Jacobs clarifies that "the master who did these things was highly educated, and styled a perfect gentleman. He also boasted the name and standing of a Christian, though Satan never had a truer follower."[5] In her 1831 autobiography, the formerly enslaved Mary Prince recalls the mercilessness of her master "Mr. D——": "Nothing

---

[4]Linda Brent, *Incidents in the Life of a Slave Girl*, in *The Classic Slave Narratives*, ed. Henry Louis Gates Jr. (Penguin, 2002), 437–665, at 516–17.

[5]Brent, *Incidents in the Life of a Slave Girl*, 495.

could touch his hard heart—neither sighs, nor tears, nor prayers, nor streaming blood; he was deaf to our cries, and careless of our sufferings. . . . Yet there was nothing very remarkable in this; for it might serve as a sample of the common usage of slaves."[6] If Christian prayer is a tool of the oppressor, an exercise meant to train the slave's body and soul to submit to such horrors, and indeed the very silencing of their cries for help and mercy, then it is an evil that ought to be abolished together with the White supremacist regimes of violence that it serves.

However, this is not what Christian prayer meant for the enslaved Afrodescendant peoples who embraced it and practiced it in secret. Jacobs recalls a Methodist prayer meeting in which she sat next to a "poor, bereaved mother" who exclaimed,

> "My Lord and Master, help me! My load is more than I can bear. God has hid himself from me, and I am left in darkness and misery." Then, striking her breast, she continued, "I can't tell you what is in here! They've got all my children. Last week, they took the last one. God only knows where they've sold her. They let me have her sixteen years, and then—O! O! Pray for her, brothers and sisters! I've got nothing to live for now. God make my time short!"[7]

This lament is reminiscent of Job's, of those in the Psalms, and of Jesus's on the cross. It is a prayer to God from the Godforsaken. It is also a request *for* prayer from a community: "Pray for her, brothers and sisters!" It is an act of speech that barely expresses the ocean of grief within: "I can't tell you what is in here!" Who would dare deprive this woman of her prayerful voice on the hasty assumption that Christian prayer is only ever an instrument of oppression? Can modern scholars hear and understand this woman's cry?

To be able to speak one's pain in prayer and be heard by a community of brothers and sisters may provide a modicum of

[6]Mary Prince, "The History of Mary Prince," in *The Classic Slave Narratives*, 249–321, at 268.

[7]Brent, *Incidents in the Life of a Slave Girl*, 519.

comfort, even if one remains in a pit of anguish too deep for words. Although the grief remains, one may find more consolation and empowerment still in the embodied experience of joining together in song. After this woman spoke her heart, Jacobs notes, "the congregation struck up a hymn, and sung as though they were as free as the birds that warbled around us." These are the words they sang:

> Ole Satan thought he had a mighty aim;
> He missed my soul, and caught my sins.
> Cry Amen, cry Amen, cry Amen to God!
>
> He took my sins upon his back;
> Went muttering and grumbling down to hell.
> Cry Amen, cry Amen, cry Amen to God!
>
> Ole Satan's church is here below.
> Up to God's free church I hope to go.
> Cry Amen, cry Amen, cry Amen to God!

Jacobs concludes, "Precious are such moments to the poor slaves. If you were to hear them at such times, you might think they were happy." *Happy*. To guard against complacency, she adds, "But can that hour of singing and shouting sustain them through the dreary week, toiling without wages, under constant dread of the lash?"[8] Jacobs offers an important reminder that it is not enough merely to pray, because the unjust system of slavery must be actively dismantled. But it is also striking just how valuable prayer is to the wounded people she describes. Christian prayer practiced as lament over the evils of slavery and communal celebration of God's tender mercies and promises of redemption is a lifeline for those in bondage. The God who through Christ endures the scourge of the Roman crucifiers also becomes present in the crucifying, hellacious circumstances of slavery and offers its sufferers the sustaining hope of freedom.

W. E. B. Du Bois expresses the quality of this black and blue

[8] Brent, *Incidents in the Life of a Slave Girl*, 519–20.

prayer tradition well when he says, "Through all the sorrow of the Sorrow Songs there breathes a hope—a faith in the ultimate justice of things."[9] To some extent, this hope in ultimate justice refers to a heavenly end where, as Howard Thurman puts it while reflecting on the slave spirituals during the Jim Crow era, "there will be no proscription, no segregation, no separateness, no sorrow, but complete freedom of movement—the most psychologically dramatic of all manifestations of freedom."[10] Although many slave songs make such final expectations explicit, they have also inspired a struggle for liberation in history. This is especially clear with the hymn "Oh Freedom":

> Oh Freedom! Oh Freedom!
> Oh Freedom! I love Thee!
> And before I'll be a slave,
> I'll be buried in my grave,
> And go home to my Lord and be free.

The singer would rather die than be enslaved. The implication is that he or she would fight for freedom even if this meant risking his or her life. Interpreted in this light, the eschatology in the prayer of the slaves does not so much suppress as enkindle a rebellious spirit. It is, therefore, unsurprising to see songs such as "Oh, Freedom" cited frequently in James Cone's Black liberation theology. Cone helpfully explains that the slaves sang about a freedom "that *included* but *did not depend upon* historical possibilities" because, although they obviously wanted their concrete oppressive circumstances to change, they did not often have the political power to effect such changes immediately.[11] Whatever

---

[9] W. E. B. Du Bois, *The Souls of Black Folk* (Simon and Schuster, 2005), 251.

[10] Howard Thurman, "The Negro Spiritual Speaks of Life and Death" (1947), in *A Strange Freedom: The Best of Howard Thurman on Religious Experience and Public Life*, ed. Walter Earl Fluker and Catherine Tumber (Beacon Press, 1998), 55–79, at 76.

[11] James H. Cone, *The Spirituals and the Blues: An Interpretation* (Orbis Books, 1991), 82.

historical transformations were or were not imaginable, spirituals such as "Oh, Freedom" empowered enslaved communities to connect with the God who created them to be free in both this life and the next.

This was the God who raised Jesus from the dead. The God encountered in the movements of the Spirit. The God about whom the ex-slave abolitionist Sojourner Truth exclaimed, "Oh God, I did not know you were so big!"[12] This was a divine mystery greater than any devilish designs of slaveholders. Those who participated bodily and communally in the singing of such spirituals desired membership in "God's free church" and experienced this through their prayer. Slavery was hell, but prayer was a hidden opening through which heaven might appear and bring comfort and strength to the afflicted. On the lips of slaveholders, prayer was death, but in the feet and hearts and lungs of the enslaved, it was new and abundant life.

Christian Prayer in the Black Freedom Struggle

After the abolition of slavery in the United States, the domination of God's precious black and blue children continued by other means: discrimination, segregation, political disenfranchisement, economic deprivation, false criminalization, lynchings and massacres, and other forms of violence. The struggle for freedom was not over. In many ways, it was just beginning. Christian prayer played a crucial role in this struggle by vocalizing suffering and hopes, providing much-needed comfort and strength, and engendering acts of nonviolent resistance.

With unparalleled clarity, Martin Luther King Jr. revealed the significance of prayer for collective, antiracist struggle. He did this in one way through his public practice of prayer. This practice could be seen not only at any given Sunday morning church service where King would lead the congregation in song and supplication, building them up after the latest experience of White supremacist

[12] *The Narrative of Sojourner Truth*, ed. Nell Irvin Painter (Penguin Classics, 1998), 45.

terror, but also in the streets, in a well-organized act of protest, indeed *as* this very act of protest. Lewis Baldwin gives the example of the 1965 struggle for voting rights: "As the demonstrators prepared for the great march from Selma to Montgomery, the media captured King and other ministers in a circle on their knees, with Ralph Abernathy, King's closest associate, praying that blacks and whites would learn to live together in peace."[13] To kneel in prayer before policemen wielding clubs and angry mobs spewing hate was, for King and his companions, a courageous form of direct action. Although we have every reason to believe that this prayer was genuine—that those on their knees were really opening their hearts to God in desperate longing for a better world—it was also a carefully crafted performance designed to move and teach those who witnessed it. The lesson was simple: Black people are humble children of God, precious human beings who do not deserve the abuse that is regularly heaped upon them. Such prayer in the light of day and in the glaring light of television cameras was meant to provoke a change of hearts, minds, and recalcitrant institutions.

Private acts of prayer have also been integral to the Black freedom struggle. Consider the justly famous episode in which King, distressed by death threats received prior to the 1956 Montgomery bus boycott, felt helpless and frightened—in a word, blue. He descended to the kitchen. The hour was late and the house still. In his solitude he began to pray. This is how he later described his experience:

> The words I spoke to God that midnight are still vivid in my memory. "I am here taking a stand for what I believe is right. But now I am afraid. The people are looking to me for leadership, and if I stand before them without strength and courage, they too will falter. I am at the end of my powers. I have nothing left. I've come to the point where I can't face it alone." At that moment I experienced the presence of the Divine as I had never experienced Him before. It seemed as

---

[13]Lewis V. Baldwin, *Never to Leave Us Alone: The Prayer Life of Martin Luther King Jr.* (Fortress Press, 2010), 80.

> though I could hear the quiet assurance of an inner voice saying: "Stand up for righteousness, stand up for truth; and God will be at your side forever." Almost at once my fears began to go. My uncertainty disappeared. I was ready to face anything.[14]

Such private acts of prayer are vital to the struggle for freedom insofar as they cast out fear and give one the strength to endure. Without laying his soul bare in this honest manner and receiving "the presence of the Divine" through "the quiet assurance of an inner voice," would King have found the courage needed to persist in the face of credible death threats? Would the civil rights victories he helped win have ever come to pass? Even when it takes place in moments of isolation and apparent inaction, prayer can facilitate social transformation by steadying and grounding its vulnerable human agents. King is part of the oft-overlooked contemplative strand in African American Christian prayer.[15] In addition to the sermons, songs, and shouts that give bold expression to Black religion, there is also the quiet reception of everyday grace without which meaningful freedom, whether personal or collective, would never fully take hold.[16]

Before King, there was Ida B. Wells (later Wells-Barnett). She similarly modeled the radical unity of a life of prayer and antiracist struggle.[17] Cornel West characterizes her as "the most courageous Black organic intellectual in the history of the country," noting that "you have to wait to get Martin King to get another courageous intellectual like that." He describes her as the leader of an "anti-terrorist movement," which "was going to call into question the bestiality and barbarity and brutality of Jim Crow and American

---

[14]Martin Luther King Jr., *Stride Toward Freedom: The Montgomery Story* (Beacon Press, 1958), 125.

[15]Barbara A. Holmes, *Joy Unspeakable: Contemplative Practices of the Black Church*, 2nd ed. (Fortress Press, 2017), 112.

[16]Kevin Quashie, *The Sovereignty of Quiet: Beyond Resistance in Black Culture* (Rutgers University Press, 2012), 80, and Katie G. Cannon, *Black Womanist Ethics* (Scholars Press, 1988), 127–43.

[17]Emilie M. Townes, *Womanist Justice, Womanist Hope* (Scholars Press, 1993), 69–106.

terrorism and lynching, but would do it in the name of something that provided a higher moral ground and higher spiritual ground given her Christian faith."[18] Wells-Barnett fought against lynching and other injustices in a nonviolent way simply by reporting the truth about them. Like King, she faced constant death threats. And like King, she found courage in the presence of God.

One story from her life particularly illuminates how she thinks about the purpose of prayer in the midst of struggle. Black sharecroppers in Elaine, Arkansas, had begun to organize in order to push for fairer pay and more just working conditions. They met in a church on the evening of September 30, 1919. A group of White men opened fire on the church, and a gunfight broke out. One White man was killed. In response, a large number of armed White men from Arkansas and surrounding states, including five hundred troops sent by the governor, began slaughtering Black men, women, and children. When the massacre ended, more than two hundred Black people and exactly five White people had been killed. The only arrests made were of Black people, and twelve Black men in particular—"the Elaine Twelve"—were tried for murder and sentenced to death. At the time, Wells-Barnett was living in Chicago, exiled from the South, but she made her way to Arkansas in secret to visit these twelve men in prison and to advocate for them. Hiding amongst their wives and loved ones, so as not to be detected by the guards, she witnessed the incarcerated ones raise their voices in prayer:

> I listened to those men sing and pray and give testimony from their overburdened hearts, and sometimes the women would take up the refrain. They shed tears and they got "happy," and the burden of their talk and prayers was of the hereafter. Finally, I got up and walked close to the bars and said to them in a low tone, "I have been listening to you for nearly two hours. You have talked and sung and prayed about dying, and forgiving your enemies, and feeling

[18] Cornel West, with Christa Buschendorf, *Black Prophetic Fire* (Beacon Press, 2014), 141.

> sure that you are going to be received in the New Jerusalem because your God knows that you are innocent of the offense for which you expect to be electrocuted. But why don't you pray to live and ask to be freed? The God you serve is the God of Paul and Silas who opened their prison gates, and if you have all the faith you say you have, you ought to believe that he will open your prison doors too. If you do believe that, let all of your songs and prayers hereafter be songs of faith and hope that God will set you free; that the judges who have to pass on your cases will be given the wisdom and courage to decide in your behalf.[19]

Although Wells-Barnett, like Jacobs before her, appreciated the "happiness" that comes from prayer even in the midst of sorrow (the heavenly hopes that momentarily comfort the oppressed), she resisted the notion that the purpose of prayer is only eschatological or palliative. She called to mind the biblical witness of Paul and Silas, and on this basis argued that the Elaine Twelve ought to pray for God to act directly in history. She pointed toward a potential effectiveness of prayer which does not rest on the moral suasion that may result from its public performance or on the personal fortitude that its private practice may impart but on God's ability to hear the cries of the poor and actively respond.

Such beliefs in divine agency may seem naïve, or even hurtful, given the grim state of the world. Certainly, they raise questions of theodicy. If God could respond to our prayers by overcoming whatever afflicts us, especially if this affliction is undeserved, then why is no such response usually forthcoming? How can God be almighty and just if God lets the innocent suffer? With good reason, unanswered petitions often give way to cries of lament. For some Black intellectuals, such as William R. Jones and Anthony Pinn, this line of thinking culminates in a form of protest atheism, where the prayer of complaint finally morphs into a decision

[19]Ida B. Wells, *Crusade for Justice: The Autobiography of Ida B. Wells*, ed. Alfreda M. Duster (University of Chicago Press, 1970), 402–403.

against the existence of God.[20] However, this is not the path that Wells-Barnett took. Although her circumstances were incredibly daunting, she remained undeterred in both her activism and her prayer. She wrote *The Arkansas Race Riot* to raise awareness about the massacre and the unjust court proceedings following it.[21] Thanks to the legal action of the NAACP, of which she was a founding member, and other social justice organizations the case eventually made its way to the Supreme Court, which ruled in favor of the falsely accused on the grounds that they were denied due process (*Moore vs. Dempsey*). One of the twelve later visited Wells-Barnett in Chicago and attributed his freedom to the kind of historically focused prayer that she exhorted them to practice: "We never talked about dying anymore, but did as she told us, and now every last one of us is out and enjoying his freedom."[22] Was this man's liberty the result of divinely answered prayers or direct human efforts, such as honest reporting and sound legal strategy? Wells-Barnett would suggest *both*. She refused to choose.

Just as unanswered prayers rightly give way to lament, so too answered ones rightly occasion gratitude and rejoicing. Recall the stirring final lines of King's "I Have a Dream" speech at the 1963 March on Washington for Jobs and Freedom:

> When we allow freedom to ring—when we let it ring from every village and every hamlet, from every state and every city, we will be able to speed up that day when all of God's children, black men and white men, Jews and Gentiles, Protestants and Catholics, will be able to join hands and sing in the words of the old Negro spiritual, "Free at last, free at last, thank God Almighty, we are free at last."[23]

---

[20]William R. Jones, *Is God a White Racist? A Preamble to Black Theology* (Anchor Press, 1973), and Anthony B. Pinn, *Why, Lord? Suffering and Evil in Black Theology* (Continuum, 1995).

[21]Ida Wells-Barnett, *The Arkansas Race Riot* (Createspace Independent Publishing, 2013).

[22]Wells, *Crusade for Justice*, 404.

[23]King, "I Have a Dream," in *A Testament of Hope: The Essential Writings and Speeches*, ed. James M. Washington (HarperCollins, 1986), 217–20, at 220.

This Christian prayer of thanksgiving belongs to the indefinite time of the already and the not yet. King quotes a hymn from his spiritual forebears in order to anticipate a future that he only dreamt of and that we must still await. The examples of King and Wells-Barnett challenge Christians today to be grateful for God's liberative presence in the struggle to abolish slavery and to achieve equal rights for all human beings and grateful, too, for the many courageous actors in this struggle, including those remembered and forgotten. At the same time, these holy examples demand that Christians remain expectant and unyielding in the fight for a more grace-filled world, drawing on all their resources of prayer and protest to engage the fight, because the lives of God's black and blue children are continuing to be destroyed well into the twenty-first century. The hour is too soon for gratitude alone.

Christian Prayer at Mother Emanuel

It had seemed an ordinary, peaceful Wednesday evening at Mother Emanuel, a historic African Methodist Episcopal (AME) church in Charleston, South Carolina. Several people, young and old, were gathered for the weekly Bible study. Then a cataclysmic eruption of violence occurred:

> Felicia's Bible fell to the floor. A bullet pierced it.
>
> Beneath the table next to her, she spotted her old friend Polly Sheppard cowering, as yet unhit. The killer's heavy boots marched toward her.
>
> Felicia prayed silently, Polly prayed out loud.
>
> The gunman stopped shooting when he reached Polly, dead eyes looking down at her, his heavy black pistol pointed at her feet.
>
> "Shut up!" he snapped.[24]

[24]Jennifer Berry Hawes, *Grace Will Lead Us Home: The Charleston Church Massacre and the Hard, Inspiring Journey to Forgiveness* (St. Martin's Press, 2019), 17.

Members of the church were praying together before the shooting started. The prayer continued during the carnage, and it continued afterward. This prayer at Mother Emanuel demonstrates the vitality and the importance of the long, ongoing tradition of Christian prayer in "black and blue." The resurgent culture of anti-Black, White supremacist violence that the world is presently witnessing wants to put a stop to such prayer. It yells, "Shut up!" It murders, it burns down,[25] and it desecrates. But it cannot stifle the Holy Spirit that moves in the hearts and bodies of this resilient people.

June 17, 2015, was not the first time Mother Emanuel fell victim to White supremacist attack. In the early months of 1822, after years of racist harassment and persecution, Denmark Vesey, an ex-slave and a leader of the church's Bible study, began organizing free and enslaved members of the church for a slave revolt and an Exodus experience. Like the Hebrews of old, they planned to flee Egypt (i.e., the United States) and make their way to the promised land (in this case, Haiti, which after the Haitian Revolution of 1791–1804 was the only Black-led country in the Western hemisphere). Their plans were exposed before they could be enacted, and thirty-five people including Vesey were executed. The church was burned to the ground, and the surviving members were scattered, forced to go elsewhere or meet in secret until the end of the Civil War.[26] During the freedom struggle of the 1950s and '60s, Mother Emanuel was a site of activism. Both Martin Luther King Jr. (1962) and Coretta Scott King (1969) spoke there, and many members participated in local boycotts and peaceful demonstrations.[27] That the killer decided to target this particular church was no accident.

The biblical text being studied that evening was the parable of the sower. This was Myra Thompson's first time leading the Bible study. "She described a world of sin in which hatred and

---

[25]Richard Fausset, "3 Black Churches Have Burned in 10 Days in a Single Louisiana Parish," *New York Times* (April 5, 2019).

[26]Herb Frazier, Bernard Edward Powers Jr., and Marjory Wentworth, *We Are Charleston: Tragedy and Triumph at Mother Emanuel* (W Publishing Group, 2016), 68–70.

[27]Frazier, Powers, and Wentworth, *We Are Charleston*, 123–39.

worldly desires had hardened hearts, leaving too many people unable to nourish the seeds of God's grace within themselves." Dylann Roof's heart was already too hardened to appreciate just how aptly this parable described his own situation. In his case, the seeds of grace had fallen on the inhospitable ground of White supremacy. Though he was a stranger, the twelve Black Christians in the church welcomed him, gave him a Bible, let him join their intimate prayer meeting, let him sit next to the pastor, Reverend Clementa Pinckney. As a child, Dylann had played with a biracial, Black friend. He had attended Sunday school at a Lutheran church. None of these seeds of grace was a match for the toxic soil of White supremacist web content in which he found his malignant sense of purpose. Reports indicate that he immersed himself in a slew of hateful websites after watching news coverage of the murder of the unarmed, Black, seventeen-year-old Trayvon Martin on February 26, 2012, and Googling "black on white crime" (already a telling search term).[28]

While at prayer, Myra and Clementa were shot to death. So, too, were Cynthia Hurd, Susie Jackson, Ethel Lance, DePayne Middleton-Doctor, Tywanza Sanders, Daniel L. Simmons Sr., and Sharonda Coleman-Singleton. These are the "Emmanuel Nine," each a precious child of God gone too soon. Polly, Felicia Sanders (Tywanza's mother), and Felicia's granddaughter were present at the Bible study but did not get hit. Clementa's wife, Jennifer, and their daughter Malana, who huddled together in an adjacent church office, also survived. After the shooting, these five shaken survivors, other church members, family and friends, press, and government officials congregated in a nearby hotel. "Some cried, some prayed, some paced." Receiving the news on her cellphone that her mother Ethel was one of those killed, Nadine Collier screamed aloud in her car. While everyone awaited the coroner's report, the Reverend Norvel Goff Sr.

> asked people to gather and hold hands. For those too overcome to stand, people knelt to wrap themselves in

[28]Hawes, *Grace Will Lead Us Home*, 14, 182, 185, 248.

> arms of comfort. Goff's voice rose in prayer, then in song. He began the first lines of an old Christian hymn, and the group joined him.
>
> My hope is built on nothing less
> than Jesus' blood and righteousness
> I dare not trust the sweetest frame,
> but wholly lean on Jesus' name.
>
> The people sang together, hundreds of human voices converging in a somber river of shock and grief.[29]

Such prayers of mourning and togetherness continued almost unceasingly in the coming days. There were prayer vigils of solidarity in churches throughout Charleston and many other U.S. towns and cities. Twenty-five thousand people joined together for a march dubbed the Bridge to Peace, in which "there were nine minutes of silence, spontaneous singing, and prayers—always prayers."[30] President Barack Obama gave a eulogy at Rev. Pinckney's funeral and sang "Amazing Grace."[31]

These prayers in the immediate aftermath of the massacre were significant in countless ways known only to those who voiced them or held them in their hearts, and perhaps their meaning remained partly hidden even for such persons. What were these prayers doing? In response to such violence, many agreed it was not enough merely to offer "thoughts and prayers," as the rote expression goes. There was a need for action of other sorts, such as removing the Confederate flag from the state capitol, seeking greater gun control measures, and continuing to struggle for an end to White supremacy in all its forms. Yet these prayers after the shooting were doing something very real and irreplaceable that is not easy to categorize. One can see this clearly by considering what happened when the prayers began to subside. After the news cycle had shifted, and most people had moved on with their

[29]Hawes, *Grace Will Lead Us Home*, 35, 44, 50.
[30]Frazier, Powers, and Wentworth, *We Are Charleston*, 8–9.
[31]Hawes, *Grace Will Lead Us Home*, 287–94.

busy lives, the survivors still ached. Felicia felt neglected by the leaders of her church, who had stopped visiting. "She desperately needed a person of the cloth to say, 'God didn't leave you. He's still with you.' That was all she wanted, an assurance that God would pull her through this." Praying together was a way to feel connected with God's abiding love and presence in times of agony, and without it, there was bitter isolation. She eventually found some spiritual support by speaking and praying with a minister at a nearby Presbyterian church. "At one point [in this meeting] she cried, 'I don't know what my purpose is!' " Prayer is a way to express questions borne of grief and confusion, a time to be oneself without pretense or polish, a chance to let everything go and let everything out. It is a space for wounded bodies and souls to be heard and to heal.[32]

For many survivors of violence, prayer may also eventually be a context in which to explore the possibilities of forgiveness and to find the power to forgive. The only conditional petition in the Lord's Prayer is "Forgive us our trespasses as we forgive those who trespass against us." Such forgiveness is a lofty expectation when one is faced with a coldblooded, racially motivated killer such as Roof, who has not shown even an inkling of remorse. On the contrary, he has said, "I would like to make it crystal clear. I do not regret what I did. I am not sorry. I have not shed a tear for the innocent people I killed." Moreover, his hardened heart is only one individual inflection of what seems to be an increasingly hard-hearted culture that stubbornly refuses to repair the harms done by five centuries of institutionalized racism and, in fact, seems intent on exacerbating them.

Nevertheless, some of the survivors and family members of the deceased stunned the world by publicly offering forgiveness to Roof at his bond hearing. Nadine spoke the words first. Looking at him, she said,

> I just want everybody to know, to you, I forgive you! You took something very precious from me. I will never talk to her ever again. I will never be able to hold her again. But

[32]Hawes, *Grace Will Lead Us Home*, 142, 143.

> I forgive you! And have mercy on your soul. You. Hurt. Me! You hurt a lot of people. But God forgives you. And I forgive you.

Myra's husband, Reverend Anthony Thompson, made a similar statement:

> I forgive you. And my family forgives you. But we would like you to take this opportunity to repent. Repent. Confess. Give your life to the one who matters most—Christ—so that he can change it, can change your ways no matter what happens to you.

Felicia added her voice too:

> We welcomed you Wednesday night in our Bible study with open arms. You have killed some of the most beautiful people that I know. Every fiber in my body hurts! And I'll never be the same. Tywanza Sanders is my son, but Tywanza was my hero. Tywanza was my hero! But as we say in the Bible study: We enjoyed you, but may God have mercy on you.[33]

What should observers make of such statements of forgiveness, which call on the names of God and Christ, which convey unspeakable grief, and yet which express kindness and request divine mercy for an unrepentant White supremacist murderer?

One important point to remember is that not everyone touched by the massacre responded in this manner or found it appropriate to do so. For example, "DePayne Middleton-Doctor's cousin, Waltrina Middleton, [was] upset about the way the statements of forgiveness were immediately used to interpret the larger meaning of what happened at Emanuel Church: it 'took away our narrative to be rightfully hurt. I can't turn off my pain.' "[34] Similarly, Nadine's sister Sharon was angry about such a quick offer of

---

[33]Hawes, *Grace Will Lead Us Home*, 74–75, 272.
[34]Frazier, Powers, and Wentworth, *We Are Charleston*, 172.

forgiveness: "before Sharon could think about forgiving in any honest way, she needed to know more. She needed to be angry and cry and know exactly what happened." Yet for Sharon it was a question of time. After the trial ended, she felt God move her heart in a new way: "She could forgive Roof, at least for now. Forever? Time would tell." Everyone's path is different on such questions, and for some deeply prayerful Christian people forgiveness may never come in this life because the hurt is just too great and the injustice too persistent. At the sentencing, "some screamed at Roof, calling him evil. Several hoped he burned in hell for eternity. They called him a coward. Satan. An animal. A monster." Given the severity and remorselessness of the crime, my own view is that no one who remains in a state of righteous anger ought to be judged for this. Their outrage is warranted and may itself become the occasion for honest and meaningful prayer. It is also crucial to acknowledge that those who do forgive do not thereby condone the murderous behavior or advocate any unwarranted slackening of the Black freedom struggle. Many who spoke forgiving words were relieved to hear that Roof was given a maximum sentence (even if they had misgivings about the death penalty in general) and many have gone on to agitate for social reform in various areas.[35]

Although there is a range of perspectives on the matter which must be respected, I do believe as a Christian that it is a good and astonishing thing that the practice of prayer at Mother Emanuel has brought some of those most deeply hurt by this most recent massacre to a place where they feel empowered to forgive. Arguably this is much more than one can reasonably expect from anyone, but it is what the extraordinary tradition of Christian prayer in black and blue has made possible. This tradition has been a refuge for the racially oppressed, a site specifically set apart. But it has also been a place of welcome, strength, and healing that has grace to offer all of God's children, if they can only learn to receive it. The God worshipped in this tradition is one who seeks the lost and who accomplishes wondrous deeds in history. This

---

[35]Hawes, *Grace Will Lead Us Home*, 78, 279, 281, 283.

God heals and liberates, reserving the tenderest mercies for the most afflicted, while empowering them for renewed action. This God has not given up on anyone, not even grievously malformed White terrorists like Roof—though this God unequivocally condemns his evil ways and the larger culture of White supremacist violence he unapologetically represents.

From a certain angle, such Christian prayer in black and blue seems to do nothing. It seems helpless in the face of the seemingly endless cruelty of the world, and for this reason many have rejected it, preferring more militant forms of engagement. Yet I submit that such prayer does much more than meets the eye. Its meaning is elastic, diverse, and mysterious. For many, it means survival. It means hope. It means community. It means power. It means a passionate love that extinguishes hatred and stirs action. It means that White supremacist violence does not have the final word, that it cannot ultimately disfigure the beautiful, darkly hued creature that God made and calls me to be. What have I to fear if the Spirit is with me and Jesus is always by my side? Yes, slaveholders prayed. Perhaps even Roof prayed genuinely at some point in his life. But the slaves prayed, too. Our greatest moral heroes prayed. Mary Prince, Harriet Jacobs, Sojourner Truth, Denmark Vesey, Ida B. Wells-Barnett, Martin Luther King Jr., and James Cone prayed. So did the Elaine Twelve and the Emanuel Nine. Understanding what prayer means for these black and blue children of God is crucial if we—all of us, whatever our so-called race, whether we are Christian or not—hope to honor their memory and join with them in their struggle.

2

Interpreting Desire

Prayer in Thomas Aquinas and the Slave Spirituals

Tertullian famously posed the rhetorical question, "What indeed has Athens to do with Jerusalem?"[1] Readers of this chapter might similarly ask, "What has the Angelic Doctor to do with Black spirituality?" Given the scant attention this relationship has received, one could be forgiven for assuming that Thomas Aquinas's theology and the slave spirituals—an assortment of worship songs that emerged from the African American experience of slavery—have little to do with each other.[2] Experts in

---

A version of this chapter appears in *The Thomist* 89 (2025): 303–29.

[1]Tertullian, *Prescription Against Heretics*, chap. 7, https://www.newadvent.org/fathers/0311.htm.

[2]A note on word choice: I use the term "slave spirituals" to name that worship music that was composed under conditions of slavery. The more traditional designation, "Negro spirituals," sometimes includes postslavery adaptations of old songs and additions of new songs made by formerly enslaved persons and their descendants through the end of the nineteenth century and into the early part of the twentieth century. Moreover, after the assassination of Martin Luther King Jr. in 1968, the word "Negro" fell into disuse and other racial categories such as "Black" and "African American" rose to prominence, each with particular connotations. "Black" has pan-Africanist, nationalist, and activist roots, while "African American" emphasizes integration, multiculturalism, and geographical specificity. I use both freely, as appropriate. Some scholars prefer to speak of "enslaved persons"

one of these bodies of literature are typically not well versed in the other. One conversation requires familiarity with the context of medieval universities and apostolic religious movements such as the Dominicans, the scholastic integration of early Christian Platonism with a rediscovered Aristotelianism, and the intricacies of a centuries-long tradition of Catholic teaching that both builds toward and builds on Aquinas's extraordinary contribution. The other conversation requires detailed knowledge of the conditions of American slavery, the folk cultural blending of evangelical Christian piety with remembered African traditions, and the religious dimensions of Black freedom struggles from the antebellum era up to the present. The composers of the spirituals were denied anything resembling the classical education that Thomistic scholarship presupposes. Conversely, the study of Black sources has been so marginal to the discipline of Catholic theology that it remains rare to see them treated seriously by any Catholic theologians who are not themselves Black—and we are few.[3]

Beyond the general disconnect between these scholarly conversations, there is a more specific impediment: Aquinas accepted the institution of slavery as he knew it in his day. On the basic question of whether it could be just to enslave another person, he and the composers of the slave spirituals are sharply divided. The first section of this chapter addresses this challenge by situating Aquinas's views of slavery in their historical and intellectual context, assessing his legacy on this topic, and noting important developments in Catholic teaching. While some might find his permissive attitude toward slaveholding so objectionable that they would rather not pursue any rapprochement with him, I contend

---

instead of "slaves," in order to emphasize their full personhood and humanity. I balance this approach with a desire to name honestly what it was like to be treated as "a slave."

[3]For Black Catholic theological discussion of the spirituals, see Diana L. Hayes, *Forged in the Fiery Furnace: African American Spirituality* (Orbis Books, 2012), 70–83; M. Shawn Copeland, *Knowing Christ Crucified: The Witness of African American Religious Experience* (Orbis Books, 2018), 3–58; and Bryan N. Massingale, *Racial Justice and the Catholic Church* (Orbis Books, 2010), 107 and 138.

that other aspects of his thought are significantly more promising and make ongoing dialogue an attractive option.

Common ground is possible. This is so particularly in the area of spirituality.[4] Aquinas and the authors of these Black sacred songs were people of prayer. The living God who offers deliverance from evil was the center of their lives. In a world full of suffering, they found comfort in their memory of the crucified and risen Lord and in their belief that God would provide. They knew their happiness did not ultimately consist in worldly goods but in sanctifying grace and the gift of eternal life. Although there are differences of emphasis in these two spiritual traditions, the same Spirit of truth was at work in them both. The approach I take in this chapter is to read Aquinas's teachings on prayer in light of the slave spirituals (second section) and then to read the spirituals in light of his teachings (third section). This method of mutual illumination preserves their differences while highlighting genuine connections.

In addition to being possible, such common ground is also necessary, in a particular sense. As the Catholic Church has grown in its recognition of the wrongness of slavery, it has also endeavored to increase its solidarity with the poor and oppressed throughout the world, including the still-mistreated descendants of slaves in the Americas. If it is serious about such values, it cannot afford to ignore the wisdom of Black spiritual traditions. At the same time, it continues to revere Aquinas as an indispensable source of many doctrines and practices, and with good reason. Consequently, it must seek some form of reconciliation between these two commitments. Catholics of the twenty-first century need the Angelic Doctor and Black spirituality to have *something* to do with each other.

---

[4]In addition to spirituality, another possible locus, which lies beyond the scope of this chapter, is natural law. See Martin Luther King Jr., "Letter from Birmingham City Jail," in *A Testament of Hope: The Essential Writings and Speeches of Martin Luther King, Jr.*, ed. James M. Washington (Harper & Row, 1986), 289–302, at 293; Vincent W. Lloyd, *Black Natural Law* (Oxford University Press, 2016), 88, 149; and Thomas S. Hibbs, "Aquinas and Black Natural Law," *Nova et Vetera* 21, no. 3 (Summer 2023): 943–70.

Reckoning with Aquinas and Slavery

Aquinas was no abolitionist. His embrace of the institution of slavery as it was practiced in his day—and in the ancient world that shaped the writings of Greek philosophers, church fathers, and the sacred scriptures themselves—fails to meet the antislavery standards of present social ethics. His shortcomings in this regard are hardly unique. The practice was so deeply woven into the fabric of language, law, and religion that very few classical sources questioned it (whether Christian or not). In Aquinas's medieval Europe, practical distinctions had appeared between chattel slavery and serfdom, though laws often used the same Latin word *servus* for a person in either state. Serfs who owed allegiance, rents, and other obligations to their lords were not considered freepersons, but neither were they reduced to the status of possessions. Yet trafficking in human property did occur. Non-Christians, persons considered heretical, and captives brought from Eastern Europe, Central Asia, and in some cases sub-Saharan Africa were sold and kept as chattel (i.e., capital) in places that we would now call Italy, France, and Spain.[5] Aquinas does not restrict the meaning of *servus* to nonchattel conditions, and his account of slavery entails some sort of ownership.[6]

Certain passages in Aquinas's works suggest a limited awareness of the fallenness of this institution and a desire to curb its worst excesses. For example, he argues that slavery was not part

[5]Marc Bloch, *Slavery and Serfdom in the Middle Ages*, trans. William R. Beer (University of California Press, 1975), 33–91; Sally McKee, "Domestic Slavery in Renaissance Italy," *Slavery and Abolition* 29, no. 3 (September 2008): 305–26; Juliane Schiel, "Slavery in the Western Mediterranean," in *The Palgrave Handbook of Global Slavery throughout History*, ed. Damian A. Pargas and Juliane Schiel (Springer Nature/Palgrave Macmillan, 2023), 179–92; and Christopher J. Kellerman, SJ, *All Oppression Shall Cease: A History of Slavery, Abolition, and the Catholic Church* (Orbis Books, 2022), 33.

[6]*STh* II-II, q. 61, a. 3, corp. Unless otherwise noted, my references to Aquinas come from the parallel Latin and English texts in the Aquinas Institute's online collection: aquinas.cc.

of humanity's prelapsarian condition because it involves a type of "pain" (*poena*) inappropriate to the "state of innocence."[7] He does not suggest that any specific "race" is by nature meant for servitude (a largely anachronistic notion).[8] Nor does he deny that slaves are human beings. In fact, he affirms that they are "rational animals" capable of thought and free will.[9] Perhaps most importantly, he acknowledges that the obedience that he assumes slaves owe their masters is limited. Echoing Augustine, he clarifies, "if the emperor commands one thing and God another, you must disregard the former and obey God."[10] The same preeminence of divine authority over human authority would check the deference owed not just to emperors but all earthly masters. In like manner, citing Seneca, Aquinas stresses that the jurisdiction of a slaveowner extends only to the body, not the soul, and therefore, "in matters touching the internal movement of the will man is not bound to obey his fellow-man, but God alone."[11]

Nevertheless, these qualifications do not amount to a rejection of slavery. Indeed, other pieces of textual evidence show Aquinas's comfort with it. His commentary on Aristotle's *Politics* presents slavery as an essential ingredient of a household and raises no objections to the claim that it is natural for some people to be subjected to this state because of their allegedly inferior minds.[12] Nuancing Aristotle's position on the "natural slave," Aquinas else-

---

[7] *STh* I, q. 96, a. 4, corp.

[8] Some scholars argue that race has roots in the medieval period (Heng) and even earlier (Isaac). Others attribute its origins to the trans-Atlantic slave trade (Jennings) and even later to Enlightenment-era philosophy (Eigen and Larrimore). The question of when and how race emerges is complicated. In any case, Aquinas's account of slavery does not explicitly rely on any racial divisions. See Geraldine Heng, *The Invention of Race in the Middle Ages* (Cambridge University Press, 2018); Benjamin Isaac, *The Invention of Racism in Classical Antiquity* (Princeton University Press, 2004); Willie James Jennings, *The Christian Imagination: Theology and the Origins of Race* (Yale University Press, 2010); and Sara Eigen and Mark Larrimore, eds., *The German Invention of Race* (SUNY Press, 2006).

[9] *STh* II-II, q. 47, a. 12, ad 2; II-II, q. 50, a. 2, corp.

[10] *STh* II-II, q. 104, a. 5, corp.

[11] *STh* II-II, q. 104, a. 5, corp.

[12] *Sentitia libri Politicorum* I, 1/A.

where contends that slavery is not natural absolutely but only in a secondary sense related to utility. He asserts that if a man can make good use of a piece of land, it is natural that he should have it. In like manner, he reasons, if a wise man can use another's physical powers for a good purpose, it is natural (in the sense of fitting or agreeable, not strictly necessary) that this individual should be his slave.[13] This purpose-relative and nonracial sense of slavery's naturalness is morally problematic on its own terms, because, as rational creatures, human beings have an innate dignity that differs dramatically from the mere economic value of a plot of land or other usable property. Moreover, Aquinas's account was easily racialized by later authors, since modern racial divisions between White Europeans and the more darkly hued peoples of the world were often drawn (falsely and violently) along the very mind-body lines he invokes.[14] Related ideas about the naturalness of slavery were taken up in the sixteenth century to justify the enslavement of Natives and Africans in the Americas.[15]

Even if Aquinas had clearly disavowed Aristotle's theory of the "natural slave," this would not necessarily have changed his view of slavery as a social hierarchy requiring dutiful submission from its subjects. Appeals to nature were not necessary for him to hold that "a slave is a kind of possession" (*servus est possessio quaedam*),[16] that "inducing a slave" to leave his or her master is a type of "theft,"[17] and that "to strike" (*verberare*) a slave is a legitimate means of discipline.[18] The evils of slavery could not have

[13] *STh* II-II, q. 57, a. 3, ad 2.

[14] By the eighteenth century, a common racist assertion was that "*Negroes* are Creatures destitute of Souls." This rebarbative remark is quoted in Robert Bernasconi, "The Philosophy of Race in the Nineteenth Century," in *Critical Philosophy of Race: Essays* (Oxford University Press, 2022), 51–75, at 54.

[15] The first to do this seems to have been the theologian John Mair. See Joseph E. Capizzi, "The Children of God: Natural Slavery in the Thought of Aquinas and Vitoria," *Theological Studies* 63 (2002): 31–52, at 33, and Anthony Pagden, *The Fall of Natural Man: The American Indian and the Origins of Comparative Ethnology* (Cambridge University Press, 1982), 38.

[16] *STh* II-II, q. 61, a. 3, corp., translation modified.

[17] *STh* II-II, q. 61, a. 3, corp.

[18] *STh* II-II, q. 65, a. 2, corp.

been undone simply by shifting the question of its legitimation from a natural to a conventional register, since both canon law and Roman civil law permitted the practice.[19] Nor is the much-discussed distinction between medieval theories of right (*ius*) and modern theories of rights (*iura*) the decisive issue, because defenses of slavery occurred on both grounds: the institution's apologists have deemed it an integral part both of an ontologically right social order and a slaveowner's individual property rights.[20]

To make real progress, the idea of slavery itself had to become repugnant. It had to be exposed as something unnatural, antisocial, and radically contrary to the will of God. Catholic teaching is much clearer on this matter now than it has been at any other time in its history. A recent pastoral letter of the U.S. bishops acknowledges the horrors of American slavery and its aftermath in the following words:

> As this country was forming, Africans were bought and sold as mere property, often beaten, raped, and literally worked to death. This form of slavery, known as chattel slavery, was different from and far more brutal than the slavery known in ancient times. Racial categories, which classified different ethnic communities as different races, some even as subhuman, were used to justify this new form of slavery. The injustices of chattel slavery were horrifying and lasted for generations. Families were separated, marriages were forbidden or dishonored, and children were maltreated and forced to work. After slavery ended, many former slaves faced continued servitude in the evolving economies that once relied upon their labor, and blacks encountered new

[19]Kellerman, *All Oppression Shall Cease*, 42.

[20]For further discussion of this distinction, see Paul J. Cornish, "Marriage, Slavery, and Natural Rights in the Political Thought of Aquinas," *Review of Politics* 60, no. 3 (Summer 1998): 545–61; David Lantigua, "The Image of God, Christian Rights Talk, and the School of Salamanca," *Journal of Law and Religion* 31, no. 1 (March 2016): 19–41; and Stephen F. Brett, *Slavery and the Catholic Tradition: Rights in the Balance* (Peter Lang, 1994).

> forms of resentment and violence. In freedom, millions of blacks lived in constant fear for their lives. Most resided in extreme poverty and endured daily indignities in their interactions with whites. Efforts to advance out of poverty by working a small farm, owning a business, building a school, or forming a trade union generally met fierce resistance throughout the country. For so many, the right to participate in the political process would be withheld or severely hindered for another century.[21]

The bishops are right to recognize the particular brutality of modern, racialized, chattel slavery and its Jim Crow offshoots. However, overlooking the reality of premodern chattel slavery leads them to underestimate troubling continuities in the practice as well as to downplay the ways in which theological attitudes toward it have themselves drastically changed. To hold another in bondage is now regarded as a morally intolerable act and a very grave sin, but it was not always so. Although racialization changed the institution for the worse, slavery is not wrong just because it was imposed on particular races. Nor was it a trivial matter for those who endured it in antiquity. It has always been morally flawed at its core. The church now recognizes that no human being should be made to suffer in such a state.[22]

If Aquinas were writing today, he would likely follow the bishops' lead in such judgments, but since he died over 750 years ago, scholars are compelled to reckon with his mixed legacy in relation to slavery. It has not been wholly negative. Dominican friars familiar with Aquinas's theology were among the first Catholic leaders to denounce the enslavement of Natives and

---

[21] United States Conference of Catholic Bishops, *Open Wide Our Hearts: The Enduring Call to Love—A Pastoral Letter Against Racism* (2018), https://www.usccb.org/resources/open-wide-our-hearts-enduring-call-love-pastoral-letter-against-racism.

[22] *Gaudium et Spes*, no. 27 (December 7, 1965), and Pope John Paul II, "Discours de sa Sainteté Jean-Paul II à la communauté Catholique de l'Île de Gorée dans l'eglise de Saint Charles Borromée" (Voyage Apostolique au Sénégal, en Gambie, et en Guinée) (February 22, 1992).

Africans by Spanish and Portuguese colonizers. The Dominican Bartolomé de las Casas is justly celebrated for his defense of the human dignity of Indigenous persons throughout much of his adult life and especially during his debate with Juan Ginés de Sepúlveda at Valladolid, Spain, in 1550–1551. Yet it is telling that both theologians relied on the authority of the Bible, Aristotle, and Aquinas to formulate their contrasting positions. Sixteenth-century Thomism did not so much settle the Catholic fight about slavery as set its terms and parameters. One could use Aquinas to argue in favor of either the equal respect owed to every rational creature or the rightful domination of some by others.[23]

Given this ambiguity, it should perhaps come as no surprise that, well into the nineteenth century, many U.S. Catholic leaders still regarded slavery as a legitimate and even good thing, under certain conditions. They had the backing of theological tradition and had thoroughly accommodated themselves to a culture shaped by the practice. Although Pope Gregory XVI's 1839 bull *In Supremo Apostolatus* condemned the slave trade, these leaders interpreted this papal teaching narrowly to prohibit only further transporting of new slaves from Africa, not the institution of slavery as it already existed in America, let alone the idea of slavery itself. Many American Catholic religious communities, including Dominicans, owned slaves and profited from their unpaid labor. Prior to the Civil War, individual U.S. bishops either opposed the abolitionist movement or remained silent about it. None publicly supported it. At this time, the typical Catholic position in the country was pro-slavery.[24]

---

[23]Bartolomé de las Casas, *In Defense of the Indians*, trans. and ed. Stafford Poole, CM (Northern Illinois University Press, 1992); Luke Glanville, David Lupher, and Maya Feile Tomes, eds., *Sepúlveda on the Spanish Invasion of the Americas* (Oxford University Press, 2023); Thomas F. O'Meara, "The Dominican School of Salamanca and the Spanish Conquest of America: Some Bibliographic Notes," *The Thomist* 56, no. 4 (October 1992): 555–82, especially 577; and Kellerman, *All Oppression Shall Cease*, 61.

[24]Cyprian Davis, OSB, and Jamie Phelps, OP, eds., *"Stamped with the Image of God": African Americans as God's Image in Black* (Orbis Books, 2003), 35–40; Cyprian Davis, OSB, *The History of Black Catholics in the United States* (Crossroad, 2004), 28–66; Kellerman, *All Oppression Shall*

While Aquinas is not uniquely to blame for Catholic complicity in slavery, hindsight makes clear that he should have taken a much more critical stance toward it. Prior to modernity, such a stance was not unheard of: Antislavery views were expressed by Gregory of Nyssa and John Duns Scotus, among others.[25] It was possible, even in the ancient past, to recognize the sinfulness of slavery. It is tempting to wonder how history might have unfolded differently had Aquinas perceived the theological necessity of abolishing this evil institution. But, of course, such counterfactual speculations have limited value. The more important work for current students of Aquinas is to think constructively with him in hopes of achieving a better future. Given that his account of slavery is not viable in any respect, I suggest instead turning our attention to other aspects of his thought that may help clarify the theological meaning of the lives and hopes of the enslaved.

Aquinas on Prayer

One promising avenue that has not yet been pursued is to put Aquinas's understanding and practice of prayer into conversation with the slave spirituals. This approach is attractive because it builds on the recent recovery of Aquinas as a "spiritual master" (in the sense of teacher or guide)[26] and because it focuses on a

---

Cease, 125–49; and Seymour Drescher, *Abolition: A History of Slavery and Antislavery* (Cambridge University Press, 2009), 385.

[25]Ilaria Ramelli, "Gregory of Nyssa's Position in Late Antique Debates on Slavery and Poverty, and the Role of Asceticism," *Journal of Late Antiquity* 5, no. 1 (Spring 2012): 87–118; Anthony Soto, "The Structure of Society according to Duns Scotus (Continued)," *Franciscan Studies* 12, no. 1 (March 1952): 71–90, at 79–82; and Kellerman, *All Oppression Shall Cease*, 21–25, 41–46.

[26]On the role that prayer plays in this spiritual reframing of Aquinas, see Jean-Pierre Torrell, OP, *Saint Thomas Aquinas*, vol. 2, *Spiritual Master*, trans. Robert Royal (Catholic University of America Press, 2003), 330–36; Jean-Pierre Torrell, "The Interpreter of Desire: Prayer according to St. Thomas Aquinas," in *Christ and Spirituality in St. Thomas Aquinas*, trans. Bernhard Blankenhorn, OP (Catholic University of America Press, 2011), 65–73; Dominic Legge, OP, "Christ's Prayer to the Father (and Ours)," in *Thomas Aquinas as Spiritual Teacher*, ed. Michael A. Dauphinais, Andrew

dimension of his work that connects well with the limited data we have of enslaved African Americans' thoughts and experiences.[27] Although these oppressed persons were not trained scholastic theologians, many were people of prayer who knew how to express their holy desires to God, and this is how Thomists should see them.

This section summarizes some of Aquinas's key teachings on prayer, while focusing on potential connections with the prayerful songs of enslaved Black persons. It demonstrates that Aquinas's understanding of prayer as that virtuous activity by which rational creatures interpret their desires and offer them worshipfully to God applies to the spirituals. It presents his positive assessment of vocal and musical prayer. It discusses the kinds of desires that he thinks ought to form the basis of prayer, including those for eternal life, the virtues needed to attain it, and the temporal things that support our physical and spiritual well-being, while noting that these desires are reflected in the spirituals. It explains how his incorporation of prayer into the doctrine of divine providence encourages a high degree of confidence like that found in the spirituals. And it concludes by considering some of his own prayers as examples.

The longest question in the *Summa Theologiae* is the treatise on prayer: II-II, q. 83. The first of its seventeen articles introduces the idea that prayer is "an interpreter of desire" (*desiderii interpres*).[28] With this turn of phrase, Aquinas indicates that prayer is not simply a desire. It is a desire that has been translated into a meaningful act of speech. Prayer turns a feeling of want or need into a rational act of petition addressed to an agent capable of response. In more technical terms, Aquinas argues that prayer

Hofer, OP, and Roger W. Nutt (Sapientia Press of Ave Maria University, 2023), 261–74.

[27]For a classic overview of the spirituality of enslaved African Americans, see Albert J. Raboteau, *Slave Religion: The "Invisible Institution" in the Antebellum South* (Oxford University Press, 2004).

[28]*STh* II-II, q. 83, a. 1, ad. 1. This is also the title of what may be the most comprehensive study of Aquinas's teachings on prayer: Lydia Maidl, *Desiderii interpres: Genesis und Grundstruktur der Gebetstheologie des Thomas von Aquin* (Verlag Ferdinand Schöningh, 1994).

belongs among the rational powers of the soul, not the appetitive. More specifically, it is an act of practical reason that, as such, does not only behold an intellectual object but also causes an effect. The manner of causation in this case is not "commanding," as when the mind immediately moves one of the body's limbs, but rather "disposing," that is, making a nonbinding request of someone with the power to act.[29]

According to this way of thinking, prayer is something that can only be done by beings of a rational nature.[30] The fact that enslaved persons prayed should have laid to rest any demeaning questions about the fullness of their humanity. In the *Summa Theologiae*, prayer is categorized as one of the acts of religion, which is itself understood as an aspect of the moral virtue of justice—again something only rational beings possess. Religion is the part of justice that "pays due worship to God."[31] Prayer is one type of such worship: By asking God for things, one acknowledges a profound dependence on God's goodness and power and thereby shows proper reverence to God.

In this text, religion is distinguished from the theological virtues of faith, hope, and charity.[32] As a practice of justice, religion does not exclusively consist of such supernaturally graced features of Christian life but also involves actions and habits that are at least partly developed from principles inchoate to humanity's rational nature.[33] Aquinas acknowledges that prayer may be a sign of the infused theological virtues at work in one's life insofar as "they cause the act of religion,"[34] but he also implies that it is a practice whereby any human being can seek to render God what is

---

[29] *STh* II-II, q. 83, a. 1, corp.

[30] The Franciscan tradition analogically extends the capacity for prayer even to nonrational creatures, insofar as they too participate in songs of praise and cries of lament. Pope Francis draws on this tradition in his ecological encyclical, *Laudato Si'* (May 24, 2015). By contrast, Aquinas limits his analysis to that sort of spiritual activity that only rational beings can do. In my opinion, both approaches are beneficial.

[31] *STh* II-II, q. 81, a. 5, corp.

[32] *STh* II-II, q. 81, a. 5, ad 2.

[33] *STh* I-II, q. 63, a. 1, corp.

[34] *STh* II-II, q. 81, a. 5, ad 1.

due. Being a Christian—and, more decisively, someone actually transformed by grace—is not a prerequisite for prayer. To be able to pray is a human capacity discernible in anyone who elevates their desires to God, including African captives both *before* and after they underwent any process of Christian initiation.

Quoting Psalm 9, Aquinas highlights the prayer of the poor that the God of Israel hears prior to the coming of Jesus.[35] Moreover, although Aquinas critiques what he takes to be the ancient Egyptian understanding of prayer as causing changes in fate, he grasps that this culture too was one of prayer.[36] He knows, as well, that sinners pray, and he argues that in some cases God may kindly answer them: "God hears the sinner's prayer if it proceeds from a good natural desire, not out of justice, because the sinner does not merit to be heard, but out of pure mercy."[37] Prayer, then, is not exclusively the act of a sanctified Christian person perfectly conformed to God's will, though it is exclusively the act of a rational creature.[38]

By making these points, I am not suggesting that enslaved persons were necessarily sinful in any particular respect or that those among them who professed Christian faith were insincere. Indeed, many people in bondage (whether Christian or not) may have received graces of sanctification comparable to those of the holiest saints. If we are to doubt anyone's virtue, it should be that of every baptized and believing Christian who became a "dealer in human flesh."[39] What I am arguing is that prayer, as Aquinas understands it, is a highly accessible activity, which requires little

---

[35] *STh* II-II, q. 83, a. 1, obj. 1.

[36] *ScG* III, qq. 95–96.

[37] *STh* II-II, q. 83, a. 16, corp.

[38] Whether the persons of the Trinity pray to each other and how to understand the prayer of Christ in view of his divine nature are complicating factors, which have been addressed well by others. See Michael Joseph Higgins, "Aquinas on Prayer in the Eternal Trinity," *Modern Theology* (published online 2024): 1–16, and Legge, "Christ's Prayer to the Father (and Ours)." However, my focus in this chapter is on human prayer.

[39] In Catherine of Siena's mystical locutions, God tells her that becoming a "dealer in human flesh" is a sign of great sin and cruelty. See Catherine of Siena, *Dialogue*, trans. Suzanne Noffke, OP (Paulist Press, 1980), sec. 7, p. 35.

more than a human nature in order to be practiced. There are no grounds to suspect that enslaved Africans lacked something necessary to pray, in Aquinas's sense of the word. The fact that they were often denied education and adequate Christian formation is not disqualifying,[40] nor is the fact that many retained connections to traditional African lifeways.[41] These persons were human, therefore rational. They had the capacity for prayer, and they used it.

The mere fact that such enslaved persons prayed is noteworthy, but how they did so also deserves further theological attention. To the question about whether prayer must be vocal, Aquinas offers a characteristically nuanced response. He retains the possibility of praying silently to God in the solitude of one's individual mind, something that enslaved persons did as well.[42] At the same time, he emphasizes that the Latin term for prayer (*oratio*) is derived from words that mean "spoken reason" (*oris ratio*).[43] He recognizes that public, liturgical settings require the officiant to pray out loud. More significantly, he constructs a threefold argument for the positive value of vocal prayer, which applies to individual and communal contexts alike. He notes that such outward ex-

[40] Although conversion to Christianity was frequently cited as a rationalization for enslaving non-Christians, including Africans, the religious instruction to facilitate such conversion was often lacking. Reasons for this included the unwanted expense, racist assumptions that Blacks had inferior minds, and fears that Christianized slaves would "think themselves equal to white folks" (Raboteau, *Slave Religion*, 102). When education was given, the central message was to be docile and submissive, but enslaved Africans discovered other, more liberative meanings in the Bible that inspired their songs and prayers (Copeland, *Knowing Christ Crucified*, 22).

[41] According to the bishops at the Second Vatican Council, "The Catholic Church rejects nothing that is true and holy in [non-Christian] religions" and urges its members to "recognize, preserve and promote the good things, spiritual and moral, as well as the socio-cultural values found among [them]." This includes African traditions. See *Nostra Aetate*, no. 2 (October 28, 1965).

[42] *STh* II-II q. 83, a. 12, corp. Barbara A. Holmes recovers the silent, contemplative dimension of Black spirituality, arguing that "we must find the stillness at the core of the shout." See her *Joy Unspeakable: Contemplative Practices of the Black Church*, 2nd ed. (Fortress Press, 2017), 22.

[43] *STh* II-II, q. 83, a. 1, corp.

pression helps to "excite interior devotion," allows the body to participate in paying God what is due, and manifests "a certain overflow from the soul into the body, through excess of feeling."[44] This argument emphasizes a strong sense of body–soul unity that could remind one of Black spirituality.

Aquinas's mention of devotion (*devotio*) recalls his discussion of this topic in the previous question of the *Summa Theologiae*, where he defines it as "the will to give oneself readily to things concerning the service of God."[45] A broad sense of the word "prayer" could include such a willing gift of oneself, but Aquinas identifies prayer more narrowly with petition.[46] He treats devotion as another act of religion that, though closely related to prayer, more properly belongs to the will than to reason.[47] However, devotion is not therefore irrational. Aquinas explains that it is caused by an act of "contemplation" (*contemplatio*) or "meditation" (*meditatio*). He uses these words more or less synonymously here to designate a consideration of divine greatness and human frailty, which moves the will to surrender itself to God.[48] As we shall see, the spirituals show ample evidence of both prayer and devotion, understood in these senses.

The spirituals do not merely vocalize these acts of religion. They express them in song. Aquinas wholeheartedly approves of such a practice. Drawing on Aristotle, Boethius, and Augustine, he maintains that "the human soul is moved in various ways according to various melodies of sound," and he concludes that "the use of music in the divine praises is a salutary institution, that the souls of the faint-hearted may be the more incited to devotion."[49] In his replies to objections, he does argue that preaching should be prioritized over singing—not a surprise given that he belongs

[44] *STh* II-II, q. 83, a. 12, corp.
[45] *STh* II-II, q. 82, a. 1, corp.
[46] Brian Davies, "Prayer," in *The Oxford Handbook of Aquinas*, ed. Brian Davies and Eleanor Stump (Oxford University Press, 2012), 467–74, at 467.
[47] *STh* II-II, q. 82, a. 1, corp. and ad 3.
[48] *STh* II-II, q. 82, a. 3, corp.
[49] *STh* II-II, q. 91, a. 2, corp.

to the Order of Preachers.[50] He cares more about truth than aesthetics. Nevertheless, he also acknowledges the value of musical worship even when its content is lost on some participants: "even if some of them understand not what is sung, yet they understand why it is sung, namely, for God's glory: and this is enough to arouse their devotion."[51] On Thomistic grounds, the musicality of the spirituals is a major plus.

Aquinas explains that the goodness of an act of prayer largely depends on the kinds of desires it conveys. A beautifully sung prayer that sought the wrong things would be a bad prayer. Citing Romans 8:26, he acknowledges that humans often do not ask for what they ought and that, in such cases, their petitions will not be answered.[52] Nevertheless, commenting on the same passage from Romans, he maintains that the Holy Spirit helps us pray rightly "by inspiring us with holy desires."[53] Moreover, he argues that the Lord's Prayer offers us a perfect template for purifying and ordering our desires.[54] As he says elsewhere, "in this prayer the entirety of what we desire is contained."[55]

As a general philosophical principle, Aquinas holds that we should pray for intrinsically good things that we "cannot ill use, because they cannot have an evil result." This criterion excludes "riches," "honors," "powers," "splendid marriages," and other external status symbols that may increase vice and lead to moral ruin. At the same time, it encourages prayers for goods that are "the object of beatitude and whereby we merit it: and these the saints seek absolutely when they pray, as in Ps. 79:4, 'Show us Thy face, and we shall be saved,' and again in Ps. 118:35, 'Lead me into the path of Thy commandments.' "[56] One is on sure ground, then, when praying for the vision of God, eternal beatitude, and

---

[50] *STh* II-II, q. 91, a. 2, ad 3.

[51] *STh* II-II, q. 91, a. 2, ad 5.

[52] *STh* II-II, q. 82, a. 5, obj. 1.

[53] *STh* II-II, q. 82, a. 5, ad 1 and sed contra.

[54] For a thorough discussion, see Paul Murray, OP, *Praying with Confidence: Aquinas on the Lord's Prayer* (Continuum, 2010).

[55] *Super Evangelium S. Matthaei Lectura*, ch. 6, lect. 3.

[56] *STh* II-II, q. 82, a. 5, corp.

total conformity to God's will. Such desires are undeniably holy.

Between morally ambiguous worldly things for which one should not pray and the morally transcendent hopes of complete sanctification and everlasting union with God for which one certainly should pray, Aquinas acknowledges a third category of temporal goods that are acceptable to seek insofar as they are instrumental toward attaining such lofty ends. He considers it appropriate, then, to pray for worldly things that are needed to sustain "the life of the body" and support "acts of virtue."[57] Depending on one's circumstances, this category might include food, clothes, shelter, safety, health, livelihood, and—I would add—deliverance from the unjust institution of chattel slavery, which was detrimental to both body and spirit.

Studying the sequence of petitions in the Lord's Prayer, Aquinas argues that it fittingly asks first for God to be praised ("Hallowed be Thy name"), then for our everlasting inclusion in this worship ("Thy kingdom come"), then for the meritorious character by which we may attain this end ("Thy will be done on earth as it is in heaven"), and then for the sacramental and material means that we need to develop such a character ("Give us this day our daily bread"). Praying rightly means desiring God above all else, but it also involves asking for gifts that humans need to survive, flourish, and grow in charity. Aquinas interprets the final petitions of the Lord's Prayer as requests to be freed from "obstacles" such as sins, temptations, and all the evils of this fallen world.[58] If slavery is recognized as the terrible evil that it is, then prayers seeking its abolition correspond perfectly with Jesus's final plea, "Deliver us from evil." The Lord's Prayer is an abolitionist text.

Some scholars have thought that the desires articulated in the spirituals are mainly for a heavenly life to come, while others have argued that such eschatological references are coded language pointing to historical aspirations that the enslaved community was not free to express openly.[59] My view, in keeping with Aquinas's

[57] *STh* II-II, q. 83, a. 6, corp.

[58] *STh* II-II, q. 83, a. 9, corp.

[59] For a discussion of this spectrum of views, including a critique of Ben-

list of appropriate desires in prayer, is that these songs function at both levels simultaneously. They are polysemic works of art and worship, which express a holistic longing for freedom. Aquinas's theory of the multiple senses of scripture may be extended analogically to the spirituals, insofar as they, too, signify things with words (e.g., by referring literally to heaven) and signify things with things (e.g., by using heaven as a symbol for all the types of deliverance they desire, including sociopolitical).[60]

In Aquinas's treatments of prayer in the *Summa contra Gentiles* and the *Compendium Theologiae*, he emphasizes that prayer is part of God's providential governance of the universe. He explains that our petitions neither communicate information God lacks nor change God's will, since God is omniscient and immutable. Nevertheless, this does not mean that prayer does nothing. God's ability to fulfill those requests from us that speak the very desires that God inspires in us is included within God's providential care for creation and in no way contradicts it. Going beyond the common idea that prayer only works transformatively on us, Aquinas goes so far as to say that "prayers and pious desires are the cause of some of the things done by God." Righteous prayers exercise a secondary causality that is created and sustained by God's primary causality. Aquinas sums up his logic with a convincing analogy: "To say, therefore, that we must not pray that we may obtain something from God, because the order of His providence is unchangeable, is like saying that we must not walk in order to arrive at a place, nor eat that we may have nourishment, both of which are clearly absurd." God has made us to acquire what we need in part through prayer, and therefore praying can be effective.[61]

Believing that God is providential enables one to pray with confidence and to hope that a response will soon come. On this

jamin Mays's thesis that the spirituals are primarily "other-worldly" and "compensatory," see James H. Cone, *The Spirituals and the Blues: An Interpretation* (Orbis Books, 2008), 13–18.

[60] *STh* I, q. 1, a. 10, corp.

[61] *ScG* III, qq. 95–96. For a more detailed discussion, see Rudi te Velde, "Thomas Aquinas's Understanding of Prayer in Light of the Doctrine of *Creatio ex Nihilo*," *Modern Theology* 29, no. 2 (April 2013): 49–61.

basis, Aquinas declares that "all diffidence should be banished from our lives."[62] He urges us to remember that all things are possible for God and that God has a special care for human beings. The spirituals reflect a similarly high degree of trust in God. Amid the horrible conditions of slavery, which could give one ample reason to despair, these songs reveal an almost incredible hope in God's protective, loving action. Yet this point must be held in tension with the apparent failures of providence, the just prayers for liberation that have gone unanswered, the sorrows too deep for words that instead find expression in screams and moans, and the devastating feelings of Godforsakenness comparable to Jesus's on the cross,[63] which are evident in the same songs. The spirituals are at once hope and pain.

Many of the prayers and hymns attributed to Aquinas,[64] particularly those in *The Office of the Feast of Corpus Christi*,[65] are connected to the Mass. They praise the "hidden Deity, / Under these appearances concealed" and rejoice in "this supper of our new King."[66] Since the spirituals are typically composed outside the context of Catholic liturgy, they do not share the same Eucharistic focus.[67] However, when Aquinas prays for virtue and eternal

---

[62] *Compendium Theologiae*, chap. 6.

[63] In his commentary on the Gospel of Matthew, Aquinas clarifies that, although Jesus's cry of dereliction shows him speaking "according as he is a man," it should not be understood in an Arian or Nestorian sense, as implying a separation from the divine nature (*Super Evangelium S. Matthaei Lectura*, chap. 27, lect. 2).

[64] Any mystical or ecstatic experiences attested in early hagiographies are difficult to verify historically. See M. B. Crowe, "On Re-Writing the Biography of Aquinas," *Irish Theological Quarterly* 14, no. 4 (1974): 255–73. For this reason, I limit my account of Aquinas's personal spirituality to prayers and hymns that are thought to have been his direct compositions.

[65] For background on this liturgical feast and Aquinas's contribution to it, see Paul Murray, OP, *Aquinas at Prayer: The Bible, Mysticism, and Poetry* (Bloomsbury, 2013), 167–75.

[66] *The Aquinas Prayer Book: The Prayers and Hymns of St. Thomas Aquinas*, trans. and ed. Robert Anderson and Johann Moser (Sophia Institute Press, 2000), 69, 103.

[67] To be clear, Black Catholics have long blended a Eucharistic faith with Black spirituality. We might consider the Venerable Augustus Tolton, the former slave whom God called to the priesthood on the Feast of Corpus

life in the same sacramentally oriented texts, strong thematic connections with the spirituals are discernible. For example, in his "Longer Prayer after Communion" (*Gratias tibi ago*), he asks that Christ's presence may "remove my vices / and increase in me / charity, / patience, / humility, / obedience, / and all virtues" and that it may "give me final happiness."[68] Such desires appear in Aquinas's less Eucharistically specified prayers, as well such as "For Ordering a Life Wisely" (*Concede mihi*) and "For the Attainment of Heaven" (*Te Deum totius consolationis*).[69] Such requests for a sanctified life and heavenly bliss resonate both with Aquinas's teachings on the proper desires to voice in prayer and, as we shall see, with the lyrical content of many spirituals.

Even so, we must acknowledge another significant difference: Aquinas's prayers are not written from a condition of oppression and do not express an urgent longing for social change. Although he teaches that it is good to pray for certain necessities of life, they do not figure prominently in the prayers written by his hand (at least the ones we have). In one case, he prays for all "transitory things" (*transitoria*) to pass away, and there is little reason to think he intends this apocalyptic hope to be read as a metaphor for historical liberation. In another case, he does recognize "temporal goods" (*temporalia*) as gifts from God but only in very general terms.[70] By contrast, the spirituals are suffused with very specific experiences of suffering, which lead them to seek a very particular deliverance that would be both eschatological and historical.[71] In theory, Aquinas is not opposed to this sort

---

Christi, the same day he received his first communion. We might also think of the spirituals that are included in *Lead Me, Guide Me* (1987), the hymnal used by many historically Black Catholic parishes. See Caroline Hemesath, *From Slave to Priest: A Biography of the Rev. Augustine Tolton (1854–1897): First Afro-American Priest of the United States* (Franciscan Herald Press, 1973), 27, and M. Shawn Copeland, "*The African American Hymnal* and the African American Spiritual," in *Black Catholic Studies Reader: History and Theology*, ed. David J. Endres (Catholic University of America Press, 2021), 141–61.

[68] *Aquinas Prayer Book*, 83.

[69] *Aquinas Prayer Book*, 5, 53.

[70] *Aquinas Prayer Book*, 7, 19.

[71] This spiritual struggle for deliverance did not end with the abolition

of prayer. In practice, his interests lie elsewhere. This difference indicates that the Thomistic tradition of spirituality has much to learn from the Black tradition about what prayer means in contexts of injustice.

Prayer in the Spirituals

Viewed from Aquinas's perspective, the spirituals are prayerful songs of rational creatures seeking to enunciate, interpret, and realize their holy desires. To be sure, they are full of pathos. Their words and melodies evoke powerful feelings that range from sorrow to joy. Commenting on this emotional spectrum, an early twentieth-century anthologizer James Weldon Johnson contrasts the lines "Sometimes I feel like a motherless child" and "Sometimes I feel like an eagle in de air."[72] These sentiments are not unreasonable, given the circumstances. They are appropriate responses to the agony of life under slavery, on the one hand, and the community's awesome experiences of God's presence and promise, on the other. However, these songs evince more than such emotional intelligence (vital as that is).

Analyzing the themes favored by many of their lyricists, Johnson detects a rigorous form of theological reasoning: "as God saved Daniel in the lion's den, so would He save them; as God preserved the Hebrew children in the fiery furnace, so would He preserve them; as God delivered Israel out of bondage in Egypt, so would He deliver them."[73] These examples show a clear pattern: A premise supplied by biblical faith supports a practical conclusion about what hopes are right to vocalize for one's community now. Finally, their distinctive style also bespeaks a certain artistic genius

---

of slavery. Black freedom fighters have continued to use these songs for strength and inspiration into the twentieth century and beyond. For this story of ongoing reception, see Cheryl A. Kirk-Duggan, *Exorcizing Evil: A Womanist Perspective on the Spirituals* (Orbis Books, 1997).

[72]James Weldon Johnson, "Preface," in *The Books of American Negro Spirituals*, ed. James Weldon Johnson, musical arrangements by J. Rosamund Johnson (Da Capo Press, 2002), 11–50, at 41.

[73]Johnson, "Preface," 20.

and hard-won folk wisdom, which should not be underestimated. Johnson describes the use of traditional African rhythms, call-and-response structures, and verbal repetitions, which intentionally encourage full bodily and communal participation, and marvels at how seamlessly they are combined with Christian motifs that bring practical solace and strength in the midst of oppression.[74] The creative blending of these elements makes the full and brilliant humanity of the spirituals' composers unmistakable.

The Black theologian James Cone makes a similar point when he observes that "there is a complex world of *thought* underlying the slave songs."[75] This "thought"—a work of the rational powers of the soul—largely takes the form of interpreted desire, which is to say, prayer. Enslaved persons made sense of the longings of their hearts by voicing them to God. To understand their minds, it is helpful to consider what they sought through song. As in Aquinas, so too in the spirituals, desires for moral sanctification and everlasting beatitude are evident. In the case of the spirituals, however, these desires are more explicitly connected with a comprehensive hope for deliverance from evil that had concrete, abolitionist implications. *To be free*—that was the fundamental yearning: free from the weight of personal sin by means of virtue, free from the sting of death through the gift of a happy afterlife, and free from all the hardships and injustices that constituted the system of slavery. If one only enjoyed the last possibility in another world beyond the grave, then so be it, but the desire was for slavery to end now, or as soon as possible, through the cooperative action of God and humans in history. This Black spirituality of freedom both coheres with Aquinas's spirituality in

---

[74]Johnson, "Preface," 21–28. John Lovell Jr. demonstrates the aesthetic originality of this music in his *Black Song: The Force and the Flame: The Story of How the Afro-American Spiritual Was Hammered Out* (Macmillan, 1972). Lauri Ramey analyzes the poetic quality of the spirituals in her *Slave Songs and the Birth of African American Poetry* (Palgrave Macmillan, 2008). There is no denying the artistry of these songs.

[75]Cone, *Spirituals and the Blues*, 19, italics in the original. For a fuller treatment of Cone's approach to prayer, see my *Thinking Prayer: Theology and Spirituality amid the Crises of Modernity* (University of Notre Dame Press, 2015), chap. 6.

many crucial respects and develops spirituality in new directions by highlighting its socially transformative power.

As an example of prayer for an improved moral character, consider the spiritual "Lord, Make Me More Patient."[76] This first line is repeated three times, followed by the clause, "Until we meet again." A footnote indicates that, as the song continues, the word "patient" is replaced by additional adjectives "expressive of the virtues," such as "holy, loving, peaceful, etc." Other examples abound. The spiritual "Just Now" repeats the request "Sanctify me" upward of five times, asking for a moral reformation that would come through the gracious power of God.[77] Making a Christological connection, the spiritual "Lord, Remember Me" features a verse in which everyone singing expresses a personal longing to imitate the Son in his final hour: "I want to die like-a Jesus die, and he die wid a free good will."[78] This last phrase, "a free good will," demonstrates that the principal desire here is not for more suffering. It is for Christlike holiness and the interior freedom it implies. Finally, although it is styled more as an exhortation than a petition, the spiritual "You Must Be Pure and Holy" indicates a desire for that meritorious ordering of one's life that would facilitate one's reunion with God.[79]

Such virtue-seeking songs are intermingled with many, such as "In the Mansions Above," that anticipate a glorious life after death. Those singing this spiritual cry out, "My Lord, I hope to meet my Jesus in de manshans above." They want to be present with the risen Lord in this exalted place and thereby find freedom from the "many crosses an' trials" they have suffered "here below."[80] There is no need to doubt the literal, eschatological meaning of the desires voiced in this song in order to appreciate

[76]William Francis Allen, Charles Pickard Ware, and Lucy McKim Garrison, eds., *Slave Songs of the United States: The Classic 1867 Anthology* no. 71 (Dover, 1995), 52. Among collections of the spirituals, this very early one has the advantage of preserving lyrics and melodies obtained through direct contact with enslaved persons on plantations.

[77]Allen, Ware, and Garrison, *Slave Songs*, nos. 85, 67.

[78]Allen, Ware, and Garrison, *Slave Songs*, nos. 15, 12.

[79]Allen, Ware, and Garrison, *Slave Songs*, nos. 129, 107.

[80]Allen, Ware, and Garrison, *Slave Songs*, nos. 79, 59.

that it also offers its participants an emancipatory image, which could inspire struggles for greater material freedom prior to death.

Other spirituals more obviously work at both levels. The one called "Many Thousand Go," which the collectors note "had been sung in secret to avoid detection" by slaveowners who would not have condoned its message, proceeds through a litany of repeated "No more" verses: "No more peck o' corn for me," "No more pint o' salt for me," "No more hundred lash for me," "No more mistress' call for me." The editors clarify that these measures of corn and salt were "slavery's rations."[81] Every lyric in this passionate hymn is tied to details of the slave experience. The spiritual "I Want to Go Home" similarly calls for "no sun to burn you," "no hard trials," "no whips a-crackin'," "no stormy weather," "no tribulation," "no more slavery," and "no evil-doers." When it concludes by repeating the line, "all is gladness in de kingdom," it seems to speak literally of eternity and figuratively of historical possibilities that God may fulfill in this world.[82] In either case, it clearly condemns slavery as something antithetical to the coming kingdom and the will of God that is supposed to be done on earth as in heaven. Echoes of the Lord's Prayer are everywhere—and, in fact, it was sometimes sung as a spiritual by the Fisk Jubilee Singers.[83] The final petition, which seeks deliverance from evil, can be heard indirectly in the spiritual "O Daniel," which culminates with the plaintive lines, "O my Lord delivered Daniel, O why not deliver me too?"[84]

I have claimed that the spirituals are songs of both prayer and devotion, as Aquinas uses these terms. A good example of devotion—that is, a willing gift of oneself to God—can be found in the spiritual "I Wish I Been Dere," which emphasizes the singer's desire for the whole community ("mother," "sister," "brother," and "I") to "follow Jesus," "fight" alongside him, and wear his

[81] Allen, Ware, and Garrison, *Slave Songs*, nos. 64, 48.

[82] Allen, Ware, and Garrison, *Slave Songs*, nos. 61, 46.

[83] J. B. T. Marsh, *The Story of the Jubilee Singers with Their Songs*, 3rd ed. (Hodder and Stoughton, 1875), 222.

[84] Allen, Ware, and Garrison, *Slave Songs*, nos. 114, 94.

"crown."[85] In like manner, the spiritual "Hold Out to the End" repeats this titular phrase many times and concludes with the line, "It is my 'termination for to hold out to the end." This song is not so much a request for God's grace as an expression of a soul determined to persist in doing what God commands. Its author's admirable goal is to have the whole community ("all dem Mount Zion member") stay on the right path through life's "ups and downs" and regardless of whether "the cross come or no come."[86] These songs, and others like them, reveal a devout people striving to surrender themselves completely to God.

Although their suffering was great, they tried not to lose hope. Honestly expressing their griefs to God seemed to help. The spiritual "Nobody Knows the Trouble I've Had" names the mysterious depths of anguish enslaved African Americans bore in their spirits and flesh. The pain was so deep no one could understand it, except the crucified Lord: "Nobody knows but Jesus."[87] There is nothing quite like this raw confession of hurt in Aquinas's works. His discussion of the Psalms—including ones involving desperate pleas and laments, such as 21, 26, 39, and 54 in the Vulgate numbering—might offer some basis for connection,[88] but his account of such prayers mainly proceeds in the doctrinally expository fashion typical of his biblical commentaries. We never hear Aquinas report about himself, as this spiritual's author does, "Sometimes I'm down, / Sometimes I'm almost on the groun'."[89] His hymns could never be dubbed "Sorrow Songs."[90]

What difference does it make to pray from such depths? It does not, as one might expect, decrease the level of trust that one is able to place in God's providence. The spiritual "Jehovah, Hallelujah" gives voice to a salient theme in these songs when it

[85] Allen, Ware, and Garrison, *Slave Songs*, nos. 39, 29.

[86] Allen, Ware, and Garrison, *Slave Songs*, nos. 76, 57.

[87] Allen, Ware, and Garrison, *Slave Songs*, nos. 74, 55.

[88] *In Psalmos Davidis Expositio*, Psalms 21, 26, 39, 54, and Murray, *Aquinas at Prayer*, 131–42.

[89] Allen, Ware, and Garrison, *Slave Songs*, nos. 74, 55.

[90] See the classic essay on the "Sorrow Songs" in W. E. B. Du Bois, *The Souls of Black Folk* (Simon & Schuster, 2009), 240–54.

proclaims, "De Lord is perwide" (i.e., the Lord will provide).[91] While the experience of oppression does not necessarily reduce confidence in God's omnipotent goodness, it does give this confidence a more critical edge vis-à-vis the powers of the world. It inspires politically charged apocalyptic rhetoric, as the spiritual called "The Day of Judgment" attests: "And de moon will turn to blood. In dat day—O-yoy, my soul!"[92] To pray, sing, and shout in such a way is to give rightful worship to the God who ultimately will not tolerate such evil. The prayers *de profoundis* lifted up by enslaved Black persons were rational acts of religion that simultaneously praised the crucified and risen Lord and challenged an unjust social order.

Conclusion

It is impossible to know exactly what Aquinas would pray for if he were alive today or somehow transported into our world. What desires would move his heart? How would he interpret them before God? I would like to think that the spirituals—and all the tender memories of suffering and hope they preserve—would inform his spirituality. He would bring them before the Blessed Sacrament, as he laid his soul bare and sought a deeper contemplation of the mystery of God. Perhaps when reciting his prayer "For the Forgiveness of Sins" (*Ad te fontem*), as he reached the part where he confesses his own faults, he would think of his defense of slavery and experience remorse: "For in sinning, / I have offended you, my God; / I have harmed my neighbor; / I have not even spared myself injury."[93] Catholics would do well to say this prayer with Aquinas as they reflect on how deeply their church has been involved in slavery, racism, and other injustices.

It is not too late for Thomistic spirituality and Black spirituality to develop a real synergy—not unlike that which Aquinas (*pace* Tertullian) powerfully orchestrated between Athens and Jerusa-

[91] Allen, Ware, and Garrison, *Songs*, nos. 2, 2.
[92] Allen, Ware, and Garrison, *Songs*, nos. 72, 53.
[93] *Aquinas Prayer Book*, 47.

lem. He showed that wisdom traditions from different cultural and historical contexts can come together to form a whole that is greater than the sum of its parts. In addition to his teachings on prayer, we ought to retrieve his synthetic prowess and apply it in those new dialogical circumstances that our epoch imposes on us. The conversation in theology today is not just about how Athens relates to Jerusalem but also about how Europe and America relate to Africa, how the Global North relates to the Global South, how the university relates to social movements, how the memory of the Middle Ages relates to humanity's collective hopes for the future. This chapter has contributed to such discussions by indicating various respects in which Aquinas's understanding and practice of prayer illuminate the slave spirituals, and vice versa, but more work remains to be done in spirituality and other theological and philosophical areas. Aquinas's genius for integrating diverse elements can be a guiding light in such labors. Moreover, as we do this thinking, it remains necessary to pray with the unknown authors of the spirituals: no more slavery, no more oppression, no more abuse, no more dehumanization, no more hatred, no more segregation, no more evil, because "all is gladness in de kingdom."[94]

[94] Allen, Ware, and Garrison, *Slave Songs*, nos. 61, 46.

3

Spiritual Resistance to Race-Related Sexual Violence

Black and Native Perspectives

In North America today, the term "race" simultaneously conceals and reveals two world-shattering facts and their aftermath. Serving as a euphemism, it enables one to allude to these historical realities in polite conversation without really facing their horrors. These facts are, first, the genocidal conquest of Indigenous peoples by European settler colonists and, second, the trans-Atlantic slave trade—the trafficking of human beings mainly from West Africa to meet the colonists' demands for unpaid agricultural labor. Land was stolen, bodies were shackled, and countless lives were destroyed so that a privileged few could increase their private capital.[1] Conquest and slavery are the original sins of this continent.

A draft of this chapter was first presented on March 31, 2022, as a keynote lecture at a conference hosted by Gonzaga University in Spokane, Washington. The theme of the conference was, "'Our transgressions before you are many, and our sins testify against us' (Is 59:12a): Re-Imagining Church in Light of Colonization and Catholic Sexual Abuse."

[1]David E. Stannard, *American Holocaust: The Conquest of the New World* (Oxford University Press, 1993); George E. Tinker, *Missionary Conquest: The Gospel and Native American Cultural Genocide* (Fortress Press, 1993); and Nicholas Radburn, *Traders in Men: Merchants and the Transformation of the Transatlantic Slave Trade* (Yale University Press, 2023).

Their aftermath includes lynchings, massacres, displacements, disenfranchisements, deprivations, incarcerations, exclusions, commodifications, and intergenerational traumas. These forces have affected not only people whose genealogies are exclusively African or Native but also people who have mixed ancestry, whether they identify as Black, Indian, creole, *mestizo/a*, or in some other way. Immigrants from Asia, Oceana, the Middle East, and other parts of the world who do not meet the current standards of Whiteness, which have shifted over time,[2] and more recent immigrants from Africa whose ancestors were not brought as slaves, find themselves swept up into the whirlpool of this violent North American history and must struggle to find their bearings within it. These are the indelicate facts behind the word "race."

With the phrase "race-related sexual violence" I mean to indicate a dense cluster of complicated problems. I am thinking, for example, about the ways that White supremacy has been propelled by lust, greed, and other disordered forms of eros; the ways that the bodies of Black, Native, and other people of color have been exotified and objectified, including in pornographic and other demeaning pop cultural representations; the ways that some women in these communities have been coerced into conditions of sexual and reproductive servitude or subjected to forced sterilization; the ways that some racially oppressed men have engaged in sexually abusive behavior in unhealthy attempts to resist racist forms of emasculation and dehumanization; the ways that the supposed need to protect White women's sexual purity has been used to justify lynching, as well as legal and cultural norms against miscegenation; and the ways that darkly hued people have been made to feel ashamed of their bodies, sexually inadequate, ugly, dirty, or unworthy of love.[3] To this list, one

[2]David R. Roediger, *Working Toward Whiteness: How America's Immigrants Became White* (Basic Books, 2005).

[3]Marianne O. Nielsen and Karen Jarratt-Snider, eds., *Indigenous Justice and Gender* (Arizona University Press, 2023), 7–12; Sarah Deer, *The Beginning and End of Rape: Confronting Sexual Violence in Native America* (University of Minnesota Press, 2015); Bryan N. Massingale, "The Erotic Life of Anti-Blackness: Police Sexual Violation of Black Bodies," in *Anti-*

must add the instances in which representatives of the church, whether at residential schools, parishes, or in other contexts, have molested or raped vulnerable children of color, often seeking them out precisely because their racially marginalized status made it less likely that a clerical or legal authority would intervene.[4] This is not a complete list. These are just a few salient examples that reveal a pervasive linking of the violence that is called racial with the violence that is called sexual. As Cornel West puts the point, "Everyone knows it is virtually impossible to talk candidly about race without talking about sex."[5]

I do not intend to define what "sexuality" means in any exact sense. I prefer, rather, to suggest in a more general way that it is associated with desires, bodies, intimacies, vulnerabilities, and hopes for fulfillment. To harm this aspect of our humanity or to use it to harm others is a very serious sin and an offense against God. God has made these things. They are among the best and most beautiful mysteries in creation, and they reflect something of the divine nature, insofar as it too goes outside of itself to risk deep communion with another. Sexuality is meant to be an image of divine love.[6] And yet, in the hands of what has been called

---

Blackness and Christian Ethics, ed. Vincent W. Lloyd and Andrew Prevot (Orbis Books, 2018), 173–94; Traci C. West, *Wounds of the Spirit: Black Women, Violence, and Resistance Ethics* (New York University Press, 1999); Delores S. Williams, *Sisters in the Wilderness: The Challenge of Womanist God-Talk* (Orbis Books, 2003), 67–71; M. Shawn Copeland, "'Wading through Many Sorrows': Toward a Theology of Suffering in Womanist Perspective," in *A Troubling in My Soul: Womanist Perspectives on Evil and Suffering*, ed. Emilie M. Townes (Orbis Books, 1993), 109–29; Emilie M. Townes, *In a Blaze of Glory: Womanist Spirituality as Social Witness* (Abingdon Press, 1995), 68–88.

[4]Jack Lee Downey, "Colonialism Is Abuse: Reconsidering Triumphalist Narratives in Catholic Studies," *American Catholic Studies* 130, no. 2 (2019): 16–20; Tiffany Stanley and Lea Skene, "In the U.S., Black Survivors Are Nearly Invisible in the Catholic Clergy Sexual Abuse Crisis," *Associated Press*, November 29, 2023; and Sari Horwitz et al., "In the Name of God," *Washington Post*, May 29, 2024.

[5]Cornel West, *Race Matters*, 25th anniversary ed. (Beacon Press, 2017), 83.

[6]Kelly Brown Douglas, *Sexuality and the Black Church: A Womanist Perspective* (Orbis Books, 1999), 112–20; Marvin M. Ellison, "Reimagining

"race," sexuality has become a site of cruelties so severe they make one think of the devil. The sexual violation of Black and Native bodies is a nightmare in which all that happens is the polar opposite of what it should be. Where there should be warmth, there is cold-heartedness. In place of embodied pleasure and joy, there is lasting trauma and disassociation. In lieu of trusting, life-giving relationships, one finds only manipulations, cover-ups, and codes of silence.

We must resist this demonic force with all our heart, all our soul, all our mind, and all our strength (cf. Mark 12:30), for to love God and to combat this great evil are, in a sense, one and the same. However, the possibility of a specifically *spiritual* resistance to race-related sexual violence is fraught. This is so for at least two different reasons. First, there is the problem of Christian complicity in this violence. The difficulty here is not only that individuals who have considered themselves Christian have been perpetrators. A more devastating fact is that Christian institutions, teachings, and practices have abetted such wrongdoing to the point that resistance to race-related sexual violence could meaningfully be understood as a fight against Christianity as it has actually existed (which can be distinguished from how it should ideally exist).

The second reason that the prospect of a specifically spiritual resistance to race-related sexual violence is fraught has to do with a prevailing sense that what is needed, above all, is collective political action. This action aims to take power away from the persons, groups, and churches that are causing the harm. These entities must be compelled to stop their violence and be held accountable in public ways, such as by criminal or civil courts. There is also a need for new policies, programs, and investments oriented toward public safety, economic reparations, and tribal sovereignty, among other pressing agenda items. A suggestion that spirituality is the

---

Good Sex: The Eroticizing of Mutual Respect and Pleasure," in *Sexuality and the Sacred: Sources for Theological Reflection*, 2nd ed., ed. Marvin M. Ellison and Kelly Brown Douglas (Westminster John Knox Press, 2010), 245–61; and Rowan D. Williams, "The Body's Grace," in *Theology and Sexuality: Classic and Contemporary Sources*, ed. Eugene F. Rogers Jr. (Blackwell, 2002), 309–21.

answer could seem to imply that prayers, sacraments, or rituals of healing are an adequate substitute for legal proceedings and structural changes, which, of course, they are not.

These concerns must be taken seriously in any account of how spirituality contributes to the practice of resistance. They do not so much delegitimize a spiritual approach as demonstrate that it must be pluralistic, politically engaged, and victim- and survivor-centered. In the remainder of this chapter, I highlight the perspectives of some Black and Native writers who show that spirituality plays an important role in the struggle against race-related sexual violence. I first discuss several Black perspectives, then several Native ones. I cannot promise to be representative, let alone comprehensive in my analysis. My hope is merely to shed light on the complexity and severity of various forms of race-related sexual violence and to gesture toward some of the spiritual traditions that have contributed to efforts of resistance.

Some of these sources, such as Alice Walker and Inés Talamantez, reveal that the most helpful spiritual traditions are not always Christian. As a Catholic theologian, I accept this fact with humility. Because Christianity has been tied to race-related sexual violence, it can be an impediment to healing for many people. Moreover, to insist on the universal superiority of Christian spirituality would repeat the very dominative mind-set that has fueled Christian complicity from the start. Other sources, such as M. Shawn Copeland and Marie Therese Archambault, describe positive ways that the God of Christian revelation has been experienced and mediated through African and Indigenous cultures, and their voices deserve our attention as well. Appreciating these creative inculturations of the gospel allows one to honor the embodied choices of Black and Native Christians who have found something other than violence in their Christian faith. Many people of color perceive the life, death, and resurrection of Jesus as a precious symbol of divine love, which affirms their human dignity and empowers them to resist oppression. Spiritual resistance to race-related sexual violence draws on diverse religious and nonreligious traditions, and each of these must be respected for the good work it does to overcome evil and promote justice and well-being.

A politically engaged spirituality of resistance must wrestle with persistent tensions that affect Black and Native communities in different ways. For example, there is a tension between a need for public justice and a learned distrust of the U.S. justice system. There is a tension between the demand for White institutions to do more and the assertion of self-determination and sovereignty on the part of Black and Native peoples. And there is a tension between fighting enemies that come from the outside and struggling with internal challenges in oneself, one's family, or one's racial group. There is no simple, uniform answer to this great cluster of problems, but a new synthesis of spirituality and political action can help each person discern how best to engage them. Amid the evil of race-related sexual violence, spirituality can become a source of incalculable good if it takes on a holistic, antiracist, decolonial, and reparative agenda that prioritizes the agency and flourishing of those who have been harmed and affirms that the divine Creator is with them.

Black Perspectives

In *The Cross and the Lynching Tree*, the Black liberation theologian James Cone notes that between the years 1880 and 1940, there were nearly five thousand documented lynchings of Black women, men, and children in the United States. This number does not include the lynchings of Native, Latine, and Asian persons that also occurred during this violent period of U.S. history. Lynchings were acts of brutality. They often took place in the light of day, as spectacles enjoyed by crowds. Their mode of attack varied. It could involve hanging, beating, shooting, stabbing, or burning. In many cases, it included the mutilation of sexual organs. Cone explains, "It was a family affair, a ritual celebration of white supremacy, where women and children were often given the first opportunity to torture black victims—burning black flesh and cutting off genitals, fingers, toes, and ears as souvenirs."[7]

This theatrical display of very real cruelty was regarded as a

[7] James H. Cone, *The Cross and the Lynching Tree* (Orbis Books, 2011), 3, 9.

type of vigilante justice. It was touted as a communal effort to punish dangerous criminals who had transgressed the religious, moral, and legal codes prohibiting the mixing of races. No such punishment was meted out when White men raped Black women. In such cases, authorities and White citizens looked the other way. But any insinuation of a romantic liaison between a Black man and a White woman, even if the claim were false or the relationship were fully consensual, was prone to cause a ferocious backlash. Rape was the immediate accusation, and it was hurled at Black men whenever a White person wanted a pretext to humiliate and violate them. Lynching was a symbolic means of protecting the supposed sexual purity of the White race and of White women in particular. However, Black men were not its only victims. Cone tells the chilling story of a Black woman from Georgia named Mary Turner who protested her husband's lynching for a crime he did not commit and was herself arrested and given over to the mob. She was stripped naked and set on fire and her unborn child was cut from her womb and trampled to death.[8]

Cone argues that Black people found the strength to resist such race-related sexual violence through prayer, song, and community. He writes, "For most blacks, it was the blues and religion that offered the chief weapons of resistance. At the juke joints on Friday and Saturday nights and at churches on Sunday mornings and evening week nights blacks affirmed their humanity and fought back against dehumanization." Blues music allowed Black people to express and feel their emotions, to love their erotic bodies, and to develop "a cultural defiance against white supremacy." At the same time, spirituals and gospel hymns sung in Black churches emphasized the crucified Christ's solidarity with suffering people and his promise to deliver them from the forces of evil and death. As Cone puts the point, "the spirituals and the church, with Jesus's cross at the heart of its faith, gave birth to the black freedom movement . . . [and gave] people courage to fight."[9] Even if the world was against them, the story of Jesus helped them trust that

[8]Cone, *The Cross and the Lynching Tree*, 7, 120.
[9]Cone, *The Cross and the Lynching Tree*, 12, 28.

God was on their side, and the hope they gained from this conviction enabled them to survive and struggle for a better tomorrow.

The Black Catholic womanist theologian M. Shawn Copeland builds on Cone's perspective by drawing particular attention to the unjust suffering and spiritual agency of poor, despised women of color. In her Madeleva Lecture in Spirituality, called *The Subversive Power of Love*, she discusses the nineteenth-century Catholic free woman of color Henriette Delille, who founded the Sisters of the Holy Family and thereby resisted the sexually coercive practice of concubinage (or *plaçage*) that oppressed many free women of color in her context. Copeland suggests that Delille's spiritual witness, expressed through her establishment of a celibate community devoted to love, prayer, and service, disrupted violent ways of representing Black women's bodies as passive objects of property and exploitation. She argues, "In founding a religious congregation, Henriette Delille asserted black women as fully capable of chastity, as chaste—as fully capable of possessing, choosing, and disposing of themselves and their own bodies." In this context, chastity was an assertion of bodily autonomy. Copeland continues, "[Delille's] vision challenged commonly held readings of those bodies and not only contravened slavery's vicious stereotypes of black women as impious, promiscuous, and lewd, but constructed an alternative to the nineteenth-century system of plaçage in Louisiana."[10] By opting out, Delille and her community affirmed their embodied dignity.

In the same lecture, Copeland attends to the experiences of enslaved Black women, beginning with the prurient examination of their bodies on the auction block. She explains,

> The slave market was awash in sexuality and the rituals of inspection were titillating with "white men, examining slaves, searching out hidden body parts, running hands over limbs, massaging abdomens and articulating pelvic joints, probing wounds and scars with fingers . . ." Slavery traded

---

[10]M. Shawn Copeland, *The Subversive Power of Love: The Vision of Henriette Delille* (Paulist Press, 2009), 5.

> in pornography, in the fantasy that black female bodies existed to satisfy the slaveholder's sexual desire, that her body could be bent and shaped to his appetite.[11]

This sexual objectification of Black women's bodies continued after the auction block on plantations and in master bedrooms. Against their will, enslaved women were used for the purposes of reproduction and pleasure, but above all they were used for power—a form of racial, gender, and socioeconomic domination that made White male slaveowners feel like omnipotent gods, even though in truth they were spiritually and morally warped human beings.

Copeland contends that healing from such collective, intergenerational abuse requires a deep reaffirmation of one's enfleshed freedom. It means learning to love oneself and one's body as mysteries that are sacred and free. It necessitates a "fundamental grasp of the meaning of bodily integrity and the power of eros as holy." These are goods that Delille discovers through her spiritual experiences and practices. Copeland puts the point this way: "I propose that in order to realize her freedom Henriette Delille chose *to love*: that she experienced an attraction toward divine love that blotted out all else, that she recognized, whether gradually or in a single blinding moment, that the meaning of passion and desire are related ineluctably to divine love, to the absolute love of Christ for concrete human beings."[12]

To Cone's and Copeland's Christian theological arguments for a spiritual resistance to race-related sexual violence, I want to add some reflections from the womanist novelist, essayist, and poet Alice Walker. Although she was raised Christian and retains a respect for Black Christian forms of spiritual solidarity and political struggle, she locates her understanding of spirituality mainly beyond or outside of the church. For her, the Spirit is alive in nature, bodies, relationships, and selves that are learning to love. It moves and breathes in African and Indigenous cultures that do

[11] Copeland, *The Subversive Power of Love*, 38.
[12] Copeland, *The Subversive Power of Love*, 47, 52.

not separate it from matter and flesh and that do not imagine it as a White male deity or confine it to clerically governed worship spaces. For Walker, communion with the Spirit grounds a practice of resistance against racist and sexist violence and offers the hope of holistic wellness.

Many people are familiar with her most famous novel, *The Color Purple*. This book tells the coming-of-age story of a young Black woman named Celie, who was sexually abused by her stepfather "Pa" and by her husband "Mr.," also known as Albert. Both of these abusers are Black men who are themselves victims of an oppressive social context that recognizes neither their manhood nor their humanity. The crushing discrimination they suffer is no excuse for their own violent behavior, and at least one of these characters, Albert, eventually learns this crucial lesson, but his story is not Walker's main focus. This is a narrative about Celie and her evolution from praying to a White male god in the sky to perceiving the presence of the divine in the beauty of creation and in her own embodied desires and joys. Her spiritual teacher in this process is also her love interest, the enchanting Black female singer Shug. Shug gives Celie some important theological pointers, for example, "God is inside you and inside everybody else"; "God ain't a he or a she, but a It"; "God is everything . . . that is or ever was or ever will be." Commenting specifically on sexuality, Shug says, "God love all them feelings. That some of the best stuff God did. And when you know God loves 'em you enjoys 'em a lot more." She continues, "Listen, God love everything you love—and a mess of stuff you don't. But more than anything else, God love admiration. . . . I think it pisses God off if you walk by the color purple in a field somewhere and don't notice it."[13]

Walker's naturalist, erotic spirituality might lead one to worry that, by seeming to sanctify every bodily desire, she is giving herself no grounds on which to condemn sexually violent behavior. However, her works clearly indicate that any use of sexuality to control or oppress another is unacceptable. This use—which would be better called abuse—is antithetical to the divine purpose

[13] Alice Walker, *The Color Purple* (Penguin, 2019), 194–95.

of such erotic features of our shared embodied existence, which Walker argues are meant to cultivate wonder, intimacy, and joy. Celie's ability to love her own sexuality as a divine gift frees her to make choices for the sake of her own flourishing. It empowers her to defy the unjust demands of "Mr." and to discover healing and connection.

The child abuse that Walker portrays in the context of Black domestic life has also occurred in other spaces, including churches. While lynching was performed as a public spectacle, clergy sexual abuse of children—particularly children of color—has been a tightly kept secret. The invisibility is part of the pain. The prevalence of such crimes in the Catholic Church came into public consciousness through the reporting of the Spotlight team of *The Boston Globe* in January 2002. This was a pivotal step, yet for nearly two decades afterward, the experiences of racially minoritized victims and survivors were largely sidelined in the conversation. The Black Catholic sociologist Tia Noelle Pratt notes that "to understand why it has taken so long [to address the racial dimensions of clergy sexual abuse], we have to acknowledge just how intricately systemic racism is woven into the fabric of the Church."[14]

In recent years, a clearer picture is starting to emerge of the extent to which abusive priests have preyed on racially marginalized populations and have been intentionally sent into such communities. Personal testimonies of victims and survivors are beginning to break the silence. However, significant barriers remain to reporting, accountability, and true ecclesial solidarity, in part because most dioceses do not collect demographic data on the race of accusers and perpetrators.[15] In John Patrick Shanley's 2004 play, *Doubt: A Parable*, and its 2008 film adaptation, the drama revolves around a White Catholic priest who abuses an isolated Black child. This plot point tragically rings true. There is increasing anecdotal evidence that Black children are often chosen because of their precarious racial status. Moreover, when in rare

---

[14]Tia Noelle Pratt, "Black Catholics, Racism, and the Sex Abuse Crisis: A Personal Reflection," *The Revealer*, March 2, 2020.

[15]Katie Collins Scott, "Catholic Clergy Abuse Survivors of Color Endure Compounded Trauma," *National Catholic Reporter*, September 12, 2023.

cases they do receive financial settlements, the amounts have been shown to be as much as seventeen times lower than the norm.[16] There is also the uncomfortable fact of celebrated Black priests being credibly accused. A particularly disheartening case is that of Thaddeus Posey, OFM, Cap., the founding director of the Institute of Black Catholic Studies at Xavier University of Louisiana and a prominent early leader in the field of Black Catholic theology.[17] Race-related sexual violence attacks Black communities from without and within, and our own children are among its most unacknowledged, unmourned casualties.

The womanist ethicist Emilie Townes draws on *The Color Purple* to develop a Christian spiritual response to race-related sexual violence. She addresses a prophetic challenge to the Black community:

> We have a responsibility for our future. We must decide if we are going to live in an uneasy, destructive, but comfortable acquiescence or in communal accountability. Are we going to live with some of us filling the role of colonized victims? Or are we going to realize the great gift of who we are as African Americans and begin to "git man off [our] eyeball" so that we can see a God whose spirit calls us into a spirituality that loves our bodies into wholeness as God holds us in the palm of creation and with creation itself?[18]

Townes presents a choice to Black folks: We can either succumb to the logic of colonial domination or resist the sexual violence that still plagues our homes, neighborhoods, and churches. Her challenge can be extended to include a call to resist child sexual abuse and every form of injustice that violates bodies and souls. For Townes, spirituality is about seeking a new apocalyptic vision, a transformative practice of contemplation. She invites us to "see

---

[16]Michael Rezendes, "In Mississippi Delta, Catholic Abuse Cases Settled on Cheap," *Associated Press*, August 27, 2019.

[17]"Fr. Thaddeus Posey," https://www.bishop-accountability.org/accused/posey-thaddeus-1971, and Noelle Phillips, "13 Denver-Based Catholic Friars with Credible Sexual Abuse Allegations Identified," *Denver Post*, March 28, 2019.

[18]Townes, *In a Blaze of Glory*, 86.

a God" who enables us to love our material, sensual selves in right relationship and to treat others with proper dignity and respect. For her, knowing the Spirit and seeking justice are inseparable.

Native Perspectives

There is obviously much more that could be said about Black experiences of race-related sexual violence and the spiritual means of resistance that have emerged from this community. But I want to turn now to another set of experiences and resistance practices with which, however, I am less directly affiliated. As a Black person, I can only approach Native perspectives from the outside. However, I want to lift up a few voices I have found helpful and take the risk of offering some fragmentary observations. To overcome the twin evils of conquest and slavery, I believe Black and Native communities must work together and share the spiritual resources they have found empowering.

In her groundbreaking work, *The Beginning and End of Rape: Confronting Sexual Violence in Native America*, the Muskogee (Creek) legal scholar and Native feminist activist Sarah Deer demonstrates that the more-than-560 recognized tribal nations in the United States face a widespread problem of rape and sexual assault, which by some estimates affects more than one-third of Native women. She notes that "the vast majority of rapes in the United States are intraracial, meaning that victims are usually attacked by persons of their own race. The only exception to this general rule is AI/AN [American Indian and Alaskan Native] women, who report that the majority of assailants are non-Native." She argues that there are deep connections between colonization and this crisis of racially targeted sexual violence: "Indigenous people across the world share a common experience—namely, intrusion on their lands and culture by an exterior, hostile outsider. Rape victims experience the same dynamic, but it is played out on their bodies and souls rather than on the land."[19]

The word "soul" does some interesting work in Deer's account.

[19]Deer, *The Beginning and End of Rape*, xiv, xxiii, 6, 13.

She clarifies that she "does not mean to prescribe a static set of spiritual beliefs to all Native people," but rather to use the term "*soul* almost agnostically to refer to deep, fundamental aspects of identity, aspects that will be described differently depending on cultural beliefs."[20] Although the focus of her writing and activism has been on tribal nations reclaiming their jurisdiction over rape cases from the U.S. federal government,[21] she also acknowledges that legal remedies alone may not be enough. Some survivors have legitimate fears that courts will not be able to give them relief and may further victimize them. Likewise, psychological interventions, including Western-style therapy and medication, may not fully address the spiritual needs that many survivors have to rediscover a sense of personal self-worth and identity connected with their bodies and the traditional lands, rituals, and ceremonies of their people. Ultimately, Deer suggests that some Native souls need a type of healing that can only come through communal spiritual practice.

Another voice I want to uplift is that of Marius Tungilik, the Inuit man who is remembered as one of the first to speak out about the sexual abuse of children that occurred at the Catholic-run residential school at Chesterfield Inlet in the Nunavut territory of Canada. With "help from his friends Peter Irniq and Jack Anawak . . . [he] organized a meeting of residential school abuse victims in 1992 to begin to address the effects of abuse in a real public sense."[22] Thanks to his efforts, many other victims and survivors

---

[20]Deer, *The Beginning and End of Rape*, xvi, xxiii.

[21]The problems that Deer describes were exacerbated by the 1978 Supreme Court case *Oliphant vs. Suquamish Indian Tribe*, which stripped tribal nations of their right to prosecute non-Native perpetrators, leaving Native survivors at the mercy of federal courts they typically do not trust. The Violence Against Women Act—passed in 2013 and updated in 2022—restored tribal sovereignty over criminal cases involving sexual violence against Native women. This was an important step, but more work remains to be done to address the root issues. For further analysis, see Anne Luna-Gordinier, "Restoring Tribal Criminal Jurisdiction with the Violence Against Women Act," in *Indigenous Justice and Gender*, 83–103.

[22]Marius P. Tungilik, "The Dark Side of Sex," in *Me Sexy: An Exploration of Native American Sexuality*, ed. Drew Hayden Taylor (Douglas & McIntyre, 2008), 50–58, at 51.

came forward to share their stories and seek greater healing and justice. They exposed a pattern of race-related sexual violence throughout the Canadian residential school system. From the 1880s through the twentieth century, this violent system forcibly removed Indigenous children from their homes, isolated them from their families, suppressed their languages and cultures, imposed a Eurocentric understanding of Christianity on them, and in many cases molested and assaulted them. The point was to destroy traditional ways of life and thereby to complete the conquest. Many thousands of children died at these prison-like schools, often from illnesses that were made worse by malnutrition, poor sanitation, and outright neglect. Their bodies were regularly disposed in unmarked graves.[23]

Tungilik recalls, "The people who were entrusted to care for us had no regard for human life. They could do whatever they wanted to us, and they knew it. All the while that they preached the gospel and spoke of godly things, they abused us physically, sexually, emotionally, spiritually, and culturally." He was taken from home at the age of five. He did not speak about his experiences until many decades later. Although he was silent about his trauma, it deeply affected his sense of self and his behavior. He explains this all-too-common struggle to articulate and cope with such unspeakable childhood experiences:

> When we were kids, we did not possess the language to express how we felt. We simply did not have the words yet. As we got older, the issue became too shameful and complicated to even begin to talk about. However, because it was an unresolved childhood trauma, many of us coped with it in many dysfunctional ways, from family violence, misdirected anger, addiction to drugs or alcohol and compulsive behaviour such as gambling to, sadly for some, a perpetuation of the cycle of abuse.

[23]See the final report of the Truth and Reconciliation Commission of Canada, https://nctr.ca/records/reports/.

It did not help that when he first started sharing his story, many people in the church, the government, and his own family did not believe him or minimized the severity of what happened. Although he later received public apologies from ecclesial and state officials, he suffered from the fact that his abusers were never held accountable.[24]

Tanya Tungilik, Marius's daughter, addressed Pope Francis during his papal visit to Iqaluit in July 2022. She recounted details of her father's lifelong suffering and shared painful memories of his struggles with alcoholism and domestic violence. Touching on the topic of spirituality, she explained, "My dad's parents were deeply religious. However, my dad was eventually turned off by the concept of God, thinking how could the men of God be so evil? He also later resented the church for their role in colonizing the North and assimilating Inuit into mainstream society. He resented the fact that they discredited and destroyed their spiritual values." When her father sought help with his trauma, psychologists told him to pray and ask for forgiveness, using Christian ideas to shift the blame onto him. This is a damning example of how a Christian spirituality that is not centered on resistance can be misused to cause greater harm. In view of these experiences, it is not difficult to understand why Tanya would declare, "I have never been, nor will I ever be a Christian."[25]

Actions on the part of churches and states to hold themselves and individuals accountable for crimes committed against Indigenous children—and for the broader effects of colonialism—are crucial. Efforts such as the Truth and Reconciliation Commission of Canada and Pope Francis's 2022 penitential pilgrimage are positive steps, but there continues to be a need for comprehensive reparative work, including financial settlements with individual survivors and large-scale economic contributions to Native communities and organizations. In addition to such public initiatives, health-care professionals emphasize that Indigenous persons and

[24]Tungilik, "The Dark Side of Sex," 51, 52, 54.

[25]Tanya Tungilik, "What Pope Francis Needed to Hear About My Dad, My Mother and Me," *Canadian Broadcasting Corporation*, July 29, 2022.

groups must be free to discern their own best methods of healing, which may borrow from Western therapies, but which may also include and prioritize Native traditions featuring medicine wheels, sacred circles, sun dances, sweetgrass ceremonies, and other rituals and practices appropriate to each tribal nation and their spirituality and culture.[26] Christian theologians and church leaders must not fear such spiritual traditions, but rather celebrate them for the goodness, wisdom, and love they contain. White supremacist Christian efforts to obliterate them were and remain evil.

Native communities have fought hard for generations to keep their traditions alive and to revitalize them wherever they have been diminished. Inés Talamantez, a member of the Mescalero Apache, Sun Clan, and feminist scholar of Native American and Chicana religion, laments that "many Christian churches, especially in areas largely populated by Indians, still require that their parishioners give up participating in their own religious traditions if they wish to become Christian." This insistence is not only misguided; it is culturally and spiritually genocidal. Talamantez interviewed a medicine woman from her tribe who explained, "What I feel I am doing is just being an instrument to help heal. This is what I am doing for my people to help the young children. To help them understand that there is medicine and there is Apache religion and that all of these cohere in order to be an Apache, a proud Indian." To have pride in oneself and one's community is necessary for well-being. The deep connection with nature emphasized by Apache spirituality admirably reveres the sacredness of all life: "You have to know the intricacies of equalness between earth, plant, trees, rock, clouds, . . . even the tiniest little insect."[27] Talamantez's research into Native spiritual practices highlights the intimate, experiential knowledge that

[26]Shelley Goforth, "Aboriginal Healing Methods for Residential School Abuse and Intergenerational Effects: A Review of the Literature," *Native Social Work Journal* 6 (January 2007), 11–32, at 23–24.

[27]Inés Talamantez, "Seeing Red: American Indian Women Speaking About Their Religious and Political Perspectives," in *Reading Native American Women: Critical/Creative Representations*, ed. Inés Hernández Avila (Altamira, 2005), 219–50, at 222, 229, 230.

comes from dwelling on the land and preserving ancient lifeways. All of this is very good and pleasing to the Creator.

In addition to affirming Indigenous spiritualities, Christian theologians and church leaders must listen to the voices of Native Christians, who, like Black Christians, have discovered liberative meanings in the mystery of Jesus's life, death, and resurrection and rejected imperialist Christianity as a fundamental distortion of the gospel. Marie Therese Archambault, a Catholic Franciscan sister and a member of the Hunkpapa Lakota nation from the Standing Rock Reservation in North Dakota, articulates a Christian spiritual form of resistance to colonial violence that is worth quoting at length:

> When we read the Gospel, we must read it as *Native* people, for this is who we are. We can no longer try to be what we think the dominant society wants us to be. As Native Catholic people, we must set out with open minds and hearts; then we will encounter Jesus Christ. We must learn to subtract the chauvinism and the cultural superiority with which this Gospel was often presented to our people. We must, as one author says, "de-colonize" this Gospel, which said we must become European in order to be Christian. We have to go beyond the *white gospel* in order to perceive its truth. When we do this, we shall meet Jesus as our brother and recognize him as one who has been with us all along as the quiet servant, the one who has strengthened us through these centuries. Then we will know that the cry of Jesus Christ from the cross was the cry of our people at Wounded Knee, Sand Creek and other places of the mass death of our people. He was our companion during these years of our invisibility in this society. . . . This is the heart and core meaning of the Gospel.[28]

[28]Marie Therese Archambault, "Native Americans and Evangelization," in *Native and Christian: Indigenous Voices on Religious Identity in the United States and Canada*, ed. James Treat (Routledge, 1996), 132–53, at 135.

Archambault's Christological ideas resonate with those of Cone and Copeland and disclose, once again, that Jesus and Whiteness are not the same thing, despite how they are often presented. Native spirituality is rich and diverse enough to encompass multiple traditions, including liberative Christian ones, in which Jesus is encountered as "brother," as a member of family and clan, as one sharing suffering and crying out in solidarity.

Conclusion

Once again, there is much more that could be said. I have only barely touched on the immense trove of Black and Native writings about race-related sexual violence and spiritual means of resistance. However, I hope that the few voices I have raised up here will help anyone reading this think more critically and compassionately about the histories and present realities of this North American context and enter into deeper relationships of solidarity with victims and survivors. It is impossible to love God without resisting this interconnected web of evil. If loving God is the true essence of spirituality, as I believe it is, then the true work of spirituality is precisely to dismantle these systems of unjust power and to nurture practices of personal and communal wellness.

In Black and Native communities, spirituality *is* resistance. It is strength and healing. It is music and memory, freedom and belonging, the flesh and the earth. Rooted in tradition, it is nevertheless adaptable to the singular and contemporary needs of those who pursue it. As a life-sustaining collection of experiences and practices, it is a defiant "no" to the threat of annihilation and an emphatic "yes" to new possibilities. Spiritual resistance to race-related sexual violence—in its pluralistic, politically engaged, and victim- and survivor-centered forms—is not a continuation of colonization but the ground of its undoing. It is a prayer for a different world, in which the sacredness of each precious life is honored with love and justice.

Part 2

In the Brilliant Darkness of a Hidden Silence

4

Divine Opacity

Mystical Theology, Black Theology, and the Problem of Light–Dark Aesthetics

There is a polarized aesthetics of light and darkness pervading the Christian spiritual and theological imagination and modern culture alike. According to the crudest form of this aesthetics, light symbolizes wisdom, goodness, beauty, purity, power, and all that is praiseworthy, and darkness symbolizes every corresponding antithesis: ignorance, evil, ugliness, impurity, weakness, and wretchedness of all kinds. Translated into the terms of a formal dialectic, this aesthetics construes light as positive and darkness as negative. In ontological terms, it suggests that light is being and darkness nothing. Although this simplistic metaphorization of light and darkness has not only functioned racially, it has in fact done so. Lightly colored and darkly colored bodies have been organized into hierarchized racial collectives by this divisive symbolism.[1] In a sense, White supremacy is nothing other than

I would like to thank Steven Battin, Susannah Heschel, the Boston College African and African Diaspora Studies Works in Progress Series, and the Boston College Systematic Theology Colloquium for feedback on earlier drafts of this chapter, which first appeared in *Spiritus: A Journal of Christian Spirituality* 16, no. 2 (Fall 2016): 166–88.

[1]Willie James Jennings, *The Christian Imagination: Theology and the Origins of Race* (Yale University Press, 2010), 18; Anthony Pinn, "Introduc-

this symbolism writ large—that is, this very aesthetics insofar as it forms conscious and subconscious categories of bodily perception, shapes cultural and political institutions predicated on such categories, and supports practices of violent exploitation and enforcement (slavery, segregation, lynching, profiling, and various macro- and microaggressions).[2]

Although secular streams of thought and politics emerging from the European "Enlightenment" must bear some of the responsibility for the perpetuation and globalization of this dichotomous aesthetics, especially in its racialized forms,[3] the traditional Christian acclamation of God through metaphors of light and especially the regular association of darkness with the demonic must bear some of the responsibility as well.[4] To develop Christian spirituality and theology in a way that resists the aesthetic underpinnings of White supremacy, it does not seem feasible or desirable to avoid light imagery altogether. This imagery is woven tightly into biblical and traditional theology and, as we shall see, remains beloved in certain Black spiritual traditions. We must

tion: The Black Labyrinth, Aesthetics, and Black Religion," in *Black Religion and Aesthetics: Religious Thought and Life in Africa and the African Diaspora*, ed. Anthony Pinn (Palgrave-Macmillan, 2009), 1–15; Monique Roelofs, "Racialization as an Aesthetic Production: What Does the Aesthetic Do for Whiteness and Blackness and Vice Versa?" in *White on White, Black on Black*, ed. George Yancy (Rowman & Littlefield, 2005), 83–124; and M. Shawn Copeland, "The Critical Aesthetics of Race," in *She Who Imagines: Feminist Theological Aesthetics*, ed. Laurie Cassidy and Maureen O'Connell (Liturgical Press, 2012), 73–85.

[2]Moon-Kie Jung, João H. Costa Vargas, and Eduardo Bonilla-Silva, eds., *State of White Supremacy: Racism, Government, and the United States* (Stanford University Press, 2011), and Derald Wing Sue, *Microaggressions in Everyday Life: Race, Gender, and Sexual Orientation* (John Wiley & Sons, 2010), 137–59.

[3]Andrew Valls, ed., *Race and Racism in Modern Philosophy* (Cornell University Press, 2005), and J. Kameron Carter, *Race: A Theological Account* (Oxford University Press, 2008), 39–123.

[4]David Whidden, *Christ the Light: The Theology of Light and Illumination in Thomas Aquinas* (Fortress Press, 2014); David Brakke, *Demons and the Making of the Monk: Spiritual Combat in Early Christianity* (Harvard University Press, 2006), 157–81; and Mark Scott, "Shades of Grace: Origen and Gregory of Nyssa's Soteriological Exegesis of the 'Black and Beautiful' Bride in Song of Songs 1:5," *Harvard Theological Review* 99, no. 1 (2006): 65–83.

critique light-centric expressions of Christian faith to the extent that they risk turning lightness (particularly the lightness of skin) into an idol, but it seems we cannot excise the luminous aspects of Christian aesthetics entirely. By contrast, the employment of darkness as a supposedly obvious symbol of the demonic is an avoidable option worthy of censure. There is no legitimate theological or spiritual reason to vilify darkly colored embodiment.

Sarah Coakley raises another possibility: recover the Christian appreciation for the darkness of God from the tradition of Dionysian mystical theology.[5] Several representatives of this tradition (including Dionysius the Areopagite, Angela of Foligno, Bonaventure, and John of the Cross) treat darkness as a lofty divine name, indeed as a name that may in certain respects deserve to be ranked higher than the name of light. Coakley's recommendation that we turn to this tradition to retrain our racial consciousness is an intriguing suggestion. The retrieval of mystical theology may be a welcome component of antiracist resistance to the extent that mystical theology subverts any crudely hierarchized light–dark aesthetics and offers a spiritually attractive alternative with precedents in Christian scripture and tradition.

But there is also another, more direct option: turn to a Black liberation theology and spirituality as classically elaborated, for example, by James Cone. In agreement with Cone, I would suggest that the willingness to affirm that God is Black because God is actively present in the struggles of Black communities oppressed by centuries of White supremacy is perhaps the most significant step that Christian believers need to take toward a more inclusive theological aesthetics today.[6] Nonetheless, once one takes this

[5]Sarah Coakley, "Prayer as Crucible," *Christian Century*, March 22, 2011, 32–40, at 33. See also her *God, Sexuality, and the Self: An Essay "On the Trinity"* (Cambridge University Press, 2013), in which she writes, "As currently conceived, the second volume (*Knowing Darkly*) will adumbrate my theological anthropology of the 'spiritual senses,' and at the same time turn to the vexed category of 'race' " (xiv). Coakley's argument connecting contemplative darkness and modern race is thus still forthcoming, though it is already quite suggestive.

[6]James H. Cone, *A Black Theology of Liberation* (Orbis Books, 2005), 55–81, and James H. Cone, *The Cross and the Lynching Tree* (Orbis Books, 2011), 93–119.

crucial step of recognizing God's liberative Blackness, further questions and complications remain, which make it impossible to dismiss mystical theology as a valuable antiracist resource.

Instead of opting for either mystical theology or Black theology, I propose a constructive synthesis of the two, not unlike that found in the works of James Noel.[7] There are several reasons to prefer such a unified approach. On the one hand, mystical themes of unknowing, cruciform experience, and transformative closeness with God play important roles in the Black spiritual and cultural traditions that inform Black theology. Greater attention to mystical theology could help Black theology better appreciate these aspects of its own sources. On the other hand, unlike other mystical traditions, Black theology draws needed attention to the historical tribulations of darkly colored bodies and God's loving concern for them. Moreover, Black theology emphasizes a point that mystical theology seems to leave ambiguous, namely, that God is not the secret agent behind these experiences of oppression, but rather the liberator who promises victory over them. The first section of this chapter argues that a unified approach to mystical theology and Black theology is conceivable because it is already to some extent actual, as Howard Thurman (among others) illustrates. This section makes the case that Black theology is best understood not as a tradition separate from mystical theology, but rather as a critical continuation of it that develops it in ways that are vital for the whole church.

Having identified the possibility of a unified approach to mystical theology and Black theology, I shall then turn in the second section to consider certain obstacles that arise for such an approach. First, there is a danger of equivocation. Despite some interconnections, the darkness of God that mystical theology associates with unknowing and purgative suffering is not synonymous with the Blackness of God that Black theology associates with liberating solidarity. "Dark" does not equal "Black." To address this concern, the second section investigates the similar and different ways that these traditions employ darkness and Blackness

---

[7]James Noel, *Black Religion and the Imagination of Matter in the Atlantic World* (Palgrave Macmillan, 2009), 57–75.

theologically. A second obstacle emerges from this investigation: In different ways, mystical theology and Black theology are able to affirm the darkness and Blackness of God theologically only *because* they define darkness and Blackness in terms of some sort of negation—whether this mainly means apophasis and askesis, on the one hand, or oppression, on the other. The problem is thus that the dark and the Black seem dissociable from the negative even in those Christian traditions that appear best equipped to challenge such an aesthetic assumption.

In the third section, I seek to address this problem by pursuing a phenomenological disclosure of the night and of darkly colored bodies, as well as a theological interpretation of these positive phenomena as beautiful avenues of possible encounter with God. A positive theology of this kind, which includes darkness and Blackness in its affirmative praises, is crucial to any potential overcoming of the aesthetics of White supremacy. Although mystical theology and Black theology have made strides in this direction, they have not sufficiently specified the need for such a *via positiva* of darkness and Blackness or developed it phenomenologically.

The final section of this chapter argues that, although such a *via positiva* is necessary, it remains insufficient without an interrelated *via negativa* that can give a spiritually viable interpretation to the opacities of Black life that are also phenomenally manifest. The unknowing, suffering, and oppression that have fallen on Black human beings in a very particular way because of the aesthetics of White supremacy demand theological attention. The approach to mystical theology and Black theology that I recommend seeks the liberating presence of the hidden God in these "opaque" circumstances, that is, in intersecting modes of darkness and Blackness that have been caught up in the negations of history.

Crucially this approach does not thereby reduce darkness and Blackness to negation; such a reduction would reinscribe the dichotomous light–dark aesthetics that this argument seeks to resist. Reductionism is avoided in this case by holding the *via negativa* and *via positiva* together as two indispensable forms of contemplation. Moreover, this approach does not callously construe the suffering of Black people as a secret working of divine grace, as certain mystical–theological ways of extolling passivity before the darkness of God might inadvertently encourage. Rather it insists with the Black theological tradition that God is present as a liberating force against oppression. God wants people to be free. At the same time, by drawing more explicitly on mystical theology than much Black theology does, this unified approach wrestles with the painfully unknown quality of the Black God's presence amid the terrors and abysses of racial modernity. The God of the oppressed is also the God of the opaque. We need a Christian spirituality that can struggle with the disconcerting silences of the divine liberator, which are experienced daily by those who are dark and beautiful and forsaken.

Black Theology as a Critical Continuation of Mystical Theology

A superficial treatment of mystical theology and Black theology could construe them as two separate traditions: one ancient and spiritual, the other modern and political. But this opposition is far from satisfying. Cone's use of the spirituals of the slaves as guiding sources for Black theology demonstrates the prayerful roots of his approach.[8] But we need not limit our analysis here to Cone. Other Black theologians and scholars, such as Diana Hayes, M. Shawn Copeland, Barbara Holmes, and Albert Raboteau, have reflected at length on certain spiritual, liturgical, and contemplative aspects of Black religious experience.[9] Contemplation and action are inseparable for Black theology, just as they are for much of the Christian mystical tradition.

Yet it remains possible to ask whether Black theology displays evidence not only of spirituality in various forms but also, more specifically, of some distinguishing mark of mystical theology such as an apophatic, interior, cruciform, or ecstatic union with God.

---

[8]James H. Cone, *The Spirituals and the Blues: An Interpretation* (Orbis Books, 2008).

[9]Diana L. Hayes, *Forged in the Fiery Furnace: African American Spirituality* (Orbis Books, 2012); M. Shawn Copeland, *Enfleshing Freedom: Body, Race, and Being* (Fortress Press, 2010), 107–28; Barbara A. Holmes, *Joy Unspeakable: Contemplative Practices of the Black Church* (Fortress Press, 2004); and Albert J. Raboteau, *A Sorrowful Joy* (Paulist Press, 2002).

One intriguing candidate for this possibility in the canon of Black theological sources is Howard Thurman—the renowned spiritual mentor of Martin Luther King Jr. and the one-time student of Quaker scholar, mystic, and activist Rufus Jones, with whom he studied Meister Eckhart, Francis of Assisi, and Madame Guyon.[10] Thurman understands mysticism as a path toward a deep interior experience of God. He argues that the mystic becomes "at home *within* by locating in his own spirit the trysting place where he and God may meet." Becoming aware of this inner divine meeting place requires ascetical detachment from what Thurman calls "the traffic of the surface life."[11] It involves "solitariness," which may in certain cases be tinged with some degree of Christlike suffering.[12] Thurman sees the condition of being detached from the world and exposed to the inner presence of God as the primary foundation of the great personal and social transformation that God wants to enact through us. All meaningful ethics and politics depend upon it.

The title of Thurman's 1963 text *Luminous Darkness* is tantalizing. Is Thurman locating himself in the Dionysian tradition? The text does not offer any discussion of Dionysius. Instead, the most direct commentary on the title is a prologue containing a story of a diver who plunges into the darkness of the ocean: "As he drops deeper and deeper into the abyss, slowly his eyes begin to pick up the luminous quality of the darkness; what was fear

---

[10]Howard Thurman, *With Head and Heart: The Autobiography of Howard Thurman* (Harcourt Brace, 1979), 77. Although Thurman makes clear contributions to mystical theology, a question may still arise about whether his work counts as Black theology, since his focus on racial integration differs somewhat from Cone's emphasis on Black empowerment. In response, I would contend that we must appreciate diverse perspectives within the Black theological tradition, including but not limited to Cone's, and that a particular sort of racial integration born from Black liberation is a major goal of Cone's project.

[11]Howard Thurman, *Mysticism and the Experience of Love* (Pendle Hill, 1961), 4 and 8.

[12]Howard Thurman, "The Negro Spiritual Speaks of Life and Death," in *A Strange Freedom: The Best of Howard Thurman on Religious Experience and Public Life*, ed. Walter Earl Fluker and Catherine Tumber (Beacon Press, 1998), 55–79, at 65 and Thurman, "Suffering," in *A Strange Freedom*, 35–54, at 37.

is released and he moves into the lower regions with confidence and a peculiar vision." Then Thurman immediately quotes Psalm 139, verses 11–12: "If I say, 'Surely the darkness shall cover me / Even the night shall be light about me,' . . . / The darkness and the light are both alike to Thee."[13] The remainder of the text is a detailed description of segregation as a social evil that is harmful to both White and Black persons. Although Thurman does not explain his prologue, the message seems clear enough: The ocean depths symbolize both the experience of Black life in U.S. society, which segregationists fear, as well as the infinite mystery of God for whom light and darkness are one.

On the basis of Thurman and others, one can conclude that mystical theology and related Christian practices of prayer and spirituality already form a vital part of the Black theological tradition. At the same time, Thurman leaves room for further reflection on the relations between darkness and Blackness. He shows that Black theology does not merely inherit the wisdom of mystical theology; it also refines it by reinterpreting its contemplative-and-active practices from the perspective of Black experience. But his writings remain suggestive rather than conclusive.

To encourage further development in this area, it is important to recognize that Black theology does not confine mystical theology to a narrow context that would be relevant only to a few; rather, it makes enhancements that are relevant to Christians in general. First of all, there has never been a mystical theology whose articulation did not depend on a host of contextual factors, which the best historians of Christian mysticism recognize.[14] Furthermore, to the extent that Black theology is characterized by a context, we should not define this context too narrowly. There

---

[13]Howard Thurman, *The Luminous Darkness: A Personal Interpretation of the Anatomy of Segregation and the Ground of Hope* (Friends United Press, 1989), vii–viii.

[14]Bernard McGinn, "The Letter and the Spirit: Spirituality as an Academic Discipline," in *Minding the Spirit: The Study of Christian Spirituality*, ed. Elizabeth Dreyer and Mark Burrows (Johns Hopkins University Press, 2005), 25–41, and Walter Principe, "Broadening the Focus: Context as a Corrective Lens in Reading Historical Works in Spirituality," in *Minding the Spirit*, 42–48.

was no "Enlightenment" without the construction of Blackness as its supposed antithesis. While expanding into colonial territories worldwide, the fantasized glory of Europe reproduces itself through contrast with the fascinating yet terrifying darkness of its imagined other: Africa.[15] Contestations must therefore occur everywhere in this globalized age. Furthermore, persons of darker complexion who must bear the ambiguous effects of a racialized name have a diasporic, transnational presence.[16] The capacity of their variously colored bodies to experience and reflect the divine mystery cannot be confined to any one region or culture. How persons with darker bodies are treated ought to be a pressing concern for the whole Christian community. Black theology is, therefore, a crucial aspect of the catholicity of mystical theology, that is, a critical development of the mystical tradition as such.

Darkness, Blackness, and Negation

Having established the possibility of a unified mystical theology and Black theology, we must now take a closer look at each as a distinct tradition, centered on darkness and Blackness, respectively. By demonstrating that darkness and Blackness are not identical, this section avoids any potential equivocity. However, the main goal of this section is to consider how these traditions similarly and differently run into a second obstacle in the struggle against White supremacist aesthetics, namely, the difficulty of affirming darkness and Blackness theologically without reducing either term to some sort of negation.

The tradition of mystical theology first uses darkness as an epistemological category. By singing the praises of a brilliantly dark God, mystical theologians in line with Dionysius point to an exalted kind of experience and knowledge that can only be reached through the particular sorts of nonexperience and nonknowledge that come with a creature's self-denying passage into

---

[15] Achille Mbembe, *On the Postcolony* (University of California Press, 2001), 1–9.

[16] Ronald Segal, *The Black Diaspora: Five Centuries of the Black Experience Outside Africa* (Farrar, Straus and Giroux, 1995).

divine union. Granting some Neoplatonic influences, one may nevertheless note Dionysius's explicit dependence on Gregory of Nyssa's biblical exegesis.[17] Dionysius argues that atop Mt. Sinai Moses "plunges into the truly mysterious darkness of unknowing. . . . Here, being neither oneself nor someone else, one is supremely united to the completely unknown by an inactivity of all knowledge, and knows beyond the mind by knowing nothing."[18] Dionysius speaks of darkness as a paradoxical kind of knowing-as-unknowing, which takes place in sublime heights of divine union and self-dispossession.

Some later formulations of mystical theology, such as those found in Bonaventure, Angela of Foligno, and John of the Cross, underscore more strongly the agonistic, purgative, and cruciform characteristics of the creature's journey into God. In these sources, an epistemological interpretation of darkness ("I do not see; I do not know") is supplemented by a passiological interpretation ("I am in anguish; I have been forsaken"). The cognitively darkened Neoplatonic and Mosaic ascent of Dionysius does not disappear, but it becomes incorporated into a more overtly Christocentric way of thought and life that treats participation in Jesus's passion and death as painful means toward healing transformation. Bonaventure writes, "Let us, then, die and enter into the darkness. . . . With Christ crucified let us pass *out of this world to the Father.*"[19] God speaks similarly to Angela: "It is when it seems to you that you are most abandoned by God that you are most loved by him, and he is the closest to you." Like Dionysius, Angela approaches God "in darkness precisely because the good that he is, is far too great to be conceived or understood," but she also experiences in the sixth stage of her journey "a veritable passion and martyrdom" in a "most horrible darkness caused by demons"

---

[17]Denys Turner, *The Darkness of God: Negativity in Christian Mysticism* (Cambridge University Press, 1999), 11–18.

[18]Pseudo-Dionysius, *The Mystical Theology*, in *The Complete Works*, trans. Colm Luibheid (Paulist Press, 1987), chap. 2.

[19]Bonaventure, *The Soul's Journey into God*, in *Bonaventure*, trans. Ewert Cousins (Paulist Press, 1978), chap. 7, sec. 6.

in which it seems "there is nothing I can hope for."[20] This is her mystical Calvary.

For his part, John of the Cross gives us poetry and commentary concerning a "dark night," which he defines as a "purgative contemplation, which passively causes in the soul this negation of self and of all things." For John, nocturnal darkness means not only the successive losses of sensation and discursive understanding; it also means intense experiences of agony, abandonment, and condemnation. The soul "feels vividly indeed the shadow of death, the sighs of death, and the sorrows of hell, all of which reflect the feeling of God's absence, of being chastised and rejected by him, and of being unworthy of him, as well as the object of his anger."[21] This inner torment resembles that of Christ's on the cross. Clearly darkness signifies more than epistemic breakdown here. It also names the context of a soul-crushing humiliation.

Mystical theology construes the two sorts of negation symbolized by the image of darkness—namely, ignorance and suffering—as productive of salvific encounter. A "god" who would be perfectly accessible through perceptible or intelligible light or who would grant sinful creatures only lighthearted experiences of consolation is, from the standpoint of these mystical theologians, no true God at all, but rather a self-serving and self-deceiving fiction. This tradition holds that it is necessary to think of God as dark in order to overcome such idolatries. Darkness is thus an indispensable *via negativa*, a negative path toward greater intimacy with God.

The dichotomous evaluation of light as positive and darkness as negative is, in one sense, kept intact by the mystical employment of these terms. Darkness almost exclusively means nescience and pain. The reasons mystics give for valuing darkness are principally apophatic and ascetical.[22] Conversely, light continues to enjoy a

---

[20] Angela of Foligno, *The Memorial*, in *The Complete Works*, trans. Paul Lachance, O.F.M. (Paulist Press, 1993), chaps. 6, 8, 9.

[21] John of the Cross, *The Dark Night*, in *The Collected Works of St. John of the Cross*, trans. Kieran Kavanaugh, O.C.D., and Otilio Rodriguez, O.C.D. (ICS, 1991), bk. 1, sec. 1, and bk. 2, chap. 6, sec. 2.

[22] Jeffrey Vogel, "Growing into the Darkness of God: The Inseparabil-

privileged finality. Vladimir Lossky illustrates this point well.[23] The mystics' loss of vision and affective participations in Christ's passion are not ends in themselves. The transcendent glories of beatific vision and radiant resurrected life remain centrally motivating. The light may be experienced as flame, hence as an ecstatic state beyond intellect or spiritual sight—as Bonaventure says, "not light but the fire that totally inflames and carries us into God"[24]—but this does not confer a definitively positive meaning on darkness. There may be, as John says, "substantial touches of divine union between God and the soul," which are appropriate to the spousal intimacy of this "glad night," but these gentle caresses will also be lit by divine "lamps of fire / in whose splendors / the deep caverns of feeling, / once obscure and blind, / now give forth, so rarely, so exquisitely, / both warmth and light to their Beloved."[25] The glory of light has in no way been tarnished, and the darkness, "glad" though it may be, has not shed its negative meaning.

In another sense, however, the mystical teaching that the highest form of positivity (namely, divine union) is unattainable without passing through some radical experiences of negation (both epistemological and passiological) complicates matters considerably. This mystical ordering of the *via negativa* after the *via positiva* repositions darkness as a superior phase of divine mystagogy. In Dionysius, negative theology surpasses affirmative theology. In Bonaventure, the contemplation of the cross surpasses the contemplation of divine attributes, however sublime. In both respects, darkness signifies a loftier stage of the Christian spiritual path than does any more readily accessible created or uncreated light. Darkness raises one to hitherto inconceivable peaks of Christological wisdom and practice. Accordingly, although mystical theology preserves an aesthetic dichotomy between darkness and light on one level, on another level it encourages theologians

ity Between Apophatic Theology and Ascetical Practice," *Spiritus* 15, no. 2 (Fall 2015): 214–30.

[23]Vladimir Lossky, *The Mystical Theology of the Eastern Church* (St. Vladimir's Seminary Press, 1957), 217–35.

[24]Bonaventure, *The Soul's Journey into God*, chap. 7, sec. 6.

[25]John of the Cross, "The Living Flame of Love," in *The Collected Works*, 52.

to interpret darkness as much more than a simplistically odious phenomenon. In the dark, one may be closer to God than one is in the light. Moreover, it is impossible to possess the fullness of light without venturing through darkness.

Although there are some similarities, Black theology's understanding of Blackness is quite different from this mystical tradition's understanding of darkness. When Cone asserts that God is Black his main point is not to stress that we cannot see or comprehend God, nor to argue that God purifies the soul through suffering. He perceives no divinely hidden purpose behind racial affliction. Rather, for Cone, to affirm God's Blackness is precisely to recognize God's liberating presence among Black communities who are struggling to survive in the midst of White supremacist societies. God is Black because God enters into solidarity with Black human beings and empowers them to be free. God is Black because God does not tolerate the oppressive dynamics and self-serving idolatries of any slaveholding or ghettoizing societies.[26]

For White and Black persons, adoring a Black God may require an admission of some ignorance and a painful turning away from disordered attachments. Hence, apophasis and asceticism have important roles to play in this tradition too (for more on this point, see chapter 7). Yet, although Black theology demands *metanoia* from everyone affected by White supremacy, it lays this demand especially on those who stand to profit most from such injustice. Cone urges White Christians particularly toward a Christlike *kenosis*: a letting-go of power and privilege. By contrast, for the darkly colored victims of White supremacy, the turn toward divine Blackness mainly functions as a positive source of hope and empowerment. Cone proclaims the God-given being of Black people in order to defy racist efforts to reduce their existence to nonbeing. He celebrates the aesthetic quality of dark embodiment by declaring, "black is beautiful." In these ways, he introduces the possibility of a Black theological *via positiva* (which we shall investigate below). Here it is important to note that Cone thinks White persons, too, will ultimately be empowered by divine Blackness insofar as it calls them to a truer freedom beyond

[26]Cone, *A Black Theology of Liberation*, 63–66.

White supremacy. Although the experiences and obligations may differ significantly for White and Black communities, both are therefore meant to share in the negative and positive operations of divine Blackness.[27]

Nevertheless, the positive meaning of Blackness is obscured somewhat by the way that Cone argues for the Blackness of God. He contends that Christians must affirm that God is Black because the Bible shows a God who becomes present in liberating ways among the oppressed (particularly in the Exodus and in Christ's life, death, and resurrection), because this very God remains active in the world today, and because Black people are still oppressed. The syllogism is straightforward: If these three premises are correct, then God must be Black. This is a cogent theological argument, as far as it goes, but a problematic consequence of it is that Blackness begins to function mainly as a symbol of oppression. It must for the argument to work.[28]

The Black God does not use oppression as a painful instrument of spiritual transformation (a role that unknowing and suffering sometimes acquire in mystical theology). Rather, the Black God appears in the midst of oppression in order to combat and defeat it. This politically resistive shift in the Christian tradition's understanding of God's role in relation to certain negative conditions in which God becomes mysteriously present is a significant theological development. God enters into negative experiences in both mystical theology and Black theology. But for Black theology God enters the negative experience of oppression as its antagonist rather than its hidden agent who would seek to use it for good. This clarification of God's role contributes to the positivity of the doctrine of divine Blackness relative to that of divine darkness. However, this clarification of God's role does not remove the conceptual link between Blackness and oppression that Cone's Christian theological argument for the Blackness of God requires. The Black God is against oppression; yet to be Black is to be oppressed. As in dichotomous light–dark aesthetics, so, too, in Black

[27] Cone, *A Black Theology of Liberation*, 103, and James H. Cone, *God of the Oppressed* (Orbis Books, 1997), 215–25.

[28] Cone, *A Black Theology of Liberation*, 7, 119–23.

theology, Blackness largely symbolizes an antithesis: unfreedom.

Cone's interpretation of Blackness as a symbol of oppression has provoked accusations of essentialism. In this regard, Victor Anderson's critique is perhaps the most pointed. Womanist theologians such as Copeland and Delores Williams discuss the ways that Black women endure sexually violent kinds of oppression that differ significantly from the more recognized kinds of oppression suffered by Black men,[29] but Anderson's objection is more fundamental insofar as it targets the very assumption that Blackness and oppression can be so closely linked. By pointing toward ambiguities and pluralities in Black experience that interfere with any reductive interpretations of what it means to be Black, Anderson recasts Blackness more apophatically than other Black and womanist theologians typically do. In effect, he suggests that there is a certain degree of irreducible epistemic darkness in the phenomenality of Black life—a darkness that he seeks to express through an aesthetics of the "grotesque."[30] Although Anderson's apophatic turn makes a helpful intervention in the Black theological tradition, it does not resolve the problem of a negatively defined Blackness with which this section has been grappling. Whether Blackness is negative because it is a symbol of oppression or negative because it cannot be comprehended, the challenge of avoiding a negative association remains. Can the dark or the Black ever escape their assigned roles as metaphors of antithesis?

Via Positiva: Toward a Phenomenological Contemplation of Darkness and Blackness

As a first way to address this problem, I suggest that a unified practice of mystical theology and Black theology should not move immediately to a *via negativa* but instead dwell for a time on a *via positiva*, a positive path toward God mediated to some

[29]Delores Williams, *Sisters in the Wilderness: The Challenge of Womanist God-Talk* (Orbis Books, 2004), 143–77, and Copeland, *Enfleshing Freedom*, 19–22.

[30]Victor Anderson, *Beyond Ontological Blackness: An Essay on African American Religious and Cultural Criticism* (Continuum, 1995), 118–58.

extent by the positive phenomenalities of darkness and Blackness. The legibility of darkness and Blackness as mere metaphors for negation decreases the more one acquires a detailed awareness of their concrete modes of appearance. Phenomenological analysis likewise shows that light and Whiteness are not as simplistically positive as often assumed. Light, dark, White, and Black are complex, mixable, and variously inflected phenomena, which cannot be adequately reduced to one meaning or another. A rigorous, presupposition-bracketing attention to these phenomena demonstrates that Black human beings can claim corporeal and spiritual experiences of light as their own. Moreover, it shows that White and Black persons can learn to cherish the darkness of the night sky and of variously colored human bodies as theophanous gifts of the loving Creator.

How do darkness and Blackness appear? First, it is necessary to recognize that they do appear. They are not the absence of manifestation, but rather certain kinds of manifestation. The phenomenologist and poet Jean-Louis Chrétien demonstrates this point in *L'antiphonaire de la nuit*. Chrétien studies the subtle forms of the night's visibility as found in certain Christian theological, spiritual, and poetic traditions. The night has rich modes of presence, which give it the capacity to symbolize much more than ignorance, suffering, or oppression. The night also evokes prayer, love, grace, eternity, and countless other cherishable possibilities. Moreover, Chrétien argues that the night merges and comingles with the day in the crepuscular hours of evening and morning, which reveal its permeability and ever-changing density. Sight depends on a mixture of light and darkness, never just one or the other.[31]

Whereas the darkness of the night has a certain all-enveloping quality to it, blackness tends to refer to the dark color of localizable bodies or things.[32] With respect to things, such as tuxedo pants or piano keys, the meaning of blackness can be rather exact.

---

[31] Jean-Louis Chrétien, *L'antiphonaire de la nuit* (Édition de l'Herne, 1989). See also Karl Rahner, "Holy Night," in *The Great Church Year: The Best of Karl Rahner's Homilies, Sermons, and Meditations* (Crossroad, 1999), 57–60.

[32] I use the lowercase "blackness" here to indicate a broader meaning that goes beyond the racial category.

There are different shades and textures of this objective blackness, but its range of applicability is not nearly as expansive as that of racial Blackness. When racialized human bodies are the referent, Blackness almost inevitably becomes an exaggeration. The colors one sees range from light beige to dark ebony, but the race one perceives is called "Black." Such an exaggerated dichotomization of racial colors (White vs. Black) was meant to produce, and still reflects, vast disparities in the social standing of separated people groups. There is a certain historical honesty in the use of Blackness as a racial category, honesty about how sharp the lines of segregation and "moral exclusion" have been.[33] But there is also a phenomenological dishonesty: a refusal to welcome the spectral visibility of human skin as a beautiful reality worthy of enunciation.

Like Blackness, Whiteness is also a somewhat politically accurate yet phenomenologically misleading term, but the range of its usage has tended to be much narrower than that of Blackness because of the structural asymmetry of the "one-drop rule."[34] Marshall Bruce Gentry's analysis of the skin-color imagery in Flannery O'Connor's short stories reveals the richness that an artistic eye can capture when observing racialized bodies. As they appear, O'Connor's characters are not "white" or "black" but rather "cinnamon," "coffee," "gray," "pink," "purple," "yellowish," and more.[35] Like the night, which comingles in countless beautiful ways with the day, forming an endlessly diverse abundance of celestial vistas, so, too, human skin is wondrously polychromatic and variable. The beauty of Blackness is a shareable and mixable beauty, like a deep primary color of a painter's palette.

Linda Martin Alcoff argues that race is a "visible identity"

---

[33]For the concept of "moral exclusion," see Steven J. Battin, *Intercommunal Ecclesiology: The Church, Salvation, and Intergroup Conflict* (Cascade, 2022).

[34]Naomi Zack, *Race and Mixed Race* (Temple University Press, 1993), 19–32.

[35]Marshall Bruce Gentry, "O'Connor as Miscegenationist," in *Flannery O'Connor in the Age of Terrorism: Essays on Violence and Grace*, ed. Avis Hewitt and Robert Donahoo (University of Tennessee Press, 2010), 189–200, at 190.

which as such is not only claimed verbally by individuals and groups but also perceived. Alcoff draws on the phenomenologist Maurice Merleau-Ponty to contend that such racial perception is a "learned ability."[36] Race largely depends on visible, bodily features but also on a socially fabricated set of rules about how to interpret this sensory input. Racial perception is thus an acquired practice of reductively categorizing varying modes of bodily appearance. We need phenomenological investigations of such racial perception in order to disentangle what is given phenomenally from the modes of politically linked intentionality that shape our interpretations of what is given. The sort of awareness I propose would not be limited to the way visible bodies appear in the light of day but also treat bodies in photography, film, and other modes of artistic representation.[37]

One welcome outcome of greater phenomenological awareness is the ability to see clearly that Black human beings are not averse to light. Black bodies shine in the sun like everyone else's; they are rendered luminous by the flash of a camera and glow radiantly in glossy pictures. Light is God's gift to the whole world, not merely to those with lighter skin. Along these lines, Cone tellingly remembers that his mother's favorite hymn was "This Little Light of Mine." He explains that when she sang this song "she was affirming much more than what was apparent in the lines. . . . The 'light' was what illuminated her existence, an alternative view of life, different from the current estimations of her being in the world."[38] Although the typical Christian metaphorization of light and darkness cannot be entirely dissociated from the aesthetics of modern racism, here we find evidence of a Black woman who found strength to resist racism and love her own being precisely through such Christian metaphorization. She saw no contradiction in affirming that she, as a Black woman, participated in the light of God and was called to let this light shine in the world.

[36]Linda Martin Alcoff, *Visible Identities: Race, Gender, and the Self* (Oxford University Press, 2006), 186.

[37]Nicole Fleetwood, *Troubling Vision: Performance, Visuality, and Blackness* (University of Chicago Press, 2011).

[38]Cone, *God of the Oppressed*, 12.

The distinct modes of visibility of darkness and light may be employed to represent distinct kinds of experiences and values. My argument is not that one should disregard the potential that these terms have to function symbolically or metaphorically. Yet I do want to insist that only the most simplistic sort of imagination would associate light categorically with positive values and darkness with negative. As we have seen, the night can be a refuge, a time of contemplation, an escape from worldly cares and troubles, a place of loving intimacy. By contrast, the day can be experienced as a context of misery, toil, unthinking conformity, and unrelenting chaos. The noon sun burns and bleaches and dries out. There are kinds of light that lack warmth, lights which oppress with their unfeeling fluorescent gleam.

All of these metaphorically usable variations in the actual experiences of light and darkness are, in turn, distinct from the manifest experiences and behaviors of differently pigmented bodies. In such a bodily register, the question of the potential for symbolism is more fraught. Nothing certain about the moral character of a person is disclosed through the color of his or her skin. No immediate knowledge of anyone's ways of relating to themselves, to others, or to God is given through the enfleshed apparitions of pink or brown or any other color that meets the eye. Such snap judgments, if they occur, are added by the perceptual training of racialized and racist societies. Joseph Conrad's classic *Heart of Darkness*, for instance, is rife with symbolism that is dangerously predictable for a racialized colonial mind.[39] A more phenomenologically honest discourse would go a long way toward elevating contemporary culture above its problematic tendencies to elide the dark, the Black, and the negative.

The glory of God can be revered just as much by the contemplation of atmospheric and corporeal darkness as by the contemplation of atmospheric and corporeal light. This way of thinking calls forth a theological aesthetics congruent with the Priestly hymn of creation in Genesis 1, a paradisal vision in which night and day

---

[39]For criticism of Conrad's racial and colonial imagination, see Nicolas Tredell, ed., *Joseph Conrad: Heart of Darkness* (Columbia University Press, 1998).

exist together harmoniously and the human being (of whatever color) naturally bears the *imago Dei*. A contemplative approach of this kind does not support any strict prioritization of darkness and Blackness as divine names; nor, however, does it prioritize light and Whiteness. Instead, it makes the positive theological use of all these names an attractive option simply in view of their manifest presence within the already concretely graced *analogia entis* that is creaturely existence.[40]

Rethinking the *Via Negativa:* Contemplating the Opacities of Black Life

However, without diminishing the significance of such a *via positiva*, it is necessary also to embark on a *via negativa* that would seek the liberating presence of God amid certain negative conditions of darkness and Blackness that have been imagined and produced by modernity's racialized light–dark aesthetics. Drawing on the works of W. E. B. Du Bois, Charles Long, and Édouard Glissant, I shall adopt "opacity" as a technical term for the particular conditions of unknowing, suffering, and oppression that appear in modern Black life. To be sure, it is possible to use "opacity" more generally to refer to the non-narratability of human life as such, as Judith Butler indicates.[41] But there is also a literary and scholarly tradition that plays with the apparent double entendre in the term, using it to mean both negative darkness (that is, veiledness and anguish) and racial Blackness (dark bodily color). This is the tradition that I engage here, albeit in an explicitly theological mode that is not very prevalent within it. My interest is in contemplating *divine* opacity: the God who may be sought in such opaque circumstances.

The *via positiva* above suggests that phenomenal darkness (whether celestial or physical) analogically expresses the beauty of God, just as phenomenal lightness does. There was no basis

[40]For the understanding of *analogia entis* that I presuppose here, see Hans Urs von Balthasar, *The Theology of Karl Barth*, trans. Edward Oakes, SJ (Ignatius, 1992), 267–325.

[41]Judith Butler, *Giving an Account of Oneself* (Fordham University Press, 2005), 39–41.

for discrimination here. Within the present *via negativa*, however, the need to praise a dark and Black God acquires a special urgency because of the historical reality of White supremacy. From this perspective, a doctrine of divine opacity does deserve to be prioritized. Conversely, any alternative doctrine of divine transparency that would suggest that the current badly distributed order of things perfectly reflects the clairvoyant mind of a rational (solidaristically White) God must be vigorously contested. Black theology already explains the need for such a preferential affirmation of Blackness as a divine name. What mystical theology may help Black theology better articulate in such an argument is the troubling mysteriousness of the Black God and, indeed, of the very conditions of Black life in which this God promises to intervene.[42]

Let us consider Du Bois first. He does not regularly use the term "opacity," but he does famously characterize Black existence as a strange condition in which one is made to live behind "a vast veil." He writes, "After the Egyptian and Indian, the Greek and Roman, the Teuton and Mongolian, the Negro is a sort of seventh son, born with a veil, and gifted with second-sight in this American world—a world which yields him no true self-consciousness, but only lets him see himself through the revelation of the other world."[43] To be Black is precisely not to be transparent. Blackness is not transparent to others, who cannot see or understand what it is like to experience the world behind the veil; nor is the Black person transparent even to him- or herself. It is as though, in seeking his identity, Du Bois must as a Black person look in the mirror of the world only to find a veiled image reflected back.

There has been much discussion of Du Bois's idea of "double consciousness," which appears on the same page, but what I am more interested in here is his diagnosis of the inability to reach anything like an adequate consciousness of the meaning of Black life, including his own life. To be sure, he suggests that being veiled comes with an extra capacity for vision; he speaks of "second-

---

[42] Anderson's aesthetics of the grotesque already points in this direction, but other sources on opacity add helpful nuance.

[43] W. E. B. Du Bois, *The Souls of Black Folk* (Simon & Schuster, 2005), 6–7.

sight" and the veil as "gifted." But there is also tragedy in his description. Du Bois recognizes at a very young age that he must face a racially imposed impossibility for full self-possession or self-discovery. The veil is both blessing and curse: a sign of access to hidden wisdom and a lamentable state of estrangement from oneself and others. This passage from Du Bois calls to mind the spiritually fruitful apophasis of the mystics, in which unknowing becomes a privileged kind of knowing. At the same time, it is reminiscent of mystical cruciformity: The Black soul is not only unknown, it is torn in two. There is suffering in its hiddenness.

However, despite certain similarities, Du Bois does not speak here with the Christologically founded certainty of a Christian mystical theologian. Whether such an opaque life will be a site of healing encounter with God remains an unanswered question. It is significant, though, that Du Bois remains mindful of such a question and approaches it with some degree of hopeful anticipation. His state of mind comes through clearly in his chapter on the "Sorrow Songs": "If somewhere in this whirl and chaos of things there dwells Eternal Good, pitiful yet masterful, then anon in His good time America shall rend the Veil and the prisoned shall go free." Du Bois does not think of opacity as a final end, but rather as a possibly transient situation, undoable only (if ever) by divine decree and divine action of the "Eternal Good." Yet, for him, the inbreaking of such a future of transcendent freedom can already be glimpsed in the "free, free sunshine" and heard in the prayerful songs of his children.[44]

Historian of religion Charles Long introduces the category "Theologies Opaque." In one sense by this term he simply means "theologies of color," that is, reflections on God composed by theologians working from explicitly non-White perspectives. He gives the examples of Cone's Black theology and Vine Deloria's American Indian theology.[45] However, for Long, "opaque" is not

[44]Du Bois, *The Souls of Black Folk*, 253.

[45]Another discussion would be needed to investigate mystical theology in relation to American Indian experiences of conquest and genocide. Long cites Vine Deloria Jr., *God Is Red: A Native View of Religion* (Putnam, 1973).

strictly synonymous with "colored" or "of color." It also refers to the particular sorts of unknowing and suffering that have characterized the experiences of Black and Indigenous life in racist modernity. For instance, he remarks, "The slaves had to come to terms with the opaqueness of their condition and at the same time oppose it. They had to experience the truth of their negativity and at the same time transform and create *an-other reality*."[46] Opacity in this passage does not just mean darker color; it indicates the epistemological and passiological "negativity" (Long's word) of Blackness that was produced by the slave system.

Long contends that it was only natural for such oppressed communities to seek the basis of their dignity in a hidden God, to whom they could fly away or escape. He identifies a confluence of the "'hardness' of life and the ecstasy of religious worship."[47] Here the connection between opacity and mysticism (or something like it) is quite explicit. Nevertheless, although Long recognizes this connection, he does not endorse it himself. Instead, he argues that this sort of mystical–theological entanglement prevents opaque theologies from being truly liberative. By contrast, I suggest that the mystical–theological practices of the oppressed largely account for any sense of hope that they have been able to maintain amid the horrors of their situation.

The Caribbean literary theorist and philosopher Glissant shares Long's reluctance to advance an explicitly theological project. Nevertheless, both Long's and Glissant's approaches to opacity are helpful in ways that theologians can appreciate. Let me quote at length a poetically rich passage from a section called "The Open Boat" in Glissant's *Poetics of Relation*:

> For the Africans who lived through the experience of deportation to the Americas, confronting the unknown with neither preparation nor challenge was no doubt petrifying.
>
> The first dark shadow was cast by being wrenched from

[46]Charles Long, *Significations: Signs, Symbols, and Images in the Interpretation of Religion* (Davies Group, 1999), 191, 205.

[47]Long, *Significations*, 192, 210.

their everyday, familiar land, away from protecting gods and a tutelary community. But that is nothing yet. Exile can be borne, even when it comes as a bolt from the blue. The second dark of night fell as tortures and the deterioration of person, the result of so many incredible Gehennas. Imagine two hundred human beings crammed into a space barely capable of containing a third of them. Imagine vomit, naked flesh, swarming lice, the dead slumped, the dying crouched. Imagine, if you can, the swirling red of mounting to the deck, the ramp they climbed, the black sun on the horizon, vertigo, this dizzying sky plastered to the waves. Over the course of more than two centuries, twenty, thirty million people deported. Worn down, in a debasement more eternal than apocalypse. But that is nothing yet.

What is terrifying partakes of the abyss, three times linked to the unknown. First, the time you fell into the belly of the boat. For, in your poetic vision, a boat has no belly; a boat does not swallow up, does not devour; a boat is steered by open skies. Yet, the belly of this boat dissolves you, precipitates you into a nonworld from which you cry out. This boat is a womb, a womb abyss. It generates the clamor of your protests; it also produces all the coming unanimity. Although you are alone in this suffering, you share in the unknown with others whom you have yet to know. This boat is your womb, a matrix, and yet it expels you. This boat: pregnant with as many dead as living under the sentence of death.

The next abyss was the depths of the sea. Whenever a fleet of ships gave chase to slave ships, it was easiest just to lighten the boat by throwing cargo overboard, weighing it down with balls and chains. These underwater posts mark the course between the Gold Coast and the Leeward Islands. Navigating the green splendor of the sea—whether in melancholic trans-Atlantic crossings or glorious regattas or traditional races of yoles and *gommiers*—still brings to mind, coming to light like seaweed, these lowest depths, these deeps, with their punctuation of scarcely corroded balls and chains. In actual fact the abyss is a tautology: the entire

> ocean, the entire sea gently collapsing in the end into the pleasures of sand, make one vast beginning, but a beginning whose time is marked by these balls and chains gone green.
>
> But for these shores to take shape, even before they could be contemplated, before they were yet visible, what sufferings came from the unknown! Indeed, the most petrifying face of the abyss lies far ahead of the slave ship's bow, a pale murmur: you do not know if it is a storm cloud, rain or drizzle, or smoke from a comforting fire. The banks of the river have vanished on both sides of the boat. What kind of river, then, has no middle? Is nothing there but straight ahead? Is this boat sailing into eternity toward the edges of a nonworld that no ancestor will haunt?[48]

The opacity lying at the beginnings of modern, diasporic Black life becomes accessible to Glissant through a poetic narration of multiple traumatic events of near total unknowing: forced exile, brutal torture, imprisonment in the slave ship, death in the ocean, an ominous horizon of permanent alienation. He uses the precision of his historically informed aesthetic imagination to articulate memories and realities that remain incomprehensible. Glissant implicates the reader by saying "you"; he thereby makes each of us put ourselves imaginatively in the excruciating place of just one of the millions deported. His account is not merely a depiction of hell but of multiple hells: "Gehennas" in the plural. Startlingly these hells exist amid the beauties of the natural world: the seas, the sands, and the skies. They lie beneath the surface of modern life's tranquil, mundane happenings. In effect, his poetically marshaled argument is that to understand the conditions of Black existence today, one must recall (however impossibly) the abyssal passages of life and death that remain its unthinkable origin.

Elsewhere in the text Glissant uses the term "opacity" directly. He employs it in the first instance as a name for the untranslatability of certain threatened Indigenous languages, whose mysteriousness he argues must be preserved. He then expands his argument

---

[48] Édouard Glissant, *Poetics of Relation*, trans. Betsy Wing (University of Michigan Press, 1995), 5–7.

by demanding a "right to opacity"—not just the opacity of one's language but also the opacity of one's culture, history, body, and total interpersonal reality. Glissant's politics is grounded not so much in identity and recognition as in respect for what cannot be easily identified or recognized. Crucial to Glissant's way of thinking is his sense that not all opacities are the same and, in fact, that each of us bears "specific opacities" derived from our abyssal pasts and presents, and our constitutive relations with others who cannot be entirely known to us.[49]

A certain mystical–theological way of reading Glissant's "Open Boat" passage could tempt one into problematically assuming that something spiritually positive (even perhaps divine union itself) transpired in the abysses of the trans-Atlantic slave trade. The idea would be that these experiences of "the dark night" participate in Christ's passion, death, and perhaps descent into hell, and thereby possess a sanctifying power for those who endure them. On such an account, the very intellectual and affective negativity of the travails would demonstrate some sort of hidden grace at work. This is a dangerous way to seek greater unity between mystical theology and Black experience. It must be avoided because it does not respect the opacity of the events or the anguish of the persons who suffered them.

In a different vein, a certain Black theological perspective might prompt one to conclude that the liberating God is present with the slaves on their ships. Again, the extreme negativity of the given circumstances (that is, the condition of racial oppression) makes such an interpretive move feasible. This account expresses more clearly than the previous one that God does not will such oppression or wish to use it for good. Yet even this more welcome argument on the part of Black theology does not by itself seem to honor the opacity of the experience sufficiently. Although Christian revelation may give us ample reason to hope in the liberating presence of God, even amid the cruelties of this world, it does not render the incomprehensible comprehensible. It does not take away the nescience and the pain. Therefore, it leaves open a space of

[49] Glissant, *Poetics of Relation*, 119, 189, 193.

intense questioning, uncertainty, and precariousness. The God of the opaque is the liberator one desperately desires and seeks—but assuredly does not understand—while meditating on tortured brown bodies sinking into the deep indigo waters of the Atlantic.

Conclusion

In this chapter, I have argued that a certain way of uniting mystical theology and Black theology has the potential to provide a much-needed reorientation in Christian imagination. Such a theological approach can help Christians resist any simplistic aesthetic contrast between light and darkness in which light would be exalted and darkness maligned. This sort of dichotomous light–dark aesthetics has informed racial thinking in modernity and brought immeasurable harm to human beings with darkly colored bodies. Therefore, we need to strive to correct it and to free Christian spirituality and theology from its damaging influence. When developed together, mystical theology and Black theology give us a promising way to do this.

More specifically, I have contended that we need a contemplative practice that includes both a positive and a negative theology of darkness and Blackness. By seeking God's presence amid the variously colored phenomenalities of creation, the *via positiva* avoids reducing darkness and Blackness to the role of antithesis and, moreover, celebrates the mixtures, complexities, and possibilities of divine communication that are already abundantly manifest. Conversely, by seeking God's presence amid the opaque conditions of unknowing, suffering, and oppression that have afflicted darkly colored bodies in a particular way, the *via negativa* opens up a precarious space in which the abysses of wounded selves and societies expectantly yet uncomprehendingly call upon the abyss of God. I submit that liberation from the hierarchized aesthetics of light and darkness, which forms the symbolic matrix of White supremacy, depends on the individual and communal actions that would flow from such a multifaceted—mystical and Black, positive and negative—practice of theological contemplation. This is an option that the worldwide Christian community has not yet imagined, recognized, or sought to implement.

5

Love for the Annihilated

A Black Theological Reading of Angela of Foligno's Memorial

In his "Letter from Birmingham City Jail," Dr. Martin Luther King Jr. bemoaned "a degenerating sense of 'nobodiness'" that plagued the Negro community in his day.[1] Over six decades later, the problem persists. In recent years, the cry "Black Lives Matter!" has taken on King's mantle by revitalizing and reimagining his nonviolent fight against the murdering of Black bodies and souls.[2] While protesting the fact of unjust killings by police and other governmental and nongovernmental agents, this cry also combats the annihilative positioning of Blackness within contemporary society. It challenges any language, culture, or institution that explicitly or implicitly associates Blackness with nothingness. It opposes all those material and conceptual structures that pres-

---

An earlier version of the present chapter appeared in Jessica Coblentz and Daniel P. Horan, eds., *The Human in a Dehumanizing World: Reexamining Theological Anthropology and Its Implications* (Orbis Books, 2022), 143–61. This version includes some significant revisions that reflect my current thinking and emphasize connections with Christian spirituality.

[1]Martin Luther King Jr., "Letter from Birmingham City Jail," in *A Testament of Hope: The Essential Writings and Speeches of Martin Luther King, Jr.*, ed. James M. Washington (Harper, 1986), 289–302, at 293.

[2]Olga M. Segura, *Birth of a Movement: Black Lives Matter and the Catholic Church* (Orbis Books, 2021), 13–18.

sure the self-reflective Black person to confront the possibility of "nihilism," by which I mean the possibility that his or her life means nothing to this world.[3]

The annihilative force of modern anti-Blackness is only one among many interlocking forces of this type. In connection with race, one must also consider questions of class, coloniality, gender, sexuality, ability, nationality, and so on.[4] Those consigned by oppressive social forces to the status of nonbeing, nonperson, or nonhuman are everywhere.[5] They are diverse. And, arguably, they are the majority of this world's population. I am thinking of all those who are treated like their lives do not matter, like their bodies can be used for any purpose without their consent, like they are an evil to be feared and controlled, like their deaths are ungrievable, and like they do not deserve health care or clean water or a safe place to stay or opportunities to flourish—indeed, anyone who struggles every day to believe they are worthy of love. I focus on Blackness here because that is the position of nothingness to which my body, despite its caramel color and mixed genetic history, has been most regularly assigned and because this negative symbolic use of my body prior to me, and without my consent, has filled me with questions to which I have struggled to find answers, questions that are relevant to the present period of racial reckoning in the United States and abroad.

The central question of this chapter is whether sources from the Christian mystical tradition might remind us of a divine love that could bring hope and joy to such annihilated lives. To be sure, any number of mystical approaches are conceivable. I cannot hope to catalogue and evaluate them all. But for me this will be their

[3]Cornel West, *Race Matters*, 25th anniversary ed. (Beacon Press, 2017), 11–20.

[4]Patricia Hill Collins and Sirma Bilge, *Intersectionality* (Polity Press, 2016).

[5]Gustavo Gutiérrez, *A Theology of Liberation: History, Politics, and Salvation*, 15th anniversary ed., trans. Sister Caridad Inda and John Eagleson (Orbis Books, 2005), xxix, and Sylvia Wynter, "Unsettling the Coloniality of Being/Power/Truth/Freedom: Towards the Human, After Man, Its Overrepresentation—An Argument," *New Centennial Review* 3, no. 3 (Fall 2003): 257–337.

test: Do they search for this divine love, and do they retrieve it for the sake of such negatively positioned communities and persons? The Christian mystical tradition attests to the possibility of a transformative union with divine love that takes place in this very historical, corporeal life. Through a Black theological reading of one provocative source in this tradition—namely, Angela of Foligno—I aim to show that the divine love that mystics reveal to us is the same love that the annihilated of this world desperately need and desire and that, in some cases, they have already found.

Methodological Considerations

As I look back to the Christian past in this chapter, I use a Black lens forged by modern structures of racial violence and the activist movements that resist them. I ask what a self-reflective Black person who is tempted by nihilism because of a lifelong exposure to anti-Black racism might find in nearly forgotten fragments of a more theologically saturated premodern culture. With this Black retrospective my agenda remains futural. I am interested in recovering a divine love that might be consoling and energizing for people living now and for future generations. In response to critics, whether historians or contemporary theorists, who might consider this method to be unhelpfully anachronistic, I can only ask that it be judged according to its fruits.

The constructive interpretation I develop in this chapter is inspired by feminist scholars such as Barbara Newman, Grace Jantzen, Wendy Farley, Amy Laura Hall, Elizabeth Dreyer, Mary Catherine Hilkert, Sarah Coakley, and others who draw on medieval women mystics and vernacular theologians to argue for women's flourishing, authority, and other liberative ends.[6]

---

[6]Barbara Newman, *Sister of Wisdom: St. Hildegard's Theology of the Feminine* (University of California Press, 1997); Grace Jantzen, *Power, Gender, and Christian Mysticism* (Cambridge University Press, 1995); Wendy Farley, *The Thirst of God: Contemplating God's Love with Three Women Mystics* (Westminster John Knox Press, 2015); Amy Laura Hall, *Laughing at the Devil: Seeing the World with Julian of Norwich* (Duke University Press, 2018); Elizabeth A. Dreyer, *Accidental Theologians: Four Women*

A similar strategy is conceivable for Black theologians who are interested in retrieving insights from the Christian tradition's historical archive.

The feminist use of the Middle Ages is facilitated by the fact that women are prevalent in medieval sources as authors and celebrated saints and by the fact that sexual difference is an explicit topic of discussion.[7] By contrast, the peoples of Africa remain at a certain remove from the theologians of medieval Europe, and "race," in the modern sense of the term, had not yet been invented.[8] For these reasons, it is not immediately obvious with whom or with what contemporary Black readers ought to identify when reading premodern mystical texts. Should they read themselves into the figures of poverty and illness to whom some mystics show extravagant largesse? Should they read themselves into the darkness that functions as an equivocal metaphor of both evil powers and the sort of ecstatic unknowing that one experiences in contemplation (a possibility explored in the previous chapter)? In either instance, they are at risk of identifying with something that will reinforce their sense of nothingness relative to a White-dominant world derived from a supposedly normative (which is to say, premodern, European) Christianity.

One might be tempted to forgo any effort to do a Black theological reading of medieval mystics on the assumption that Black people have no place in such literature and the culture it represents. Black people could be inclined—or encouraged even—to seek divine love exclusively in their own traditions, that is, in places and texts marked as specifically Black: hush arbors, spirituals, slave narratives, independent Black churches, movements

---

Who Shaped Christianity: Hildegard of Bingen, Catherine of Siena, Teresa of Avila, and Thérèse of Lisieux (Franciscan Media, 2014); Mary Catherine Hilkert, *Speaking with Authority: Catherine of Siena and the Voices of Women Today* (Paulist Press, 2001); and Sarah Coakley, *God, Sexuality, and the Self: An Essay "On the Trinity"* (Cambridge University Press, 2013).

[7]Newman, "Gender," in *The Wiley-Blackwell Companion to Christian Mysticism*, ed. Julia A. Lamm (Blackwell, 2013), 41–55.

[8]Willie James Jennings, *The Christian Imagination: Theology and the Origins of Race* (Yale University Press, 2010).

of protest and racial uplift, or African Indigenous materials that reflect what African life was like prior to European Christian incursions. This research into Black religion, spirituality, and mysticism is crucial. Scholars such as Albert Raboteau, James Cone, Diana Hayes, and Joy Bostic reveal the power of such an approach, and I follow their lead in other chapters in this book.[9]

However, I also want to ask the following: What are the implications of assuming the impossibility of a Black theological reading of medieval mysticism? Does a White Christian living today inherit the whole tradition but a Black Christian only a racially defined and temporally recent part of it? Is there a hidden presupposition that persons of European descent are more capable of understanding and connecting with medieval mystics because of an allegedly shared geography, history, or bodily appearance, which is in fact highly dubitable? By its very existence, Black theology challenges the idea that medieval European sources provide a more authoritative witness to the gospel than comparable Africana ones do, and it questions whether they actually deserve the elevated authority they often enjoy. At the same time, Black theology must not be expected to discuss only its own designated sources—which suffer, at least in their quantity, by a racially discriminatory lack of institutional support—while the rest of theology is implicitly encouraged to offer new interpretations of whatever materials it finds valuable. Black theology is not just a way to read certain things. It is a way to read everything. By engaging sources that one might not expect it to touch, Black theology may both clarify its relevance to a wider array of theological conversations and gain insights helpful to its own aims.

At the end of *Black Skin, White Masks*, Frantz Fanon argues that the inhumanity of the anti-Black colonial order is best counteracted, not by a repristinated Black past to which Black people

---

[9]Albert J. Raboteau, *Slave Religion: The "Invisible Institution" in the Antebellum South* (Oxford University Press, 2004); James H. Cone, *The Spirituals and the Blues: An Interpretation* (Orbis Books, 1991); Diana L. Hayes, *No Crystal Stair: Womanist Spirituality* (Orbis Books, 2016); and Joy R. Bostic, *African American Female Mysticism: Nineteenth-Century Religious Activism* (Palgrave Macmillan, 2013).

would have to adhere slavishly but by the recognition of a shared, corporeal, and endlessly questionable humanity, enveloping past, present, and future and a limitless variety of cultural achievements. Fanon claims the Peloponnesian War, the invention of the compass, and Immanuel Kant's wonder at the night sky as much as he claims jazz. He refuses racially objectifying restrictions on his practices of identification and belonging. He emphasizes the freedom and responsibility to think creatively about history as a whole and to invent new ways of imagining life together. In short, Fanon—the great progenitor of Black studies and anticolonial rebellion—insists on the humanizing possibility of a Black reading of non-Black sources.[10]

The Black Catholic womanist theologian M. Shawn Copeland illustrates this possibility in her theological work, including in her creative use of medieval Christian mystics such as Catherine of Siena. In *Knowing Christ Crucified*, Copeland reads Catherine's *Dialogue*—particularly Catherine's description of a spiritual ascent from the feet of the crucified Christ to his head—through lenses provided by the Black spiritual "Jacob's Ladder" and by Josiah Henson's slave narrative. Henson identifies himself as "a poor, despised, abused creature, deemed by others fit for nothing but unrequited toil." He is one of the annihilated. Yet he finds purpose in the love that Christ shows him on the cross and in his own efforts to follow Christ's example through compassionate love of others. Copeland likens Henson's discovery of a nihilism-defeating mystical discipleship not to any poor people whom Catherine serves or any metaphors she uses but to Catherine's own interior life.[11]

In the spirit of Fanon and Copeland, I offer a Black theological reading of Angela of Foligno's *Memorial*. I hope that this reading both honors the lasting significance of Angela's Christian witness and affirms the lives of Black people who continue to face an-

[10]Frantz Fanon, *Black Skin, White Masks*, trans. Richard Philcox (Grove Press, 2008), 198–206.

[11]M. Shawn Copeland, *Knowing Christ Crucified: The Witness of African American Religious Experience* (Orbis Books, 2018), 119–23.

nihilation because of the anti-Black forces of modernity. Angela was an Italian Franciscan laywoman who lived from the middle of the thirteenth century to the early fourteenth. Despite significant differences in context, I contend that Black readers may be able to identify with her experiences of inner torment and receive encouragement through the messages of love that God speaks to her troubled soul. It is important for theologians to acknowledge that Black readers can identify with the protagonists of Christian mystical texts, and not only with marginalized recipients of charity or metaphorical uses of darkness. The fact that Angela is European is less significant, as far as the question of relatability goes, than certain facts about her inner struggles and the ways that her growing consciousness of divine love helps her overcome them. What she cared about most, namely God's empowering grace in her life, is more valuable to a Black theological reading than any contingent facts about her externally visible identity.

Angela has recently received some positive attention in Francophone postmodern theory and its Anglophone offshoots thanks to Georges Bataille's reading of her in the last part of his *Inner Experience* and thanks to the sympathetic interpretation that Amy Hollywood makes of Bataille's work in her *Sensible Ecstasy*. Bataille identifies with Angela's experiences of torment and ecstatic unknowing. To him, these experiences suggest not only the nothingness of Angela as a sinful creature but also the nothingness of the infinite darkness that transcends her knowledge and will, which she interprets theologically but he interprets atheologically. He also prizes her meditations on the crucified Christ, insofar as they seem to dramatize the dissolution of the subject, and he performs his own meditations on photos of a Chinese torture victim in search of a similar effect. Bataille's response to the annihilation that he perceives all around him at the height of the Second World War is not to seek solace in an ever-greater divine love but to seek communion with others by contemplating the condition of nothingness or radical vulnerability that he shares with them. Although Hollywood is troubled by certain aspects of Bataille's at times wildly pornographic work, she values his struggle to create a mysticism, not of totality and self-glorification but of intimate relationship through imagined self-laceration.[12]

If Bataille can read Angela within his own context, which, despite being European, differs in countless ways from hers, then Black theologians can do their own contextually informed readings of her—and, for that matter, any other sources they like. The Black theological interpretation I develop in these pages arguably remains closer to the heart of Angela's mysticism than Bataille's does, insofar as it retains her Christian faith commitments and refocuses attention on the healing words of love that God speaks to her. In contrast to Bataille's postmodern reduction of mysticism to a condition of inner-worldly communion made possible through the annihilation of subjectivity, Black theology prioritizes a type of mysticism that builds up subjects who have been torn down. Black theology does not invite human beings to plunge themselves into the decentering horrors and pleasures of the world but to seek embodied, communal ways of honoring the God of love who created the world and promises to save it. Its message to the annihilated is not that their hellacious experiences of carnal life reflect what it means to be human. Rather, its message is God loves you and wants you to be free.

The Reading

Having clarified some of my reasons for attempting such a reading, let me turn now to Angela herself. She began her mystical path as a person of enough privilege and wealth to partake in an indulgent, luxurious lifestyle. Although we have few details about her early years, we know she was of relatively high social standing and that she was part of a well-connected family.[13] We

[12] Georges Bataille, *Inner Experience*, trans. Leslie Anne Boldt (SUNY Press, 1988), 99–157, and Amy Hollywood, *Sensible Ecstasy: Mysticism, Sexual Difference, and the Demands of History* (University of Chicago Press, 2002), 60–190.

[13] For additional context, see Bernard McGinn, *The Flowering of Mysticism: Men and Women in the New Mysticism (1200–1350)*, vol. 3, The Presence of God: A History of Western Christian Mysticism (Crossroad,

also know, however, that she was unhappy. She suffered from an increasingly painful awareness of her sinfulness, and this distress prompted her to change everything about her life. The first thirteen steps of her path, as reported by her confessor and amanuensis, the Franciscan friar known in the text as "Brother A," involved feelings of intense guilt, harsh penances, anguished visions of the cross, and fledgling efforts to embrace a life of poverty, despite the wishes of her family. In the fourteenth step, she received another vision of Christ crucified, but this one was slightly different. In it, Christ invited her to drink the blood from his side and she tasted it. She recounts how she felt during this multisensory vision: "At this I began to experience a great joy, although when I thought about the passion I was still filled with sadness."[14] This is the first time in her narrative that anything like joy bursts through her grief and self-recriminations.

Going forward, a pattern emerges in which Angela is very judgmental and punishing toward herself, but God is very sweet, gentle, and loving toward her. For example, one day while washing lettuce, she begins to feel like she is unfit to do even this menial task. She says, "I am only worthy that God send me immediately to hell, and I am likewise only worthy to collect manure." She speaks at the beginning of her *Instructions* about being "plunged into an abyss of deep humility," and she exclaims, "See what a devil I am and what malice is in my heart!" She feels like a "total fraud" and sinks into a state of extreme despair.[15] This sort of abusive self-talk and its attendant feelings of lowliness and wretchedness occur frequently throughout her text, even as she advances to higher stages of prayer.

What I am struck by is that these are not the sorts of messages that God gives her. In fact, precisely the opposite is the case. On

1998), 142–51; Paul Lachance, OFM, "Introduction," in Angela of Foligno, *Complete Works* (Paulist Press, 1993), 15–117; and Mary Walsh Meany, "Angela of Foligno: A Eucharistic Model of Lay Sanctity," in *Lay Sanctity, Medieval and Modern: A Search for Models* (University of Notre Dame Press, 2000), 61–75.

[14]Foligno, *Complete Works*, 128.

[15]Foligno, *Complete Works*, 172, 219–20.

one occasion, the Holy Spirit comes to her and addresses her with these affirming words: "My daughter, my dear and sweet daughter, my delight, my temple, my beloved daughter, love me because you are very much loved by me; much more than you could love me." And again, the Holy Spirit says to her, "Your whole life, your eating, drinking, sleeping, and all that you do are pleasing to me." Similarly, at one point while she is meditating on the crucified Christ, he begins to converse with her, saying, "My love for you has not been a hoax"; "I have not served you only in appearance"; "I have not kept myself at a distance, but have always felt you close to me"; and, echoing Augustine, "I am deeper within your soul than your soul is to itself." Although Angela endures excruciating physical and mental torments for two years, she attributes these to the actions of demons, not to God. Her union with divine love does not torture her. Rather it gives her a "joy that greatly surpasses all measure." She "swims" in her experiences of such divine elevation and finds indescribable delight in them.

Insofar as such experiences prompt her to compare her weak and sinful soul to the extraordinary goodness of God, they sometimes do make her feel worse about herself, but she is the one doing this comparing. The outcome that God wants for her and that she experiences in the highest stages of her mystical path is an overwhelming condition of happiness, a feeling of being completely loved and welcomed into the triune life of God. Reflecting back on how this grace felt, she says, "I was so joy-filled, and my body felt so agile, healthy, [and] invigorated, that I had never experienced anything like it." The joyful effects of divine love are not merely spiritual or psychological for her. They also implicate her body.[16]

To be sure, when reading Angela, it is possible to worry about certain masochistic or sadistic tendencies. She makes herself suffer, and she desires it, and the institution of the Franciscan Order, represented by Brother A., and the Catholic Church more broadly, seem to endorse some measure of this self-crucifying behavior. It

---

[16]Foligno, *Complete Works*, 139, 142, 177, 198, 205, 206, 210, and 281.

would not be unreasonable to view this whole ascetical system with suspicion, critiquing it in Nietzschean fashion as a form of life-negating violence.[17] However, it may help to note that God does not encourage Angela to suffer in these ways, but rather to experience joy. It may also help to recognize that the joy Angela receives from God is given to her "without any merit" on her part.[18] She does not have to earn it through her self-mortifying asceticism, and in fact it would be impossible for her to do so, since this joy is a sheer grace.

Moreover, some of Angela's excessive behavior may be interpreted, not as an ascetical effort to win God's approval but as a divinely inspired act of intimate solidarity with those annihilated by the cruelty of the world. She participates in the love of God, not merely by enjoying it but also by sharing her life with others, especially those who have been discarded as dangerous and worthless. We can see this through her practice of washing the hands and feet of lepers and then drinking the water she used.[19] For her, to consume this water is to receive a gift of divine communion, just as she does when she receives the Eucharist. She believes herself to be united with Christ precisely in her loving, body-and-fluid sharing, though in this case strictly nonsexual relationships with these physically and socially annihilated people.

Another example of an apparently excessive behavior that may not be ascetical in a harmful sense but possibly a genuine practice of love would be Angela's distribution of her goods to the poor. Granted, she gives all of her possessions away with the explicit goal of freeing herself "to experience the riches of God."[20] She thus appears to emphasize the spiritual value that her impoverishment has for herself more than the material benefits that accrue to others. More generally, her texts do seem, like others on the more radical side of the Franciscan tradition, to presuppose a competitive Creator-creature relationship in which the creature's

---

[17]Friedrich Nietzsche, *The Birth of Tragedy* and *The Genealogy of Morals*, trans. Francis Golffing (Anchor Books, 1956), 231–99.

[18]Foligno, *Complete Works*, 140.

[19]Foligno, *Complete Works*, 163.

[20]Foligno, *Complete Works*, 129–30.

status must be reduced in order for the Creator's love to be made manifest, and perhaps that is not quite right. Perhaps God does not need Angela to lose everything and annihilate herself in order to bless her with divine joy. Perhaps this is not the right way to understand the cross or the practice of holy poverty.

Yet one cannot deny that Angela's early life of hoarding wealth and her later life of donating it are strikingly different and that the latter is much more clearly an expression of love for those treated like nonbeings. If we take Angela as an example of a privileged person who discovers the meaning of love by giving of herself to others and by entering into close relationships with them, then her practices of self-denial may be less troubling and more attractive to us. It occurs to me, for instance, that if White Christians in the United States followed Angela's lead, they would offer reparations to Black people and find communion with God by joining together in the Movement for Black Lives. They would not keep their distance; they would not cross the street or turn away in fear. They would pour themselves out in solidarity. This is not a bad way to read Angela, namely, as a model for the sort of radical conversion that a truly divine love would demand of White Christians living in White supremacist societies.

However, it may be more important for Black Christians to read Angela as someone who suffers from feelings of self-hatred and worthlessness similar to those experienced by people whom this world treats as nonbeings, people who are branded as guilty and made to feel ashamed simply because of their bodies or their social status. Angela's *Memorial* is the story of a person with an unbearable sense of her own vileness, which seems to have at least partly been instilled in her by then-dominant cultural attitudes toward her gender and her body. It is a narrative about how divine love counteracts this annihilating and culturally reinforced self-perception and gradually empowers her to see herself in a different light, as the very dwelling place of the Trinity and as one endowed with a great capacity for freedom and delight.[21] Black readers of her text need not identify primarily with the lepers whose feet she washes or the poor to whom she gives her goods.

[21] Foligno, *Complete Works*, 185, 215.

They can identify with her, the main character. They can relate to her interior yet contextually conditioned struggles. And they can find comfort and strength in the loving words that God addresses to her and in the blessings of joy that God imparts to her.

Now it may be the case that Angela was in fact sinful, that she was doing something malicious that needed correction. But the excessiveness of her negative self-descriptions suggests to me that there was very likely a great disproportion between any actual wrongdoings on her part and her ferociously judgmental feelings about herself. I think something similar could be said with respect to Black people who, precisely as people living in a fallen world, tend not to be perfect. We know that the demonization of Black life by anti-Black racism is a terrible thing. But in my mind, it would also be problematic to romanticize or idealize Black life by suggesting that it is impeccable through and through, nothing but pure goodness. This, too, is a life-negating distortion. Our goal must not be to insist on the innocence of Black people but to address the great disproportion that exists between any actual shortcomings any of them may have as fallible human beings and the annihilative ways their lives are regularly perceived by others and, perhaps to some degree, also by themselves. This great disproportion, which makes an ordinary imperfect person feel like trash, or like they deserve to die, or like they are not worthy of love, is a spiritual crisis that Angela shares, at least at a formal level, with many members of the Black community. For this reason, as a Black person, I can see myself in her troubles. I can relate to the experience of hearing one set of voices in my interior monologue that try to tear me down and another set, which seem to come from some higher truth or goodness, not simply from the world, and which lift me up, sanctify my existence, and promise me a joy greater than I can conceive. To this latter set belong the locutions of divine love.

More specifically, Angela's mysticism offers me one helpful way to resist the nihilistic conclusions of Afro-pessimist theorists such as Frank Wilderson and Calvin Warren.[22] To be clear, I do not

[22]Frank B. Wilderson III, *Red, White, and Black: Cinema and the Struc-*

think one has to turn to the mystics in order to find some such means of resistance. Afro-pessimism is vulnerable to various sorts of critique. For one, it relies on a structuralist definition of ontology, which unpersuasively suggests that the meaning of being is exhaustively determined by the ways dominant social imaginaries and discourses configure it, as though one's real and living experiences of oneself as a body that is not nothing had no ontological weight. Black life itself, Black *flesh* itself—that is, the living and breathing bodies of Black people—already defy the structuralist assumptions undergirding Afro-pessimism. One, therefore, does not need to invoke Angela's God in order to push back. A better phenomenology would suffice.

A second way to critique Afro-pessimism, more on its own terms, would be to note that even at a structural level, this theory selectively absolutizes the most negative instances of signification—the instances that identify Blackness with nothingness—leaving aside or disregarding other parts of language and culture that give Black life positive representation. Again, one need not call upon Angela's God to critique this theory. The interdisciplinary field of Black studies already offers a much richer account of the meaning of Blackness that makes such a critique possible, even inevitable. A reduction of Blackness to its most extreme determination by anti-Black racism—that is, a nihilistic interpretation of it—is not convincing to anyone who reads Black literature, listens to Black music, worships at a Black church, has relationships in the Black community, or studies Black theorists, including the Afro-pessimists themselves.

Nevertheless, I do believe that there is some truth in Afro-pessimism. This theory is correct to claim that there are structural features of White supremacist cultures that are annihilating of Black life. These structural features contribute to the murdering of Black bodies and souls. Unless resistance occurs at this fundamental level, unless Blackness is freed from its deeply ingrained

---

ture of U.S. Antagonisms (Duke University Press, 2010), and Calvin L. Warren, *Ontological Terror: Blackness, Nihilism, and Emancipation* (Duke University Press, 2018).

role of symbolizing nothingness, then no number of civil rights victories or Black cultural achievements will suffice to overcome the threat of nihilism. To the extent that the Afro-pessimists are right about the structural nothingness of Blackness, a systemic condition which negatively affects the psychological self-perceptions and physical well-being of Black people, there is a need not merely for a critique of this theory but also for a way of coping with and responding to its harshest implications.

My perhaps counterintuitive suggestion is that Angela of Foligno, a White woman before the invention of Whiteness, a mystic who knows nothing about our current racial politics, actually has a helpful message to offer here. To access this message, one must give less weight to her own disparaging words about herself, however faithfully or unfaithfully they have been transmitted by Brother A, and more weight to the consoling divine words that are given to her. These contain a powerful repudiation of nihilism. These words of love open up a nonontological ground hidden from the world, through which those who appear to be nothing may in fact be deeply united with the All-Good. Such an alternative, mystical perspective, whether articulated by Angela or by another medieval or even non-Western source, may not be the only way to fight the annihilative power of anti-Blackness, but, as a Black Christian and Catholic theologian, I have found this to be one very effective and energizing approach.

I should acknowledge that the close connection Angela draws between torment and darkness in the sixth supplementary step of her mystical itinerary does complicate my reading to some degree. If part of my goal is to overcome cultural identifications of Blackness with nothingness, then her highly negative comments about darkness in this part of her book may become a serious stumbling block. This is what she says:

> While I am in this most horrible darkness caused by demons it seems to me that there is nothing I can hope for. That darkness is terrible; vices which I knew to be dead are reawakened from the outside by demons, and along with those, some vices which had never been there before come

> alive in my soul. My body (which nevertheless suffers less than my soul) experiences such burning in those places—the shameful parts—that I used to apply material fire to quench the other fire, until you [Brother A] forbade me to do so. When I am in that darkness I think I would prefer to be burned than to suffer such afflictions. I even cry out for death to come in whatever form God would grant it. I beseech him to send me to hell without delay.[23]

In this passage, Angela uses darkness as a metaphor for her suffering and her supposed sinfulness, which she believes to be caused by demons. We find out that what she thinks of as sinful seems in fact to be mere erotic desire and that she is ashamed of her own body parts.

In addition to the likely gendered erotophobia and somatophobia that Angela experiences here, there is also a problematic act of signification whereby darkness is made to stand for diabolical affliction and evil. Angela's choice of imagery expresses a certain spiritual fear of the dark or "nyctophobia" that, within the indistinct associative flows of social imaginaries and public emotions, can easily translate into a rampant "negrophobia," as it has done in modernity. In the White supremacist Christian and post-Christian societies of the West, Blackness becomes an object of terror and fascination because it is something dark, therefore presumably dangerous, and probably in a sexual way. In such anti-Black cultures, whose effects have now spread globally, these sorts of phobic significations form the conscious and unconscious habits that make countless people of various racial backgrounds recoil from darkly colored bodies whenever and wherever they encounter them. These sorts of phobic significations, in turn, pressure Black people to feel ashamed of their bodies and to undergo interior torments and depressions similar to those endured by Angela—though, of course, some Black people may be less susceptible to these pressures than others.

Angela's seventh supplementary step in which she uses dark-

[23]Foligno, *Complete Works*, 198.

ness as a metaphor for a very high, unknowable, nonvolitional, Dionysian stage of union with God may help matters a little, but it also comes with its own problems. She explains that she sees God "in a darkness precisely because the good that he is is far too great to be conceived." Although this dark experience is a sublimely positive event, in which she beholds and is elevated into the divine nature, the meaning of darkness in this case remains at least somewhat privative. Darkness here is an image of the "negative" in negative theology. It signifies the infinite difference between Creator and creature, a difference that implies that "the light, the beauty, and the fullness that are in God" are so high above the creature that its normal perceptual and intellectual capacities must be transcended or suspended.[24]

A Black reader of this text might want to identify with such divine darkness precisely in order to escape the threat of being identified with the morally and affectively negative darkness of Angela's worst demonic tribulations. Fred Moten attempts something similar to this in his mystical response to Afro-pessimism. He does not draw on Angela, or any comparable figure in the Christian mystical tradition, but rather on the Japanese Buddhist philosopher Nishida Kitarō. Yet Moten's association of Blackness with the "paraontological," with an elusive presence beyond being and knowledge, beyond the sovereignty of the subject, beyond the world as it is ordinarily constructed in space and time, performs a similar operation. Black life is affirmed and the worst nihilism is avoided by reading the aesthetic sociality of Blackness into the exalted position of a divine darkness or, more precisely in Moten's case, a quasi-divine emptiness.[25]

Although like Moten I am inclined to use mystical sources to express love for Black life, I am wary of a strategy whereby one attempts to do this by deifying, or quasi-deifying, the nothingness that has been attributed to such life. That is, I am wary of reading Blackness into the "paraontological" position of divinity

---

[24]Foligno, *Complete Works*, 202.

[25]Fred Moten, "Blackness and Nothingness (Mysticism in the Flesh)," *South Atlantic Quarterly* 112, no. 4 (Fall 2013): 737–80.

or elaborating a poetics in which Blackness and divinity function more or less interchangeably. My hesitation about this way of employing or imitating mysticism is that Black people are not God. Nor are they any other approximately absolute reality that holds a quasi-divine place in nontheistic mystical traditions. In the perspective of theological anthropology, they are creatures in a fallen world who, like everyone in this world, must struggle to receive the transformative workings of divine grace. Blackness itself—which, for Moten, refers to the absorptive experience of Black life in music, community, and fugitivity—remains a condition of human vulnerability, a condition that leaves its bearers exposed not merely to suffering but also to a potential complicity in sinful acts and structures of violence, a condition in which grace may appear but also be refused.

What I would like to argue for, then, is not a paraontological Blackness but a paraontological love, a love that reveals its ecstasy beyond being by favoring, comforting, and empowering those who have been treated like nonbeings. The unknowable God that, in some sense, takes Angela beyond her self-seeking love is nevertheless the very source of love, that is, the All Good. This is the same God she enjoys in her less opaque union with Jesus.[26] If, as a Black person, I read myself into the *Memorial*, it seems best to do so not by identifying myself immediately with its divine darkness, but rather by relating myself to Angela herself: the fallen yet graced creature. The joy-inducing love that I might receive, if I am in her position, powerfully counteracts the potentially anti-Black signification whereby the darkness of my supposed race would be identified with demonic nothingness, and this counteraction happens without requiring the Blackness of my life to be something like the ineffable ground of all things. In Angela's place, I may become one with the divine, but the test of this oneness will not be the mere structural fact of my racial nothingness but the paraontological love that may flow into and through me, if in fact I love others who are annihilated. What elevates my body and soul is not Blackness per se but *love for*

[26]Foligno, *Complete Works*, 202, 205.

nothing—and in two senses. Love without asking the cost or seeking a reward. And love for those who have been discarded, as if they were nothing at all.

In conclusion, I want to reiterate that my Black theological reading of Angela is but one example of a more general possibility available to critically minded theologians who are busy addressing a range of intersecting forces of domination. This is the possibility of searching within the Christian mystical tradition for insights about the nature of divine love that may be politically, psychologically, and spiritually beneficial for various annihilated peoples of the world. These sorts of readings are meant to supplement, not replace, important studies into subaltern cultural traditions and their own internal mystical features. Christian spirituality is oriented toward a mystical understanding of the transformative presence of divine love. This presence—which is nothing other than grace, and which I believe is operative in our world, even if we cannot always detect it—animates the living bodies of those who resist annihilative structures of sin and calls these bodies into an experience of joy that knows no bounds. As a Black person—and, therefore, as a human being, because that is quite simply what a Black person is—I take great comfort in Angela's experience of such love.

6

Race, Gender, and Christian Mysticism

The Life of Zilpha Elaw

Zilpha Elaw is not a name that everyone knows, but her story is remarkable. As an adolescent, she lived on a farm in rural Pennsylvania. She was an orphan. Her mother had perished when she was twelve, and her father had died less than two years later. Before he passed, he had sent her to work as a live-in servant for a Quaker couple whom she later described as "kind benefactors."[1] It was the first decade of the nineteenth century. Although the State of Pennsylvania had abolished slavery shortly after the American Revolution, the practice was phased out gradually, and a small percentage of Pennsylvania's Black population remained enslaved into the nineteenth century. Some young Black women like Zilpha were held as chattel in her state, but she was not. Legally, she was a free person of color. Materially, her condition was precarious but relatively stable, thanks to the Quaker family who had given her a place to live in exchange for her labor.

This chapter was first published in *Theological Studies* 83, no. 4 (2022): 599–613.

[1]Zilpha Elaw, *Memoirs of the Life, Religious Experience, Ministerial Travels, and Labours of Mrs. Zilpha Elaw, an American Female of Colour*, in *Sisters of the Spirit: Three Black Women's Autobiographies of the Nineteenth Century*, ed. William L. Andrews (Indiana University Press, 1986), 49–160, at 53.

One ordinary evening, just like any other, she picked up her bucket and went to milk the cow. She sang a hymn to herself as she worked:

> Oh, when shall I see Jesus,
> And dwell with him above;
> And drink from flowing fountains,
> Of everlasting love.
> When shall I be delivered
> From this vain world of sin;
> And, with my blessed Jesus,
> Drink endless pleasures in?[2]

Her parents used to sing in this manner. As a child, she had learned to praise God with her voice. The silent spirituality of the Quaker community with whom she now lived did not move her in the same way. Since her father's death, she had begun to reflect anxiously on her mortality and to dream about judgment day, and sitting in silence did not help her address these feelings. Seeking greater spiritual sustenance, she had recently begun to attend Methodist prayer meetings. Wesleyan teachings about the process of conversion and sanctification began to shape her consciousness and give her a sense of the path that she too might follow: from recognizing herself as a sinner, to receiving the gift of justification through faith in Christ, to finally embarking on a life of Christian holiness guided by the Holy Spirit.[3]

And then, in the midst of her everyday prayers and labors, Jesus appeared to her and assured her of her salvation. This is how she describes the experience:

> As I was milking the cow and singing, I turned my head, and saw a tall figure approaching, who came and stood by me. He had long hair, which parted in the front and came down on his shoulders; he wore a long white robe down to the

[2]Elaw, *Memoirs*, 56.
[3]Elaw, *Memoirs*, 54–55.

> feet; and as he stood with open arms and smiled upon me, he disappeared. I might have tried to imagine, or persuade myself, perhaps, that it had been a vision presented merely to the eye of my mind; but, the beast of the stall gave forth her evidence to the reality of the heavenly appearance; for she turned her head and looked around as I did; and when she saw, she bowed her knees and cowered down upon the ground. I was overwhelmed with astonishment at the sight, but the thing was certain and beyond all doubt. . . . After this wonderful manifestation of my condescending Saviour, the peace of God which passeth understanding was communicated to my heart; and joy in the Holy Ghost, to a degree, at the last, unutterable by my tongue and indescribable by my pen; it was beyond my comprehension; but, from that happy hour, my soul was set at glorious liberty; and, like the Ethiopic eunuch [Acts 8:26–40], I went on my way rejoicing in the blooming prospects of a better inheritance with the saints in light.[4]

This experience marked the moment of her soul's conversion. It prompted her to join the Methodist Episcopal Church and begin a concerted effort to grow in the practice of her faith.

About nine years later, while attending a camp meeting in the wilderness, she had another wondrous experience that she associated with her sanctification. She recalls:

> It was at one of these meetings that God was pleased to separate my soul unto Himself, to sanctify me as a vessel designed for honour, made meet for the master's use. Whether I was in the body, or whether I was out of the body, on that auspicious day, I cannot say; but this I do know, that at the conclusion of a most powerful sermon delivered by one of the ministers from the platform, and while the congregation were in prayer, I became so overpowered with the presence of God, that I sank down upon the ground, and laid there

[4]Elaw, *Memoirs*, 56–57.

for a considerable time; and while I was thus prostrate on the earth, my spirit seemed to ascend up into the clear circle of the sun's disc; and, surrounded and engulfed in the glorious effulgence of the rays, I distinctly heard a voice speak unto me, which said, "Now thou art sanctified; and I will show thee what thou must do."[5]

Although these experiences were startling when they occurred, they also corresponded to desires she had articulated in prayer. They fulfilled hopes or expectations that had been nurtured in her by her faith community and by the larger revivalist context of the Second Great Awakening. They matched a recognizable pattern of development in the Christian life—a genre of spiritual autobiography.[6] Yet the precise circumstances and details were uniquely her own.

The work that this young Black woman went on to do was astonishing. She visited the sick, ministered to families in their homes, started a school for "coloured children," gave sermons in churches of various denominations and at ecumenical camp meetings, and took up an itinerant life of apostolic service, as she said, "like another Phoebe," a female deacon of the early church who worked closely with Saint Paul (see Romans 16:1–2). To follow her divine calling, she had to defy the wishes of her husband, who had thought it unseemly for a woman to preach. She risked her life by traveling into the Southern states of Maryland and Virginia and evangelizing Black slaves and White slaveowners, sometimes in mixed congregations, sometimes separately. On her Northern journey, she preached throughout New York and New England. The last we know of her, she had crossed the Atlantic and continued her preaching tour in England, delivering over a thousand sermons there.[7]

---

[5]Elaw, *Memoirs*, 66.

[6]Yolanda Pierce, "African-American Women's Spiritual Narratives," in *The Cambridge Companion to Nineteenth-Century American Women's Writing*, ed. Dale M. Bauer and Philip Gould (Cambridge University Press, 2001), 244–61.

[7]Elaw, *Memoirs*, 67–68, 82–85, 92, 103, 110, and 117. For a contem-

Elaw's early vision of Jesus and ecstatic experience of sanctification were significant moments on her path toward greater intimacy with God, and this intimacy only intensified with time. As long as she dedicated herself to proclaiming the gospel and following the promptings of the Holy Spirit within her, she reported that "[not] a single cloud intervene[d] betwixt God and my soul."[8] Her existence had become a continual effort to embody the grace of divine union. Her *Memoirs*, first published in England in 1846, and reprinted in William Andrews's 1986 collection, *Sisters of the Spirit*, provides just one example of the many narratives by Black Christian women that communicate practices, experiences, and theological ideas that I would consider "mystical" (I shall explain what I mean by this controversial term below).[9] Elaw might be read alongside other spiritually gifted nineteenth-century preachers and activists such as Jarena Lee, Sojourner Truth, Rebecca Cox Jackson, and Henriette Delille. She belongs to a tradition of Black women's socially engaged spirituality that inspired—and continues to inspire—Black feminist and womanist authors such as Alice Walker, bell hooks, Delores Williams, Emilie Townes, Diana Hayes, and M. Shawn Copeland.[10]

---

porary application of Elaw's homiletics, see Kate Hanch, "'How Can These Things Be?' Zilpha Elaw's Foolish Ministry," *Liturgy* 35, no. 1 (2020): 32–37.

[8]Elaw, *Memoirs*, 67.

[9]For a fuller treatment, see Andrew Prevot, *The Mysticism of Ordinary Life: Theology, Philosophy, and Feminism* (Oxford University Press, 2023), chap. 6.

[10]Sojourner Truth, with Olive Gilbert, Frances Titus, et al., *Narrative of Sojourner Truth*, ed. Nell Irvin Painter (Penguin, 1998); Rebecca Cox Jackson, *Gifts of Power: The Writings of Rebecca Jackson, Black Visionary, Shaker Eldress*, ed. Jean McMahon Humez (University of Massachusetts Press, 1987); M. Shawn Copeland, *The Subversive Power of Love: The Vision of Henriette Delille* (Paulist Press, 2009); Alice Walker, *In Search of Our Mothers' Gardens: Womanist Prose* (Harcourt, 1983), 71–82; bell hooks, *Feminism Is for Everybody: Passionate Politics* (Routledge, 2015), 105–109; Delores S. Williams, *Sisters in the Wilderness: The Challenge of Womanist God-Talk* (Orbis Books, 1993); Emilie M. Townes, *In a Blaze of Glory: Womanist Spirituality as Social Witness* (Abingdon Press, 1995); and Diana L. Hayes, *No Crystal Stair: Womanist Spirituality* (Orbis Books, 2016).

As a theologian and scholar of Christian spirituality, my goal is not to establish new historical facts about holy persons such as Elaw, but rather to find new meaning in their stories and to connect them to challenges facing the church and world today.[11] My argument follows a praxis-theory-praxis pattern sometimes employed within the interdisciplinary field of practical theology.[12] Having highlighted a contextual example of Christian praxis, in this case, the story of Elaw's conversion and sanctification, I shall, in a second step, use this example to reflect theoretically on topics such as the nature of Christian mysticism and its relation to racial and gender politics. Finally, I shall return to the arena of praxis by suggesting some ways that these reflections might inform our lives today.

My thesis is twofold. Studying Elaw should renew our hope in the transformative power of divine love. At the same time, it should remind us of the need for critical discernment, because even amazing persons such as Elaw, who are experientially and volitionally united with God, do not thereby automatically overcome all of the sinful beliefs and structures permeating their historical contexts. They, and we, remain human, therefore fallible, even as God's grace acts in and through us in powerful ways.

Elaw's Relation to Christian Mysticism

Although I read Elaw's story as an example of Christian mysticism, I recognize that some scholars understand mysticism in ways that would disincline them to consider her perspective.

---

[11]New historical work is being done by others, for example, Kimberly Blockett, "Disrupting Print: Emigration, the Press, and Narrative Subjectivity in the British Preaching and Writing of Zilpha Elaw (1840–1860s)," *MELUS* 40, no. 3 (Fall 2015): 94–109.

[12]John Swinton and Harriet Mowat, *Practical Theology and Qualitative Research*, 2nd ed. (SCM Press, 2016), 3–26; Joyce Ann Mercer, "Interdisciplinarity as a Practical Theological Conundrum," in *Conundrums in Practical Theology*, ed. Joyce Ann Mercer and Bonnie J. Miller-McLemore (Brill, 2016), 163–89; and Kathleen A. Cahalan and Gordon S. Mikoski, eds., *Opening the Field of Practical Theology: An Introduction* (Rowman & Littlefield, 2014), 1–7.

There are a few reasons for this. First, representations of a "canon" of mysticism—in introductory volumes, anthologies, and book series—organize it into broad regions of East and West, where "East" refers to materials coming from Hinduism, Buddhism, and other Asian traditions, and "West" refers to Jewish and Christian texts from the ancient Mediterranean world and from medieval and early modern Europe. Islam appears on either side of this divide, depending on how one imagines the geography. Sources from the African diaspora, including spiritual narratives of Black Christian women in the United States, do not appear on the most common maps of canonically recognized mysticism. They are invisible to a Eurocentric or Orientalizing gaze.

However, insofar as the word "mysticism" sometimes functions as code for the "other" of a modern, rationalist, patriarchal culture, a tradition of postmodern—and more specifically post-Freudian—philosophy has associated it with the so-called dark continent of Africa and of women's bodies and psyches. Although a Black woman has little chance of appearing on a canonical map of mysticism, the otherness that her racial and gender identity supposedly symbolizes defines the very essence of mysticism for some thinkers. This perspective has been developed in different ways by French feminist philosophers such as Luce Irigaray and Julia Kristeva, postmodern feminist theologians such as Catherine Keller and Sarah Coakley, and Black studies scholars such as James Noel and Fred Moten.[13] As some—but not all—of these sources illustrate, the subversive mystical alterity that a Black woman's

[13]Ranjana Khanna, *The Dark Continent: Psychoanalysis and Colonialism* (Duke University Press, 2003); An Yountae, *The Decolonial Abyss: Mysticism and Cosmopolitics from the Ruins* (Fordham University Press, 2017); Luce Irigaray, *Speculum of the Other Woman*, trans. Gillian C. Gill (Cornell University Press, 1985); Julia Kristeva and Catherine Clément, *The Feminine and the Sacred*, trans. Jane Marie Todd (Columbia University Press, 2001); Catherine Keller, *Face of the Deep: A Theology of Becoming* (Routledge, 2003), 201; Sarah Coakley, "Jail Break: Meditation as a Subversive Activity," *Christian Century* (June 29, 2004): 18–21; James A. Noel, *Black Religion and the Imagination of Matter in the Atlantic World* (Palgrave Macmillan, 2009), 68–75; and Fred Moten, "Blackness and Nothingness (Mysticism in the Flesh)," *South Atlantic Quarterly* 112, no. 4 (Fall 2013): 737–80.

body is made to represent can be deployed without giving any attention to actual works by Black women or the concrete experiences and thoughts they express.

Furthermore, there is a theological concern about the modernity, subjectivity, and doctrinal indeterminacy of the category of "mysticism." Emil Brunner voices this concern in his 1924 text, *Die Mystik und das Wort*, which juxtaposes a Schleiermacherian religion of mystical feeling with Brunner's preferred path of fidelity to the revealed Word of God. Vladimir Lossky develops a similar line of argument in his classic work from 1944, *The Mystical Theology of the Eastern Church*. He seeks to recover the dogmatically grounded mystical theological teachings of Gregory of Nyssa, Pseudo-Dionysius, and Maximus the Confessor as an alternative to the vitalist mystical philosophy of Henri Bergson. Denys Turner's 1995 book *The Darkness of God* continues this trend by distinguishing the "experientialist" mysticism theorized by the philosopher and psychologist William James from the Western medieval tradition of Christian Neo-Platonic mystical theology. Grace Jantzen's *Power, Gender, and Christian Mysticism*, from the same year, reveals the feminist stakes of such theological suspicion. Jantzen argues that a Jamesian focus on ineffable, noetic, transient, and passive religious experiences ignores the power dynamics, gender relations, and social contexts that shape Christian mystical traditions and overlooks the more holistic spiritual lives of women such as Hildegard of Bingen, Hadewijch of Antwerp, and Julian of Norwich.[14] If one wants to read Elaw as a theologically significant model of Christian life, then associating her with "mysticism" may in fact weaken one's case in the eyes of some Protestant, Orthodox, and Catholic theologians, including some with feminist commitments.

However, there are others, such as Bernard McGinn, who have

---

[14]Alistair E. McGrath, *Emil Brunner: A Reappraisal* (Wiley-Blackwell, 2014), 25–27; Vladimir Lossky, *The Mystical Theology of the Eastern Church* (St. Vladimir's Seminary Press, 1957); Denys Turner, *The Darkness of God: Negativity in Christian Mysticism* (Cambridge University Press, 1999); and Grace M. Jantzen, *Power, Gender, and Christian Mysticism* (Cambridge University Press, 1995).

demonstrated the usefulness of the term "Christian mysticism." McGinn highlights various contextually specific ways that Christians have prepared for, and been transformed by, a deepening consciousness of the presence of God. Inspired by the Quaker Rufus Jones, Howard Thurman grounds his Christian activism against Jim Crow discrimination in the mysticism of love. A positive feminist theological use of the term "mysticism" is evident in works by Beverly Lanzetta, Wendy Farley, Dorothee Soelle, and Maria Clara Bingemer, to name only a few. Michel de Certeau contends that the substantive noun "mysticism" (in French, *la mystique*) first gained currency in the early seventeenth century, as both a pejorative word for schools of thought suspected of heresy and as a name for a new theological science focused on spiritual practices of prayer, detachment, abandon, and pure love—as expressed, for example, by the Jesuit contemplative Jean-Joseph Surin and the French Oratorian Pierre de Bérulle. John Wesley, for his part, rejected any mystical doctrine that denies the value of practical means of grace or distorts spiritual life into an internal form of works righteousness. Yet he studied and published excerpts from many mystical authors such as John of Ávila, Francis de Sales, Madame Guyon, and Gaston de Renty. Wesley's Moravian-informed emphasis on an experiential assurance of salvation and his account of perfect union with God as the goal of Christian life drew deeply on the Christian mystical tradition.[15]

---

[15]Bernard McGinn, *The Foundations of Mysticism: Origins to the Fifth Century*, vol. 1, The Presence of God: A History of Western Christian Mysticism (Crossroad, 1991); Howard Thurman, *Mysticism and the Experience of Love* (Pendle Hill, 1961); Beverly Lanzetta, *Radical Wisdom: A Feminist Mystical Theology* (Fortress Press, 2005); Wendy Farley, *The Thirst of God: Contemplating God's Love with Three Women Mystics* (Westminster John Knox Press, 2015); Dorothee Soelle, *The Silent Cry: Mysticism and Resistance*, trans. Barbara and Martin Rumscheidt (Fortress Press, 2001); Maria Clara Bingemer, *The Mystery and the World: Passion for God in Times of Unbelief*, trans. Jovelino and Joan Ramos (Cascade, 2016); Michel de Certeau, *The Mystic Fable: The Sixteenth and Seventeenth Centuries*, vol. 1, trans. Michael B. Smith (University of Chicago Press, 1992); Robert G. Tuttle Jr., *Mysticism in the Wesleyan Tradition* (Francis Asbury Press, 1989); and Frank Whaling, ed., *John and Charles Wesley: Selected Writings and Hymns* (Paulist Press, 1981).

Some theologians might prefer to avoid the ambiguous term "mysticism" in favor of "mystical theology" or some other way of naming a profound intimacy with God that is more distinctly Christian, but whatever one calls it—and I think "Christian mysticism" remains a viable option—my point is that this title should not be denied to sources such as Zilpha Elaw. In fact, following the liberationist principle of the "preferential option," I claim that we ought to accord such sources—marginalized by race, gender, and other social factors—a certain priority in revised representations of a canon of Christian mysticism and in our constructive interpretations of the grace of divine union as a possibility for Christian life today.

The approach I take is inspired by Joy Bostic, whose 2013 book *African American Female Mysticism* clarifies the contributions that Jarena Lee, Sojourner Truth, and Rebecca Cox Jackson make to the understanding and practice of mysticism. Bostic argues that the contemplative and ecstatic experiences of divine intimacy enjoyed by these nineteenth-century Black women preachers helped them develop embodied agency, resist oppressive cultural norms, and seek social transformation. Drawing on fieldwork in Harlem, she finds similar forms of mystical empowerment in the spiritual lives of Black women today.[16]

Elaw's experiences of conversion and sanctification and other moments of prayer in her life involve accessory mystical phenomena such as visions, locutions, and trances, as well as the theologically essential characteristic of any Christian mysticism: loving union with God through Christ and the Holy Spirit. The distinction I make here between what is accessory and what is essential in Christian mysticism builds on the insights of Karl Rahner and Joseph Maréchal, as well as the Discalced Carmelites Teresa of Ávila and John of the Cross on whom they draw.[17] These sources suggest that psychological and bodily experiences of

[16]Joy Bostic, *African American Female Mysticism: Nineteenth-Century Religious Activism* (Palgrave Macmillan, 2013).

[17]Karl Rahner, *Visions and Prophecies*, trans. Charles Henkey and Richard Strachan (Herder and Herder, 1963), and Joseph Maréchal, *The Psychology of the Mystics*, trans. Algar Thorold (Dover, 2004).

prayer that seem out of the ordinary can be effects of the grace of divine union, but they can also result from natural human abilities or, perhaps, from sinful desires and deceptions. Therefore, it is necessary to be discerning about such experiences and not to seek them out as if they were the true prize. Instead, one's attention ought to remain on the essential thing: a surrender to divine love that, if authentic, will necessarily bear fruit in the loving manner in which one lives.

Elaw emphasizes this point in her own way. Although she recounts extraordinary experiences, for her these are signs of a deeper reality, namely, her transformation into an active vessel of God's grace. She says that a person who receives this divine gift can be sure that he "dwelleth in God and God in him; that he hath continual communion with the Father, and with his Son Jesus Christ; that he lives and walks in the Spirit."[18] It is for this reason, above all, that I read her story as an example of Christian mysticism—and what a fascinating example it is.

The Racial and Gender Politics of Elaw's Mystical Narrative

I now turn to a second area of theoretical reflection on Elaw's story by considering the question of its racial and gender politics. Scholars such as Delores Williams, Sue Houchins, Jean Humez, Joy Bostic, Sallie Cuffee, and Mitzi Smith contend that the mystical experiences of Elaw and other nineteenth-century Black women evangelists empowered them to resist the White supremacist and patriarchal norms of their societies.[19] The argument is that their

[18]Elaw, *Memoirs*, 114.

[19]Williams, "Visions, Inner Voices, Apparitions, and Defiance in Nineteenth-Century Black Women's Narratives," *Women's Studies Quarterly* 21, no. 1–2 (1993): 81–89; Humez, "Introduction," in Jackson, *Gifts of Power*; Bostic, *African American Female Mysticism*; Sue Houchins, "Introduction," in *Spiritual Narratives*, The Schomburg Library of Nineteenth-Century Black Women Writers (Oxford University Press, 1988), xxix–xliv; Sallie M. Cuffee, "Reconstructing Subversive Moral Discourses in the Spiritual Autobiographies of Nineteenth-Century African American Preaching Women," *Journal of Feminist Studies in Religion* 32, no. 2 (2016): 45–62; and Mitzi

spiritual intimacy with God was a basis for political defiance and embodied freedom. I largely agree with this mystical-political interpretation. However, I also believe we must acknowledge tensions in these works, which paint a more complex picture of their politics and remind us of the need for critical discernment even when we believe that mystical grace is operative.

Elaw adopts what I have called a "polarized aesthetics of light and darkness," according to which darkness represents ignorance, death, and estrangement from God, while both light and whiteness symbolize holiness.[20] Recalling her moment of sanctification, Elaw writes, "I clearly saw by the light of the Holy Ghost, that my heart and soul were rendered completely spotless—as clean as a sheet of white paper, and I felt as pure as if I had never sinned in all my life." On another occasion, when she had resisted the promptings of the Holy Spirit, she notes, "The Spirit of the Lord fled out of my sight, and left me in total darkness. . . . I had quenched the Spirit, and became like a tormented demon." Although one might suggest that such imagery is not explicitly about race, I have argued in the last two chapters that it fuels subconscious phobias and biases that are instrumental to anti-Blackness. Elaw refers to herself as a "dark coloured female stranger," and I cannot help but wonder whether a negative attitude toward darkness affected her self-understanding. Nevertheless, a positive experience of darkness may be found in her account of praying while walking at night to her religious formation classes. She says, "These nocturnal walks were to me seasons of sweet communion with my God."[21]

Elaw's racial politics is indicated more directly by her stories about preaching in Southern, slaveholding states. There are some troubling details in these accounts. For example, one Sunday in Annapolis, Maryland, she shared the pulpit with a local preacher who was an enslaved Black man. Citing Saint Paul, she suggests that this preacher was too worried about his worldly emanci-

---

Smith, "'Unbossed and Unbought': Zilpha Elaw and Old Elizabeth and a Political Discourse of Origins," *Black Theology* 9, no. 3 (2011): 287–311.

[20]For more discussion of this type of aesthetics, see chapter 4.

[21]Elaw, *Memoirs*, 60, 67, 87, 92.

pation. She writes, "This poor brother seemed to manifest an undue anxiety for his freedom. Certainly, freedom is preferable to bondage, as saith the apostle Paul, 1 Cor. vii. 21; who bade the Christian brethren in bondage to be unconcerned about it, unless an opportunity arrived of their attaining freedom; in which case, they were to avail themselves thereof." A short time later, this preacher who had cried for his liberty fell ill and died, and Elaw interprets this event as his true "release."[22] These comments are disconcerting.

However, throughout her book Elaw makes her moral condemnation of slavery quite explicit, calling it an "abomination," an "oppression," and the "deepest . . . wickedness." She argues that every instance of it, no matter how allegedly benign, involves a serious moral failing. While in Boston, she attended a lecture by the abolitionist George Thompson, and while in New York she went to a meeting of the American Anti-Slavery Society founded by Theodore Dwight Weld and Arthur and Lewis Tappan. Perhaps partly for strategic reasons, she seemed reluctant to use the pulpit to advocate for the political overthrow of the slave system. Nevertheless, her opinion was that it should be abolished.[23]

Elaw may have been able to find an enthusiastic reception among both Black slaves and White slaveowners because the content of her sermons was not directly about slavery or race. It was about salvation through Christ crucified. Although she challenged congregants to recognize their sinfulness and repent, this was a universal message, which did not discriminate between "high and low, rich and poor, white and coloured." All who heard her divinely empowered words were likely to be moved by them, regardless of each person's station in life. On one Christmas morning in Maryland, she gave a homily on the second chapter of Luke, and "Every heart was melted, nor was one person to be found in the entire assembly whose eyes were not suffused with tears. The gallery of the chapel was occupied by the slaves; and the body

[22] Elaw, *Memoirs*, 98.

[23] Elaw, *Memoirs*, 98, 135, 243n38.

of the building with proprietors; and all were alike affected."[24]

Despite the universal and not overtly political content of her preaching, there was something political in the very fact of her ministry. Elaw was aware of how incredible it was that a person of her racial, gender, and economic status should move about so freely and influence such a diverse multitude. To some degree, the grace that enabled her to do these things did not surprise her. It matched her view of God as one who "hath chosen the weak things of the world to confound the mighty."[25] The dominant politics of her context would have rather seen her silenced and in chains, but her spirituality gave her untold strength. Her prayers, songs, and exhortations could reach into the hearts of anyone and everyone. God granted her spiritual power over them, and she used it to bring whatever inner healing she could.

Elaw's gender politics exhibits similar tensions. She endorses a hierarchical relation between men and women. She denounces female "pride," "haughtiness," and "independent arrogance" as "the worst vices of humanity," while arguing from scripture that women are "formed . . . by nature for subordination," first to their fathers, then to their husbands. However, although she believed she owed obedience to her husband, she was clear that she owed a higher obedience to the divine voice within her. When her husband urged her not to become a preacher out of fear that she would be a "laughing stock," she resisted his pressure. She explains, "I was very sorry to see him so much grieved about it; but my heavenly Father had informed me that he had a great work for me to do; I could not therefore descend down to the counsel of flesh and blood." Elaw followed an inner spiritual calling that overruled her husband's carnal decrees.[26]

When religious leaders denied her call to preach, arguing that it is illegitimate on Pauline grounds, she addressed this resistance in a questionable yet, for her context, understandable manner. She conceded that Paul is correct to prohibit women preachers

[24]Elaw, *Memoirs*, 96, 101.

[25]Elaw, *Memoirs*, 92, quoting 1 Corinthians 1:27.

[26]Elaw, *Memoirs*, 61, 84.

in general, but she argued that the Holy Spirit is free to make exceptions to this rule, as we see in the case of many women in both the Old and New Testaments. She claimed that she has been moved to preach by such an "extraordinary direction of the Holy Ghost."[27] Preaching is a particular vocation that Elaw received as part of her experience of sanctification. Not everyone is so called, even though everyone is invited to radical union with the triune God. The point I want to emphasize here is that, in this mystical union, customary rules about gender performance, whether from society or the Bible, are not necessarily binding.

Finally, I want to touch on an issue that appears at the intersection of racial and gender politics, namely, an overriding suspicion of "the flesh." In Elaw's eyes, her husband was only a nominal Christian, a man more interested in the material delights of the world than the rigors of Christian holiness. When he took her to Philadelphia to go dancing in a ballroom, she was distressed by the scene: "The tones of the music and the boundings of the people were to me like awful peals of thunder, and all I could do was to weep before God."[28] The Pauline elevation of *pneuma* over *sarx* that empowered her, as the more spiritual partner, to defy the wishes of her husband (and thereby to disregard the Pauline patriarchal norms that she herself professed) also kept her from discovering the presence of God in secular music, dance, and any other apparently unruly movements of the flesh. That is, her spiritual life gave her both a special authority over her unsupportive male partner, an authority that feminists and womanists might celebrate, and an uncompromising aversion to bodily, creaturely pleasures that many feminists and womanists today would not consider sinful but at least potentially radiant with the divine.

There is a tension between the austere manner of divine intimacy that Elaw embodied and the more erotic, enfleshed mode envisioned by Audre Lorde, Alice Walker, Emilie Townes, Kelly Brown Douglas, and M. Shawn Copeland.[29] To be clear, Elaw

---

[27] Elaw, *Memoirs*, 124.

[28] Elaw, *Memoirs*, 63.

[29] Audre Lorde, "Uses of the Erotic: The Erotic as Power," in *Sister Out-*

was not dour. Her life was full of joy, pleasure, and sweetness, but these came exclusively from her obedience to the Holy Spirit. She believed in medical efforts to heal the body and, in this way, affirmed its dignity.[30] Yet she was critical of any use of the body that was not for the express purpose of praise or service. A more contemporary feminist or womanist perspective would encourage us to raise questions here about a type of holiness that comes at the expense of cultural and corporeal wholeness.

Despite her wariness of the flesh, Elaw defends the Black community against White Christians who would regard their habits as uncivilized. She distinguishes true Christian obedience to God from the elitist standards of "high-toned sensibility," "artificial delicacy," and "current respectability" that reflect racial and class divisions rather than the spiritually meaningful conflict between sin and grace. She affirms the cultural particularity of her "sable brethren" and insists that they need not conform to White standards of behavior in order to be united with God. She refuses the oppressive identification of sinful flesh with either Blackness or femaleness.[31] Even so, her general antipathy toward the flesh remains uncomfortably close to the (pseudo-)Christian rhetoric that has been used to rationalize the White supremacist and patriarchal domination of such groups—the very rhetoric, indeed, which she confronts in her *apologia* for the Black community and for her vocation as a female preacher.

All things considered, it is difficult to form a single judgment about the relationship between race, gender, and Christian mysticism in Elaw's text. On the one hand, as most commentators emphasize, her relationship with God was undoubtedly empowering for her, a poor Black woman living in a racist and sexist society. Without the graces she received in prayer, it is unclear whether

sider: Essays and Speeches (Crossing Press, 1984), 53–59; Alice Walker, *The Color Purple* (Penguin, 2019); Townes, *In a Blaze of Glory*; Kelly Brown Douglas, *Sexuality and the Black Church: A Womanist Perspective* (Orbis Books, 1999); and M. Shawn Copeland, *Enfleshing Freedom: Body, Race, and Being* (Fortress, 2009).

[30] Elaw, *Memoirs*, 104.

[31] Elaw, *Memoirs*, 117–18.

she would have found the strength to resist her husband, speak authoritatively, overcome fear, and recognize herself as precious in God's eyes. On the other hand, she expressed her intimacy with God in terms that maligned darkness, emphasized otherworldliness, upheld problematic Pauline views about slavery and the subordination of women, and championed an overly rigid view of the evils of the flesh. In these ways, one could rightly suggest that her Christian mysticism did not completely free her from the sinful structures of her context and, more specifically, from the White supremacist, patriarchal version of modern American Christianity she inherited. While celebrating her mystical union with God and its positive political significance, we must also acknowledge the harmful racial and gender constructs that cling to her story and reveal the need for a vigilant practice of critical discernment in our own spiritual lives.

Learning from Elaw Today

In the United States, and in other parts of the world as well, social movements are raising awareness about the violence suffered by people whose bodies are, as Copeland says, "marked" by race and gender, including women and LGBTQ persons; Black, Indigenous, Latino/a, and Asian persons; and many who live at the intersections of two or more of these identities.[32] White people and cis-het men are increasingly being marked by race and gender, too—by which I mean, they are being pressured to abandon the illusion of a panoptic view from nowhere, to acknowledge their bodily and cultural particularities, and to reckon with their complicities in structures of sin.[33] While many people are doing the work to understand how race and gender have shaped their sense of themselves and of what is right and possible—for better

[32]Copeland, *Enfleshing Freedom*, 55–84.

[33]Alex Mikulich, Laurie Cassidy, and Margaret Pfeil, *The Scandal of White Complicity and US Hyper-Incarceration: A Nonviolent Spirituality of White Resistance* (Palgrave Macmillan, 2013), and Susan Abraham, Geraldo De Mori, and Stefanie Knauss, eds., *Masculinities: Theological and Religious Challenges*, Concilium 2020/2 (SCM Press, 2020).

or for worse—others are reacting negatively to the shifts in moral values that are taking place, and they are using whatever power they have to arrest or reverse such developments. This multisided conflict has very real stakes. It is about whose lives matter, who is able to live at all, who has the freedom to exist in ways that make them feel whole and safe, who is allowed to belong and to receive opportunities that will help them flourish, and, in the final analysis, who is loved.

These social movements and the reactions to them are coinciding with a time of increasing secularity that is characterized, if not by outright atheism, at least by significant alienation from religious institutions.[34] This alienation may be explained by many factors, including tensions between religious beliefs and modern science, a greater awareness of religious and philosophical plurality that destabilizes adherence to any one tradition, and the persistent problem of theodicy: how to believe in an almighty God of love while injustice reigns in the world. However, analyzing survey data, some sociologists of religion argue that the most decisive factor is the extent to which church leaders have sided with reactionary cultural forces.[35] Insofar as Christian authority figures are not currently in the vanguard of social movements to transform the politics of race and gender, but rather in the opposition or on the sidelines, they are jeopardizing their moral credibility.

This is particularly true in the eyes of some younger Millennial and Gen Z persons who are appalled by current events in American religion such as the Catholic sex abuse crisis, Christian hostility to so-called critical race theory, and Christian bullying of trans children and their families. The open-ended sociological category "spiritual but not religious" is becoming the default condition of a young population that is not ready to give up on the

---

[34]Charles Taylor, *A Secular Age* (Harvard University Press, 2007), 1–4.

[35]Ruth Braunstein, "A Theory of Political Backlash: Assessing the Religious Right's Effects on the Religious Field," *Sociology of Religion* (2021): 1–31, and Michael Hout and Claude S. Fischer, "Explaining Why More Americans Have No Religious Preference: Political Backlash and Generational Succession, 1987–2012," *Sociological Science* 1 (2014): 423–47.

idea that there is some transcendent mystery of love at the heart of existence but that is also deeply bothered by the fact that the very institutions that claim to represent this love so often contradict it in practice.[36] I have taught many students who voice this perspective. At the same time, I have noticed that the students in my classes who continue to worship as Christians have a particular desire not to lose this source of meaning in their lives. Although some view any critical study of race or gender as a threat to their faith, most seem to be looking for positive connections between their spiritual practice and the politics of social transformation.

I find that reading Elaw's story as an example of Christian mysticism does some interesting things in this context. First, it gives concrete meaning to the sometimes vague notion of "spirituality" by reorienting it toward the goal of a mystical union with God that is ultimately a transformation in love. It suggests to Christians, and potentially to others as well, that this type of grace remains a live possibility for them, something worth seeking in their moments of prayer and their everyday labors. God is not aloof, but rather here with us ready to empower especially those whom this world treats as nonbeings. If one does not receive visions or hear locutions or experience ecstatic trances, this does not necessarily mean God is absent. Even without such phenomena, the Holy Spirit can refashion one into a Christlike vessel of God's grace. The concrete practices that embody this transformation differ from person to person. Not all will become itinerant preachers, like Elaw, but all can become fearless and free in their devotion to God and neighbor, including animal neighbors like Elaw's reverent bovine companion.

The fact that God showed such favor to a poor, Black woman, giving her the spiritual strength to move virtually everyone she addressed, regardless of their race, gender, or social status, makes this a particularly inspiring example of Christian mysticism for a contemporary world that is so mired in racial and gender troubles. Women, gender-nonconforming persons, and persons of color may

---

[36]Linda A. Mercadante, *Belief Without Borders: Inside the Minds of the Spiritual but Not Religious* (Oxford University Press, 2014).

be especially consoled by this demonstration of God's nearness to someone who, at least by outward signs, is similar to them. Elaw's story suggests that God is moving with great power in the souls and bodies of many racially marginalized and gender-oppressed people. Although they may not all write memoirs describing their experiences, they are agents of the Holy Spirit in history.

The tensions I have discussed in Elaw's work are also productive for us insofar as they encourage a deeper examination of self and society. In effect, they pose the question: How might we, even in our experiences of grace, remain complicit in oppressive structures, as she herself was, at least to some extent? Elaw's story compels us to scrutinize the ways that our spiritual practices and commitments may dampen, rather than energize, political action—specifically in the areas of race and gender. Instead of assuming that a just politics flows automatically from the experience of mystical union, we must think critically about the conditions under which such mystical–political praxis actually occurs. But we might also learn something from her occasions of rhetorical restraint. Some hearts may be moved more effectively by an affirmation of God's redeeming love than by a direct political denunciation, even if the latter is perfectly warranted. The question, for Elaw and for us, is not only how to seek the grace of divine union but how best to communicate it with others who are, like all of us, enmeshed in contexts of racial and gender-based violence.

To meet these challenges, we need to practice the very thing that Elaw calls "spirituality," namely, "a discernment of the presence and operations of the Holy Spirit."[37] This discernment must be critical, by which I mean cognizant of the contradictions and corruptions that can hide even in genuine struggles for holiness. But to be critically discerning in this fashion is not the same thing as succumbing to cynicism or despair, because what we are meant to seek and perhaps find is the very Spirit—the breath, the life, the unstoppable energy—of God, which indeed can change everything.

[37]Elaw, *Memoirs*, 118.

Part 3

Let Us Flee the Wickedness of This World

7

Black Asceticism

The word "asceticism," derived from the Greek *askesis*, which means practice or training, generally refers to material renunciations of food, sex, and wealth, as well as various interior processes aimed at achieving spiritual peace and self-control. While often described as a withdrawal from the world, its insights and techniques can also be integrated into ordinary life and influence political action. In the Christian tradition, asceticism is as much a fight as a flight. Christian ascetics perceive themselves as spiritual warriors engaged in a high-stakes battle against demonic powers. Although all Christians are supposed to avoid evil and seek the good, some Christians experiment with more dramatic forms of this struggle by becoming consecrated virgins, monks, or hermits and embracing austere lifestyles that others may regard as excessive. This Christian practice has roots in Jewish and Hellenistic ascetical traditions and takes inspiration from gospel accounts of Jesus's apocalyptic battle with demons, Paul's teachings about subordinating the flesh to the Spirit, and early Christian experiences of martyrdom. By the end of the fourth century CE, communities of Christian ascetics could be found across the Mediterranean world in places such as Egypt, Palestine, Syria, Italy, and Gaul.[1]

An earlier draft of this chapter was given as the Bellarmine Lecture at Saint Louis University in November 2022 under the title "Holy Detachment: Insights from Early Christian Asceticism and Black Theology."

[1]For more background, see Brouria Bitton-Ashkelony, "The Literature

Egypt was home to the much-vaunted Saint Antony, a founding figure of Christian monasticism known to us through Athanasius's hagiographical narrative and a small number of sayings and letters.[2] Although Antony was a resident of Roman North Africa, he was not Black according to the proto-racial aesthetic norms of his culture, which disfavored light and dark extremes of bodily color because of their ties to fearsome peoples living north and south of the empire.[3] On such grounds, Antony and other desert fathers and mothers whose appearances were unremarkable by Mediterranean standards can be contrasted with Abba Moses, who was called "Ethiopian" and "Black" and whose dark complexion was a topic of discussion.[4]

It is important to situate these race-coded references in their historical context. In Roman Egypt, there were tensions between

---

of Early Eastern Monasticism," in *The Oxford Handbook of Christian Monasticism*, ed. Bernice M. Kaczynski (Oxford University Press, 2020), 66–84; Columba Stewart, "The Literature of Early Western Monasticism," in *The Oxford Handbook of Christian Monasticism*, 85–100; Richard Finn, "Asceticism before Monasticism: What the First Monks Owed to the Early Christian Churches," in *The Oxford Handbook of Christian Monasticism*, 18–34; William Harmless, *Desert Christians: An Introduction to the Literature of Early Monasticism* (Oxford University Press, 2004); Kallistos Ware, "The Way of the Ascetics: Negative or Affirmative?" in *Asceticism*, ed. Vincent L. Wimbush and Richard Valantasis, with the assistance of Gay L. Byron and William S. Love (Oxford University Press, 1995), 3–15; J. Duncan M. Derrett, "Primitive Christianity as an Ascetic Movement," in *Asceticism*, 88–107; and Peter Brown, "Asceticism: Pagan and Christian," in *The Cambridge Ancient History*, vol. 13, ed. Averil Cameron and Peter Garnsey (Cambridge University Press, 1997), 601–31.

[2]Athanasius, *The Life of Antony and the Letter to Marcellinus*, trans. Robert C. Gregg (Paulist Press, 1980); *The Sayings of the Desert Fathers: The Alphabetical Collection*, trans. Benedicta Ward, SLG (Cistercian, 1975), 1–9; and Samuel Rubenson, *The Letters of St. Antony: Monasticism and the Making of a Saint* (Fortress Press, 1996).

[3]David Brakke, *Demons and the Making of the Monk: Spiritual Combat in Early Christianity* (Harvard University Press, 2006), 159.

[4]Tatjana Starodubcev, "St. Moses the Ethiopian or the Black: Cult and Representation in the Middle Ages," *Zograf* (January 2019): 1–22; Cyprian Davis, OSB, *The History of Black Catholics in the United States* (Crossroad, 2004), 9–10; Palladius of Apsuna, *The Lausiac History*, trans. John Wortley (Cistercian/Liturgical Press, 2015), 47–51; *Sayings of the Desert Fathers*, 138–43; and John Cassian, *Conferences*, trans. Colm Luibheid (Paulist Press, 1985), 37–80.

Hellenized cities such as Alexandria and Coptic-speaking rural areas, but inhabitants of both milieus shared an aversion to a third group consisting of more darkly colored outsiders whom they called "Ethiopians," along with other names such as "Kushites," "Nubians," and "Abyssinians." These Black Africans were not necessarily limited to the geographical terrain of modern-day Ethiopia but could have hailed from anywhere in Eastern, Saharan, or sub-Saharan Africa that Egyptians considered other. In the eyes of many fourth-century Egyptians, to be Ethiopian was to be violent, hypersexual, barbaric, and even demonic—a terrifying threat to the social order. Although there were images of "worthy Ethiopians," such as the eunuch from Acts 8:26–40, demeaning views of Ethiopians were widespread.[5] The highly influential ascetical literature produced in this context, including Athanasius's *Life of Antony* and the texts treating Abba Moses, absorbed and propagated such anti-Black prejudices. This early monastic tradition's noble quest for control over body and soul reinforced stigmatizing depictions of Blackness, and these associations had corrosive effects on the Christian imagination for centuries to come.[6]

Lovers of Black life, therefore, have good reasons to be skeptical of Christian asceticism, to say the least. I do not deny it. In fact, I offer further support for this critical position in the following pages. However, there is another story to tell: a story about how Black persons starting with Abba Moses have participated in, benefited from, and contributed to this ascetical tradition, drawing on it precisely to combat the very anti-Blackness in which it has been implicated. Liberation from the sinful structures of the world, inward habits of spiritual freedom and self-control, and single-minded focus on the coming kingdom of God become Black-life-affirming values when they are received and practiced as such. There is vital connective tissue between the *fuga saeculi* and fugitivity, *apatheia* and nonviolent direct action, *enkrateia* and

---

[5]Malvern van Wyk Smith, *The First Ethiopians: The Image of Africa and Africans in the Early Mediterranean World* (Wits University Press, 2009), 65, 390, 402.

[6]Brakke, *Demons and the Making of the Monk*, 163, 168.

Black power, and the refusal of *porneia* and Black feminist and womanist affirmations of eros. I return to each of these technical terms in the final sections of this chapter. By analyzing these connections, I argue that, beyond the negative dialectic that pits Christian asceticism and Blackness against each other, there is the possibility and actuality of a positive synthesis, which I call "Black asceticism." This hitherto unnamed concept finds expression in the story of Abba Moses, along with modern figures such as Sojourner Truth, Howard Thurman, Martin Luther King Jr., James Cone, and Keri Day, among other sources.[7]

The attainment of freedom in any theologically adequate sense of the word—that is, not mere arbitrary action with impunity but radical deliverance from evil—depends to some degree on asceticism, treated as a means not an end. This is true for Black persons who, like everyone, are vulnerable to sinful habits and disordered attachments and must strive for holiness, rather than simply taking it for granted. But Black persons are not in greater need of asceticism because they are Black. Nor is it acceptable to use Black bodies as symbols of the evil that asceticism seeks to overcome. If anything, Black life—in its impoverished, isolated, and governed conditions—has often been an involuntary mirror of asceticism, reflecting the very austerity at which it aims. When one also considers the many voluntary acts of self-sacrifice and hard-won moral integrity exhibited by the heroes of Black history and by unrecognized Black persons in their everyday circumstances, it becomes reasonable to characterize Black life as more nearly ascetical than not. Of course, no such generalization is perfectly defensible, because each life has its own particularities. Regardless, my more modest point would be that any default assumption that Black life and Christian asceticism are opposed to each other is a mistake. The early conflict that I sketched above and discuss further below does not imply any essential incompatibility.

Everyone is called to resist and withdraw from the evils of the world, including those of anti-Black racism. This is a universal vocation and one that should carry a particular urgency for Chris-

[7]For more examples, see also the Black Catholic saints-to-be treated in chapter 9.

tians, who are supposed to seek the kingdom of God before all else (Matthew 6:33). In addition to disciplining themselves and striving for their own virtue, Black people are waiting for others to take responsibility for their part. We are waiting for others to gain control of whatever cravings, resentments, and ego-fixations are preventing them from joining the fight for Black lives. The idea of Black asceticism is not only for Black people. It is also an invitation to others, a prayer asking them to prioritize costly love over the status quo.

Antony of Egypt

According to Athanasius, the eighteen- or twenty-year-old Antony made a momentous decision about six months after his parents died. Upon hearing the gospel passage in which Jesus exhorts the rich man to sell his possessions and give everything to the poor (Matthew 19:21), Antony determined to do just that. Abandoning his inherited wealth, he embarked on an ascetical way of life. Shortly thereafter, the devil began tempting him, first by stirring up memories of family and property, then by stoking his erotic passions. After appearing as a woman and being rebuffed, the devil reappeared "in the visage of a black boy" and identified himself as "the spirit of fornication." Antony was not swayed but instead replied, "You . . . are much to be despised, for you are black of mind, and like a powerless child. From now on, you cause me no anxiety, for *the Lord is my helper, and I shall look upon my enemies*."[8]

Blackness enters the narrative, not in the incarnate form of a human life, but in the ethereal form of a demonic apparition associated with erotic evil. The visibly dark face is interpreted by Antony, or perhaps we should say by Athanasius, as a sign of an interior darkness of mind, by which the text means sin or perversion. The boyhood signifies weakness. For the stalwart man, Antony, this should be an easily defeated enemy. The immediately preceding vision of a woman's body represents the same carnal threat to the integrity of the monk. Blackness, femaleness, sex,

---

[8] Athanasius, *Life of Antony*, secs. 1–6.

weakness—these are all ways of conveying the same danger of sinfully losing control, which, of course, Antony overcomes, the purpose of this narrative being to extol his virtue. Whether it is advisable to view one's sexual desire with such suspicion is one question. But assuming Antony had a true calling to celibacy and a need, therefore, to deny his erotic impulses, this would not justify such a demonization of Black and female life.

Unfortunately, the imagery involved in Antony's spiritual tests corresponds to actual, living people and positions them on the wrong side of a symbolic order that has real power to oppress. Antony's virtuous control of self is transposed through this symbolism into a racial and patriarchal control over the meaning of others' bodies, which is disseminated through the tradition of Christian asceticism that he exemplifies. Whether intentionally or not, his story teaches would-be saints to exotify, despise, and claim dominance over Black persons and women—and perhaps especially Black women. David Brakke shows that this is a pattern throughout much early Christian monastic literature. He cites another widely circulated story, in which a young monk encountered a demon "who stood before him as a female Ethiopian, so foul-smelling that he could not bear her odor."[9] While the point of this detail is to encourage a healthy aversion to sin, it also insinuates that dark female flesh is repulsive. It establishes a connection between certain types of bodies and feelings of disgust that is prone to have real-world consequences, especially when invested with the spiritual authority of a hagiography.

To some extent, early monastic sources were concerned about bodiliness in general, regardless of race or gender. Gluttony and greed were comparable to lust as potential obstacles to spiritual progress. The monastic goal was to escape bondage to corporeal appetites of all kinds, so that the soul might be free to love God and neighbor in a more authentic manner. However, attitudes toward the body were not exclusively negative in this context. On Athanasius's telling, although Antony experienced shame at his "bodily necessities" such as sleeping and eating, he regularly

[9]Quoted in Brakke, *Demons and the Making of the Monk*, 168.

did these activities "according to his body's need."[10] He cared for his body to such a degree that he lived to a very old age in good health. While he denied himself physical comforts, he did not torture his flesh. The text indicates that such torture was a favorite practice of the demons, not a proper way to resist them. Moreover, through the power of Antony's prayers and his great love, many persons found bodily healing.[11] The narrative concludes, "It was as if he were a physician given to Egypt by God."[12] The aim of his asceticism was not bodily self-hatred but radical availability to the divine will.

This appealing image of Antony as someone who had a balanced view of bodily life and cared for the well-being of others is corroborated by the passages about him in *The Sayings of the Desert Fathers*. For example, he is said to have taught, "Our life and our death is with our neighbour. If we gain our brother, we have gained God, but if we scandalise our brother, we have sinned against Christ."[13] Although he fled the world to dwell in the desert, he was not a solipsist, but rather someone who believed that all lives are interconnected. He chastised prideful monks who were more motivated by afflicting their bodies than discerning God's will, and he also recognized that "there was one who was his equal in the city," a doctor who gave generously to the poor and sang with the angels.[14] He seemed to have a certain humility about his monastic vocation and did not value ego-driven forms of extreme self-mortification.

It is difficult to know how accurate any sources are to the historical Antony, but according to Samuel Rubenson, the letters may be the surest guide, and these, too, present Antony as a body-affirming and deeply loving person. In this text, Antony characterizes the purpose of asceticism as "separating the fruits of the flesh from what is natural to the body" and leading "each member of the body back to its original condition." He speaks of a special process of purification for particular body parts:

---

[10] Athanasius, *Life of Antony*, sec. 45.

[11] Athanasius, *Life of Antony*, secs. 9, 14, 93.

[12] Athanasius, *Life of Antony*, sec. 87.

[13] *Sayings of the Desert Fathers*, "Anthony the Great," no. 9.

[14] *Sayings of the Desert Fathers*, "Anthony the Great," nos. 8, 24.

the eyes, the ears, the tongue, the hands, and the belly, orienting each toward beneficial actions that are natural to it.[15] He gives the same counsel to all persons and attributes to each the same "spiritual essence, in which there is neither man nor woman." His letters make no discriminations on the basis of gender. He beckons everyone to love, writing, "we ought to love one another warmly, for he who loves his neighbour loves God, and he who loves God loves his own soul."[16]

Black persons are neighbors. Therefore, they must be loved, and Antony's asceticism is a method precisely for achieving that end. Black persons are rational creatures of God who share the same spiritual essence as other human beings (as I have argued in a different way using Aquinas in chapter 2). Therefore, they need to be vigilant about avoiding sin and seeking what is good, and Antony's asceticism is as much a model for them as for anyone else. It should go without saying, but sadly must be said in this context, that Black persons are human beings, not demons. Monastic literature's tendency to present them as faces of diabolical evil seems to open a chasm between Black life and Christian asceticism. Yet Antony's practical wisdom about how to fight body-afflicting, neighbor-harming evil has the potential to bridge this divide.

Sexuality is not demonic either, but it can be used demonically. As we have seen in chapter 3, it has been wielded in shockingly violent ways against Black and Native communities, including children. One of the most devilish things imaginable is to vilify a person because of their race or gender, to reduce their body to a sexual object and brand it as disgusting, even while exploiting it without consent for whatever selfish purposes one likes. As I argue in the last section of this chapter, the monastic tradition's fight against *porneia* should be reinterpreted as a resounding "no" to such abuse. Despite what early Christian monastic literature suggests, Black life is not more or less sexual than other human life. Moreover, it should not be disparaged for the extent to which it is sexual, insofar as this is part of the body's natural condition and

---

[15]Rubenson, *Letters of St. Antony*, Letter One, 199–201.
[16]Rubenson, *Letters of St. Antony*, Letter Six, 216, 222.

the soul's God-given eros. However, something like asceticism is needed to curb the unrestrained lust, along with other vices such as avarice and pride, that have fueled the White supremacist assault on Black lives. With such concerns in mind, we can reclaim Antony and other desert fathers and mothers as allies.

Moses the Black

We turn now to one such desert father, who is remembered in part because of his ostensible racial identity. "He was black." "He was a slave." We learn these two facts from the first two sentences of Palladius's account of the monk he calls "Moses the Ethiopian." In *The Sayings of the Desert Fathers*, Abba Moses is identified as a "big, black man." Both texts emphasize that, early in his time as a monk in Scetis, he was plagued by erotic demons, even in his dreams. They thereby reinforce the problematic cultural association of dark skin with hypersexuality. Palladius describes Moses's life prior to his conversion to asceticism, indicating that he was emancipated from slavery because he was too violent to be kept in bondage and that he became "chief of one robber band" and "even committed murders."[17] From slavery to criminality to lust, much of his story reads as a stereotypical portrait, not only of Ethiopians as they were perceived by ancient Egyptians, but also of African Americans as they are often portrayed in the media today. How much of Abba Moses's story is historically true is impossible to know, but a more important consideration is what it means. It behooves us to interpret these texts cautiously, following two guiding principles. First, we should be wary of their negative depictions of Black life, since they reflect obvious biases. Second, we should let Moses be a person: flawed, graced, and singular. We should strive to see and feel the human being behind the anecdotes. By employing these strategies, we can rescue Moses's story from its overdetermination by anti-Black expectations, both past and present, and remember him as a complex, textured icon of Black asceticism.

---

[17]Palladius, *Lausiac History*, 19.1, 19.5, and *Sayings of the Desert Fathers*, "Moses," nos. 1, 8.

Palladius reports that, after many years of brigandage, Moses became "conscience stricken," and this prompted him to begin a monastic program of repentance.[18] The claim that he had a conscience that intervened in his life demonstrates that, even for this text, he was not a monster but a human being capable of moral feeling. One wonders if his violent behavior began as a justified revolt against the indignities of slavery, in the manner of a Denmark Vesey or Nat Turner, and what material poverty may have inclined him to steal, perhaps simply to survive. It is possible that he was listening to his conscience in these early, rougher years too. Whatever the case, the pain he was causing others eventually caught up with him. He wanted to become a person of peace. His new motto was, "Do no harm to anyone, do not think anything bad in your heart towards anyone."[19]

Dismissive attitudes toward Blackness affected Abba Moses deeply. His fellow monks scoffed, "Why does this black man come among us?" According to the narrator of *The Sayings of the Desert Fathers*, these hurtful words were meant as a "test." However, even if this had been their real intention, this would not exonerate the persons who said them, because it was not their job to verify Moses's character in this way, by singling him out for his physical appearance and humiliating him. They should have attended to their own souls. Regardless, it is likely that not all such racist remarks that may have been uttered were perfectly well intentioned. The narrator approvingly states that Moses "kept silence." This story is meant to illustrate that he was no longer the kind of person to retaliate but was now a virtuous man of self-control. However, the text also recounts him admitting, "I was grieved."[20] Evidently, he was not so stoic as to be unmoved by such slights. They got to him; they stung. Being a monk was difficult enough. Now imagine being the only Black one in such a context. Consider the extra emotional burdens this would involve.

The Sayings of the Desert Fathers describes another similarly

[18]Palladius, *Lausiac History*, 19.3.

[19]*Sayings of the Desert Fathers*, "Seven Instructions Which Abba Moses Sent to Abba Poemen," no. 7.

[20]*Sayings of the Desert Fathers*, "Moses," no. 3.

unnerving episode. When Moses was ordained a priest, he donned the customary white vestment, and the archbishop presiding over the ceremony exclaimed, perhaps half-jokingly, "See, Abba Moses, now you are entirely white." Moses replied, "It is true of the outside, lord and father, but what about Him who sees the inside?"[21] The archbishop's remark was supposed to be a clever comment about a double incongruity that both he and Moses could easily perceive. First, Moses was a darkly colored person wearing a bright garment. Second, the symbolic universe that they inhabited encouraged them to interpret his Black body as a sign of his reprobate past and his gleaming priestly attire as a sign of his new life of sanctity. In effect, the archbishop was playfully pointing out how curious it was that light had overtaken darkness at both levels. Moses corrected him by suggesting that there was still some malice in his heart, which God could see. The superficial covering of his body was misleading because he was still (at least somewhat) Black on the inside. By this, he did not mean simply that he was a sinner, irrespective of any racial designation. More precisely, he implied that he was the sinner that a Black person was rightly expected to be. He all but stated that the negative symbolic meaning of his body accurately conveyed the unholy state of his soul. The archbishop's quip and Moses's demurral relied on the same anti-Black assumptions.

The Sayings of the Desert Fathers intends to highlight Moses's admirable humility but inadvertently exposes his internalized oppression. The narrative of his ordination takes a disheartening turn when the archbishop who had jested about him becoming "entirely white" instructed his fellow priests to test Moses further by hurling insults at him and driving him out of the sanctuary. They shouted, "Outside, black man!" Then, "going out, he said to himself, 'They have acted rightly concerning you, for your skin is as black as ashes. You are not a man, so why should you be allowed to meet men.'"[22] Having their fun and pretending to be his spiritual masters, they jeered at him and made him leave. But the most crushing part of the story is the self-hating, dehuman-

[21] *Sayings of the Desert Fathers*, "Moses," no. 4.
[22] *Sayings of the Desert Fathers*, "Moses," no. 4.

izing manner in which he supposedly spoke to himself (which might remind one of Angela of Foligno's similarly exaggerated self-deprecations discussed in chapter 5). Given the circumstances of Moses's life, it is plausible that he would have absorbed such verbal abuse and, at least at some level, regarded it as justified. He was only human after all, despite what he told himself, and part of being human is receiving messages from others and incorporating them into one's self-concept, whether one intends to or not. In response to this passage, my opinion is that our task is not to emulate Moses but to empathize with him, to feel the pain he would have felt in such moments and to walk with him in his search for healing.

Yet Abba Moses can be more for us than an object of compassion. He can be a gifted—if occasionally overzealous—instructor in the ascetical methods of attaining inner and outer peace. He taught that each person should focus on their own sins so as to avoid judging others, because such judgment leads to wrath and eventually violence. He believed that the human inclination toward aggression, with which he was intimately acquainted from his criminal past, stemmed from a tendency to blame others for one's suffering and could be halted only by a penetrating look inward and an honest recognition of one's own need for mercy. He explained, "When someone is occupied with his own faults, he does not see those of his neighbor."[23] The self-scrutinizing person loses the will for vengeance.

As a morally reformed man, Abba Moses had earned a certain authority to speak on such subjects. With God's help, he had done the work to transform himself from a volatile to a tranquil person, and he knew what that radical change required, at least in his case: a disposition of indifference which he called a "dying to one's neighbour."[24] For him, this phrase did not mean ceasing to care for others. On the contrary, he was known to give generously of himself in acts of hospitality, even if this required using

[23] *Sayings of the Desert Fathers*, "Seven Instructions Which Abba Moses Sent to Abba Poemen," no. 3.

[24] *Sayings of the Desert Fathers*, "Seven Instructions Which Abba Moses Sent to Abba Poemen," no. 7.

up the last of his water or breaking a communal fast and risking the ire of his fellow monks.[25] For him, dying to neighbor meant refusing to think ill of anyone, regardless of their behavior, so that one would be freer to love them as God demanded.

Abba Moses pushed this maxim to an almost impossible extreme, declaring that we should not judge others "in any way whatever." Even slaves being beaten by their masters should not, on his reasoning, become incensed at this cruelty but instead dwell on the imperfect state of their own souls.[26] Although he introduced this example in an attempt to posit an exceptionless norm, it may instead prove why much greater caution is needed. Evil propagates itself not only through resentments that fuel cycles of violence but also through the pressure that victims feel to blame themselves. Unfortunately, Moses was not attentive to the psychological damage that occurs when victims hold themselves responsible for their own victimization. An enslaved person or anyone enduring physical or any other kind of abuse must be free to condemn and resist that behavior, and doing so in no way compromises their moral integrity but in fact demonstrates it. Moses was simply wrong to suggest otherwise (if, in fact, he did).

Nonetheless, we can acknowledge that asceticism seems to have given Moses much of the cognitive retraining he needed to become the loving person he felt called to be. By denying himself the pleasures of the flesh, he acquired habits of self-control that he applied to his thoughts and will. He quieted the turmoil of his heart and discovered the capacity to love his neighbors, even his enemies. His story may not be a model for everyone, but perhaps it can be an inspiration to some, including some in the Black community who are seeking a way out of violence. Moses was earnest in his convictions. He even died for what he believed. When barbarians raided Scetis, he did not flee but accepted a martyr's death, bearing witness to the search for peace in this brutal world.[27] If he had never tried asceticism, he could have easily been

[25] *Sayings of the Desert Fathers*, "Moses," nos. 5, 13.

[26] *Sayings of the Desert Fathers*, "Seven Instructions Which Abba Moses Sent to Abba Poemen," nos. 1, 7.

[27] *Sayings of the Desert Fathers*, "Moses," no. 10.

one of the attackers instead of one of those being slain. Yet, as he watched them rushing toward his cell, he would not have wanted to trade places with any of them, even for a second, because he had found a higher freedom.

Abba Moses is venerated as a saint and martyr by Orthodox Christians and has been a particular beacon of hope for Orthodox African Americans. Since its founding in the mid-1990s, the Fellowship of St. Moses the Black has served this faith community by hosting annual conferences that relate the African roots of early Christianity, exemplified by Abba Moses, to contemporary struggles for racial justice and reconciliation. One of the founders of this fellowship, a Black Orthodox priest named Fr. Moses Berry, spoke about the Movement for Black Lives and his organization's spiritual means of engaging with it. He noted, "We march, but as Orthodox we march with images, banners, incense and prayers," adding that "to make a change, we reach towards heaven, not to the unrighteous wisdom of this world." Echoing the ascetical teachings of his patron and namesake, he emphasized the value of prayer, fasting, and forgiveness. At the same time, he stressed a need to educate others about why we say, "Black lives matter," instead of "the painfully familiar, 'all lives matter.'"[28] The Fellowship of St. Moses the Black shows the socially critical power of Abba Moses's Black asceticism in action.

Fugitivity

Moses the Black inaugurated a long tradition of interweaving Black life and Christian asceticism, which has often gone unrecognized. This tradition continues in the modern period, from the trans-Atlantic slave trade to the present, and calls for further reflection and development. Among other modes of manifestation, it appears in the practice of fugitivity: fleeing the evils of the world. In early Christian monasticism, the paradigmatic line

[28]Quoted in Elena V. Kravchenko, "Matter of Race: Brotherhood of St. Moses the Black and the Retelling of African American History Through Orthodox Christian Forms," *Journal of the American Academy of Religion* 89, no. 1 (March 2021): 298–333, at 318. For more information about this fellowship, see https://mosestheblack.org.

of flight was from the city to the desert. In the slaveholding parts of the antebellum United States, it was from South to North. In both contexts, these spatial trajectories symbolized a passage from sin to salvation. Monks sought distance from the acquisitive and aggressive habits that plagued metropolitan society. Escaped African American slaves sought liberation from the vicious system of race-based chattel slavery of which they were victims, not perpetrators. But they also battled their own internal demons, which were tied to the slave experience in complex ways. There were inner struggles to heal from deep psychological wounds, as well as to develop the moral character that racially prejudiced persons assumed Black people could not acquire. As a freed slave and repentant sinner, Abba Moses represents the need to move away from both structural and personal evils. As we shall see shortly, *The Narrative of Sojourner Truth* conveys a similar message in a different time and place.

For both early Christian ascetics and enslaved African Americans, Exodus was a key model of fugitivity. In Ambrose's sermon called "Flight from the World" (*De fuga saeculi*), he resembles other ancient authors such as Philo of Alexandria and Gregory of Nyssa by interpreting this biblical story, or at least certain parts of it, as an allegory of the soul's path toward virtue. He preaches, "Let us not be ashamed to flee, for this flight is a glorious one, to flee from the face of sin. . . . Thus did Moses flee from the face of King Pharao [*sic*], so that the royal palace would not defile him or royal power ensnare him."[29] Ambrose reads Moses as one who overcame the temptations of wealth and power, just as any ascetically disciplined Christian is supposed to do. By contrast, the Black reception of Exodus—for obvious reasons—prioritizes a literal escape from slavery. When weary voices in the slave quarters sang, "Go down, Moses, / 'Way down in Egypt land, / Tell ole Pharaoh, / Let my people go," their prayer was for abolition or at least escape.[30] Construing the meaning of Exodus in these

[29] Ambrose, "Flight from the World," in *Seven Exegetical Works*, trans. Michael P. McHugh (Catholic University of America Press, 1970), 279–323, at 296, sec. 4.19.

[30] "Go Down, Moses," in *The Books of American Negro Spirituals*, ed. James Weldon Johnson, musical arrangements by J. Rosamund Johnson (Da

various theological ways allows it to represent a rich, multifaceted sense of fugitivity.

Ambrose's account of fugitivity interestingly draws on another biblical passage. He highlights Numbers 35 and its instructions about setting up cities of refuge for unintentional killers. He suggests that we should see ourselves in such fugitives, insofar as we too have likely participated in harmful behaviors from which we need to flee. He points out that the land for these sanctuary cities belongs to the Levites, that is to say, priests, whom he argues must also flee the world in order to dedicate themselves wholly to God. He thus distinguishes two figures of fugitivity: the repentant wrongdoers and the priests who mercifully minister to them. Both equally need an ascetical practice of withdrawal in order to do the work God asks them to do. Ambrose concludes, "It was right that a decree of the eternal law entrusted fugitives to fugitives."[31] Through his allegorical exegesis of this passage, he proposes a comprehensive ascetical ecclesiology: a vision of the church in which its ministers renounce material attachments in order to care for morally flawed and physically vulnerable persons whose redemption likewise necessitates some such renunciation.

Missing from Ambrose's otherwise useful account of fugitivity is the recognition that some fugitives, despite being hated by others and even indicted under the law, are entirely without blame. Numbers 35:11 seems to have precisely this situation in mind when it specifies that the cities of refuge are for people who have killed unintentionally. The point holds even more strongly in the case of Hebrews leaving Egypt and African Americans traveling the "Underground Railroad," who were violating the legal norms of their societies but for perfectly valid reasons. Pharaoh's tyrannical will was the law of the land. In like manner, the Fugitive Slave Act of 1850 classified escaped Black persons as criminals, demanded their immediate capture and return, and punished anyone who aided them. In both contexts, doing the right thing was illegal, and the outlaws in flight were, for the most part, not even inadvertently violent (as in Numbers) but were inoffensively

Capo Press, 2002), 51. For further discussion of the spirituals, see chapter 2.

[31] Ambrose, "Flight from the World," 285, sec. 2.7.

seeking a way out of oppression. The sin from which they were fleeing was not their own. To Ambrose's two types of fugitivity, then, we must add a third: the no-less-theologically significant fugitivity of those who renounce being enslaved or otherwise dominated. These defiant fugitives abandon the evil world they know—the hell of the plantation—for a promised land they perhaps have only imagined. To provide a place of refuge for them is as much a work of the church as is giving comfort and guidance to contrite sinners.

Sojourner Truth's life featured multiple experiences and practices of fugitivity. As an enslaved child named Isabella, she withdrew daily from the space of her coerced labor and abuse to seek communion with God in the wilderness:

> The place she selected, in which to offer up her daily orisons, was a small island in a small stream, covered with large willow shrubbery, beneath which the sheep had made their pleasant winding paths; and sheltering themselves from the scorching rays of a noon-tide sun, luxuriated in the cool shadows of the graceful willows, as they listened to the tiny falls of the silver waters. It was a lonely spot, and chosen by her for its beauty, its retirement, and because she thought that there, in the noise of those waters, she could speak louder to God, without being overheard by anyone who might pass that way.[32]

This verdant sanctuary was young Isabella's anchorage. It was her place of physical and spiritual reclusion, where she could be alone with God and escape, if only for a few minutes, the bitterness of her situation. These childhood retreats were rehearsals for what would come later.

As an enslaved adult, Isabella performed a more durable act of fugitivity by walking away from her master's house. She asked herself, "How can I get away?" and had the insight, which she attributed to God, that she should leave just before daybreak, so

[32] *The Narrative of Sojourner Truth*, ed. Nell Irvin Painter (Penguin, 1998), 40.

that darkness would conceal her departure. And so, she left on foot at that early hour, "her infant on one arm and her wardrobe on the other." While on her way, with the sun rising fast, she asked herself, "Where, and to whom, shall I go?" The point had been to get away from the evils of that house—including the brutal beating of her romantic interest Robert, the forced marriage to Thomas, sexual abuse at the hands of Mrs. Dumont, and false promises of emancipation made by Mr. Dumont—compared to which almost anything would be better. Her destination was an afterthought. Eventually, she was given refuge by a Mr. Van Wagener, who purchased her but treated her as a free person, since he regarded God alone as the master of all people.[33]

From that point onward, she no longer lived as a slave. However, like Moses the Black before her, she was not done fleeing evil. While living in New York City, she became disastrously involved with a misogynistic millenarian cult known as the Kingdom of Matthias, which left her penniless and adrift. After this debacle, she found herself disgusted by the whole place. She realized that the city was "but one great system of robbery and wrong" in which "the rich rob the poor, and the poor rob one another." Although she was not the murderous bandit that Abba Moses may have been, she did accuse herself of participating in evil, citing as evidence a selfish choice she made to take a snow-shoveling job away from a poor man who needed the money to support his family. Who could blame her for looking out for herself? After all, she was desperately poor, too. But she was not content with this me-first way of life and all the rationalizations that people use to justify it. Cooperating with a system built on greed "troubled her conscience sorely," and, once again, she sought a way out. She decided "that she must leave the city," and, indeed, "she felt called in spirit to leave it."[34]

If Isabella's only act of fugitivity had been fleeing slavery, she would not have become the feminist, abolitionist icon whom we revere today under the chosen or divinely appointed name Sojourner Truth. To reach this heroic stature, she needed to re-

[33]*Narrative of Sojourner Truth*, 28–29.
[34]*Narrative of Sojourner Truth*, 67–68.

nounce the racial and gender oppression that violated her dignity, as well as the socially corrosive egoism and avarice in which she judged herself to be complicit. She had to reject the immense wickedness of the wider world and also that small portion of it that dwelled within her, which she believed was keeping her from obeying God's simple command to love one's neighbor as oneself. Having experienced the blameless fugitivity of a runaway slave, which Ambrose overlooked, she now adopted the two types of fugitivity he recognized. She traveled eastward on a journey of both repentance and ministry, equipped with "only a few articles of clothing in a pillow-case, all else being deemed an unnecessary incumbrance."[35] Like Antony and the monks of old, she moved out of the city to seek a better setting for following the will of God, leaving all other concerns behind.

After some months as an itinerant preacher, engaging in the sort of evangelical work we have seen Zilpha Elaw do in chapter 6, Sojourner Truth settled in an ascetical community of sorts: the Northampton Association of Education and Industry (1842–1846). This short-lived utopian enclave was "started by abolitionists dedicated not only to ending slavery but to promoting women's rights and religious toleration," and it was one of very few predominantly White institutions at the time that welcomed Black persons as equals. Members aspired to a life of simplicity, modeled on the first apostles, and sought to distance themselves from the superficial, materialistic values of the broader society.[36] Although not a strict monastic enclosure, the Northampton Association was a place set apart, in which people of various ages, races, genders, and classes lived and worked together, attempting to instantiate an alternative vision of human life closer to the kingdom of God. It was in this context that Sojourner Truth began to network with abolitionists and other social reformers. This was the community that connected her with Olive Gilbert, who helped her write her *Narrative* and thereby gain lasting cultural signifi-

[35] *Narrative of Sojourner Truth*, 68.

[36] Christopher Clark, *The Communitarian Moment: The Radical Challenge of the Northampton Association* (Cornell University Press, 1995), 7, 111. See also *Narrative of Sojourner Truth*, 78.

cance. As in fourth-century Egypt, so, too, in nineteenth-century New England, withdrawing from the world and influencing it were not mutually exclusive propositions.

Nonviolence

Whatever its outer trappings, ascetism is largely an internal battle: an effort to gain control over those unruly thoughts and feelings inside each of us that can trigger violent behavior. By seeking deep inner calm (*apatheia*), ascetics aim to establish the psychological conditions necessary for a more peaceful world. It should come as no surprise, then, that the Civil Rights movement and other campaigns of nonviolent resistance in the twentieth century have strong ties to asceticism. Fasting and celibacy were not hallmarks of Martin Luther King Jr.'s activism, as they were, by contrast, in the public life of Mohandas Gandhi.[37] However, the commitment to nonviolence (*ahimsa*) on both a spiritual and social level was an aspect of Gandhi's more comprehensive ascetical regimen that King, following Howard Thurman, embraced wholeheartedly. These Black Baptist ministers selectively appropriated that part of Gandhi's politically charged practice of self-discipline that they deemed most relevant to the Negro community's fight for social change.

King and Thurman made no secret of their indebtedness to Gandhi. Reflecting back on the evolution of his thinking as a graduate student, King wrote,

> As I delved deeper into the philosophy of Gandhi my skepticism concerning the power of love gradually diminished, and I came to see for the first time that the Christian doctrine of love operating through the Gandhian method of nonviolence was one of the most potent weapons available to oppressed people in their struggle for freedom.[38]

---

[37] Veena R. Howard, *Gandhi's Ascetic Activism: Renunciation and Social Action* (SUNY Press, 2013), 12.

[38] Martin Luther King Jr., "Pilgrimage to Nonviolence," in *A Testament of Hope: The Essential Writings and Speeches of Martin Luther King, Jr.*,

Although King visited India, he did so more than a decade after Gandhi was assassinated. Thurman, by contrast, met Gandhi in person on his 1935 journey throughout the subcontinent. At the end of their three-hour conversation, Gandhi shared his perception with Thurman that "it could be through the Afro-American that the unadulterated message of nonviolence would be delivered to all men everywhere."[39]

The enthusiastic reception of Gandhi by such esteemed figures of African American history has contributed to an idealized image of his greatness, which may be overstated. Recent critics of Gandhi, perhaps most trenchantly Arundhati Roy, have raised concerns about his positions on race, caste, gender, and sexuality. Roy shows that Gandhi's efforts in South Africa (1893–1914), where he developed his philosophy of *satyagraha* (truth force) and first experimented with vegetarianism, fasting, celibacy, and voluntary poverty, were disconnected from the needs of the most subaltern people in that part of the world. His goal was to convince the colonial establishment to treat upper-caste "passenger Indians" such as himself with the same respect that White British subjects received. To make this argument, he consistently distinguished this group from Black Natives, whom he called "Kaffirs" and accused of being uncivilized. He also differentiated his set from lower-caste "indentured Indians" whom Roy argues "lived and worked in conditions of virtual slavery, incarcerated on sugarcane farms."[40] Back in India, Gandhi used *satyagraha* to seek humanizing reforms to the caste system, including an end to "untouchability," but he stopped short of supporting his Dalit rival, Dr. Bhimrao Ambedkar's call for the abolition of caste.[41] Later in life, as a test of his vow of sexual abstinence (*brahmacharya*), Gandhi slept naked in the same bed with teenage girls, including

---

ed. James M. Washington (Harper, 1986), 35–40, at 38.

[39] Howard Thurman, *With Head and Heart: The Autobiography of Howard Thurman* (Harcourt Brace, 1979), 132.

[40] Arundhati Roy, *The Doctor and the Saint: Caste, Race, and Annihilation of Caste: The Debate Between B. R. Ambedkar and M. K. Gandhi*, e-book (Haymarket, 2017), 46–48.

[41] Roy, *Doctor and the Saint*, 15–16, 97.

his grandniece, in an experimental practice that even close associates thought ill-advised.[42] For all of these reasons, his legacy has become controversial.

None of this changes the fact that Gandhi's innovative use of asceticism as a means of social protest—particularly the renunciation of violence—had a decisive impact on the strategies employed by King and the Southern Christian Leadership Conference. Writing from a jail cell in Birmingham, King enumerated "four basic steps" of their method of agitation, which were to be completed in order: "(1) collection of the facts to determine whether injustices are alive, (2) negotiation, (3) self-purification, and (4) direct action." Although seldom emphasized, the third, purificatory step was indispensable. It was the training ground in which participants in the struggle prepared mentally and spiritually to use their violated bodies to appeal to the collective conscience of the country. They had to cultivate a certain inner fortitude, asking themselves questions such as, "'Are you able to accept blows without retaliating?' 'Are you able to endure the ordeals of jail?'"[43] To be struck and humiliated without fighting back required something resembling the saintly character of a Moses the Black. Perhaps it was possible for some to remain composed while seething on the inside, but King and Thurman warned that any such hatred was toxic, even when one did not act on it. Nonviolence was more than a practical strategy. It was an ideal disposition closely aligned with Christian love, which had its first and most reliable effect on the "souls of those committed to it."[44] The Civil Rights movement promoted an interior striving for peace that would spill over to the outside world.

Although King and Thurman attributed many of their insights about nonviolence to Gandhi, precedents for them can also be

---

[42] Roy, *Doctor and the Saint*, 57–59, and Vinay Lal, "Nakedness, Nonviolence, and Brahmacharya: Gandhi's Experiments in Celibate Sexuality," *Journal of the History of Sexuality* 9, nos. 1–2 (January/April 2000): 105–36.

[43] King, "Letter from Birmingham City Jail," in *A Testament of Hope*, 289–302, at 290–91.

[44] King, "Pilgrimage to Nonviolence," 39.

found in early Christian asceticism. The fourth-century monastic theologian Evagrius Ponticus is remembered for identifying eight "evil thoughts" that stand in the way of peace: gluttony, lust (*porneia*), love of money, sadness, anger (*orgé*), listlessness, vainglory, and pride. He grants that we have no ability to stop these ideations from troubling us, but we can learn to exert power over them so they do not stir up passions that lead us to act in harmful ways.[45]

Regarding anger in particular, Evagrius advises us not to suppress it altogether, but rather to redirect its combative energy toward its natural target, which are the forces of evil that he calls demons. He explains that the angels help us keep our anger pointed in the right direction, while the demons seek to reroute it toward human beings:

> The nature of anger is to fight the demons and to struggle on behalf of any sort of pleasure. For this reason, the angels suggest spiritual pleasure to us, and the blessedness it yields, and they urge us to direct the angry part against the demons. The latter, however, dragging us back toward worldly desires, violently compel our anger, against its nature, to fight human beings, so that the mind, now darkened and fallen from knowledge, becomes a traitor to the virtues.[46]

Although Evagrius classifies anger as an evil thought, this description applies only when anger is unconstrained by the divine wisdom that the angels communicate and is instead motivated by worldly ambitions stirred up by demonic influences. As a Hellenistic thinker, he assumes a tripartite model of the soul, which divides it into "rational," "desiring," and "angering" parts. In this schema, the rational part is supposed to govern the desiring part by moving it toward the enjoyment of transcendent goods, above all, God. It is also supposed to govern the angering part

---

[45]Evagrius Ponticus, *The Praktikos & Chapters on Prayer* no. 6, trans. John Eudes Bamberger (Cistercian, 1972), 35. The subsequent tradition of "seven deadly sins" draws on this list but absorbs vainglory into pride and substitutes envy for sadness.

[46]Evagrius, *Praktikos* nos. 24, 49.

(*thymos*) by keeping it focused on its proper role as a defender of justice. When rightly ordered, anger does not inhibit the inner peace that Evagrius calls *apatheia*.[47]

Thurman's *Jesus and the Disinherited* (1949), a book that King is said to have carried with him on many of his journeys, conveys a similar ascetical teaching when it confronts hate, along with fear and duplicity, as three "hounds of hell" (i.e., demons). While Evagrius diagnoses eight evil thoughts that can afflict anyone, Thurman pinpoints three self-defeating "techniques by which the weak have protected themselves against the strong."[48] Thurman explains why these mental states are attractive to the dispossessed but also why they must be overcome. He argues that the underprivileged, including those like himself whom he calls Negroes, have work to do if they want to conform themselves to the way of Jesus. Like Black persons, Jesus belonged to a dominated, impoverished, and minoritized group whose suffering seemed not to matter to the world: first-century Jews under Roman occupation. However, Jesus's precarity was not all that defined him. He also had a vision for how to live together in harmony with God that required extraordinary self-discipline and even self-sacrifice. At least at a psychological level, Jesus prescribed an ascetical program that was supposed to reshape his followers into models of faith, sincerity, and love.[49]

Following Jesus's lead, Thurman contends that Black persons should not nurture hatred for their enemies, even when it is warranted. He recognizes that feelings of antipathy can be a form of "righteous indignation" and even serve a "creative purpose" for those suffering injustice. By explaining the legitimate reasons for such anger, he subordinates it to reason, just as Evagrius recommends. But Thurman is not convinced that this is enough. Distinguishing Jesus from the Zealots, he argues that it is better to resist evil through a practice of unconditional love that will never resort to violence instead of a morally justified rage

[47]Evagrius, *Praktikos* nos. 86, 88.

[48]Thurman, *Jesus and the Disinherited* (Beacon Press, 1996), 35, 36, 58, 74. See also the Foreword by Vincent Harding.

[49]Thurman, *Jesus and the Disinherited*, 11–35.

that easily could. Neither passive nor accommodating, Jesus's method of nonviolent resistance applies unrelenting pressure to the consciences of others, seeking to convert them from enemies to persons-in-community.[50] By emphasizing the resistive power in Jesus's approach, Thurman retains the antagonistic energy that one might associate with Evagrius's properly ordered anger, while insisting, as Evagrius and Abba Moses do as well, that it must never be directed hatefully against any human beings, even evildoers. In effect, he is asking Black persons to act and feel interiorly like monks. Many courageous women, men, and children who were attacked by dogs, firehoses, and batons endeavored to answer this lofty calling, at least for a time.

Power

The mood changed dramatically after King was murdered by a White supremacist. The moral suasion and universalist ethics of the New Negro era seemed to die with him, and a younger, more militant generation rose to prominence, preferring to speak not of love but Black power. One might conjecture that this shift severed the already tenuous thread tying Black life to Christian asceticism. From its origins, this relationship had been fraught, as we have seen, and serious misgivings about it, most famously voiced by Malcolm X, were on the rise during King's lifetime. King's death only cemented such concerns. However, the truth is that the synthesis I am calling Black asceticism did not so much end with King's passing as take on new forms.

For starters, we should recall that the Nation of Islam, which Malcolm X represented for much of his public career, had a strong ascetical bent resembling those found in other Abrahamic and non-Abrahamic religions, including Christianity. Like the desert fathers and mothers, W. D. Fard Muhammad, the founder of the Nation of Islam, had a practice of eating only once per day. He favored specific foods such as fresh vegetables and avoided others such as pork and sugary treats. He and his successor, Elijah Muhammad, urged their followers to do the same as well as engage

[50]Thurman, *Jesus and the Disinherited*, 27, 79, 85, 95, 100.

in regular fasts. The Nation of Islam began as a racially defined religious movement for African Americans that deviated significantly from traditional Islam by, among other things, promoting the highly unorthodox teaching that Fard was divine. But the idea that religious devotion was linked to specific dietary rules had Islamic roots. The practical argument, which had some truth to it, was that being intentional about what food one put into one's body would benefit the lives of people in the Black community.[51]

The fact that the Nation of Islam considered White people to be devils is highly problematic, as other radical Black thinkers at the time recognized,[52] but we should also note that such an association of one racial group with diabolical forces mirrors the early Egyptian treatment of Ethiopians. By drawing this parallel, I do not mean to endorse such dehumanizing rhetoric in either context but merely to reject a double standard. If Athanasius can be read charitably despite such missteps, so can Malcolm X. It is also useful to situate the Nation of Islam's practice of demonizing White persons in the historical context of slavery, lynching, segregation, and other forms of brutality that made it credible to some Black people—which is not the same as justifying it. In any case, near the end of his life, Malcolm X distanced himself from this racial ontology and embraced a more traditional view of Islam, along with a more expansive vision of humanity. His true cultural legacy is not anti-White, but it is pro-Black. His bold, charismatic spirit inspired countless admirers to love Black life, art, consciousness, and power in ways they never had before.[53]

Despite what one might assume, the concept of power championed by Malcolm X and other Black theorists and activists is not foreign to asceticism but in fact integral to it. It builds on the ancient tradition of rational self-governance (*enkrateia*), which,

---

[51]Nils Duranton, "Life in Abundance: Diet, Black Health, and Spirituality in the Nation of Islam, 1930–1975," *Studies in Religion/Sciences Religieuses* 53, no. 4 (2024): 593–611. See also the discussion of Malcolm X's "self-mortification" in Biko Mandela Gray and Ryan J. Johnson, *Phenomenology of Black Spirit* (Edinburgh University Press, 2023), 219–48.

[52]James Baldwin, *The Fire Next Time*, e-book (Vintage, 1991), 31–47.

[53]James H. Cone, *Martin & Malcolm & America: A Dream or a Nightmare* (Orbis Books, 2007), 51, 205, 290.

prior to being adapted by Christian ascetics, was developed by Plato and other philosophers he influenced.[54] According to Plato, this form of virtuous self-mastery is achieved by subordinating the supposedly lower, more passionate parts to the higher, more enlightened ones, both in the mind and in the city-state. Evagrius follows this thinking in his account of a peaceful soul in which desire and anger are ordered by reason. The political expression of this idea, which Plato articulates in *Republic*, subjects "children, women, slaves, and (among so-called free men) the rabble who constitute the majority of the population . . . who evidently experience the greatest quantity and variety of forms of desire, pleasure, and pain" to the rule of the "philosopher king," that nontyrannical monarch who has been illumined by the Good.[55] In this worldview, ascetical power over self corresponds exactly to political dominion over others.

This correspondence might justly revive Black suspicions of asceticism, because it seems obvious where such a hierarchical imaginary will situate us, namely, in the inferior position of something dangerous that needs to be controlled. However, when confronted by such a philosophy, Black persons do not have to identify with the "rabble" who are thought to be so thoroughly driven by their irrational instincts that they allegedly deserve to be treated like slaves, whether this is their legal condition or not. We can reject this pitiful status, so regularly assigned to us, and instead become our own philosopher kings, so to speak—discerning for ourselves what is good and beautiful and life-sustaining for our communities and managing them accordingly. We can take responsibility for our inner and outer lives, working to overcome any self-destructive impulses in our psyches, while defending ourselves against the disordered drives of others that prompt them to demean, harm, or kill us. Black people who refuse the role of representing and inciting others' carnal passions and instead claim the self-governing humanity that they already innately possess

---

[54]Louis-Andre Dorion, "Plato and *Enkrateia*," in *Akrasia in Greek Philosophy: From Socrates to Plotinus*, ed. Christopher Bobonich and Pierre Destrée (Brill, 2007), 119–38.

[55]Plato, *Republic*, trans. Robin Waterfield (Oxford University Press, 1993), 431b–c, 520a.

are on the road to attaining what Kwame Ture (formerly Stokely Carmichael) memorably called "Black Power." Their self-mastery is a form of *enkrateia* and should be acknowledged as such.

The analogy between Plato's *Republic* and the social philosophy of Black power breaks down on one crucial point, however. Unlike Plato, Black power advocates are not interested in dominating any supposedly inferior classes of people. The goal is simply self-determination for those who have been historically disenfranchised. The analogy remains helpful only to the extent that the leaders of such initiatives, like Plato's philosopher kings, are typically guided by clear-eyed reasoning and concern for the well-being of their communities. Despite how they are regularly portrayed (I am thinking, for example, of the Killmonger character in Marvel's *Black Panther* franchise), Black power advocates are not inclined to settle scores through indiscriminate killing. As Ture and his coauthor Charles Hamilton show in their groundbreaking work, *Black Power* (1967), the primary concerns of this movement are improving education through parental involvement in the leadership of predominantly Black schools; increasing housing safety and affordability through tenant associations in Black neighborhoods; promoting economic independence through investments in Black businesses; and strengthening political representation, not merely through voting, but also by establishing alternative political parties, platforms, and community-based institutions.[56]

Cone cites this text as a key source in his first book, *Black Theology and Black Power* (1969).[57] He embraces Ture and Hamilton's proposals and combines them with existentialist philosophical and Christian theological reflections to produce his own account of Black power as a practice of morally responsible freedom. He writes, with emphasis in the original, "Simply stated, freedom is *not doing what I will but becoming what I should. A man is free when he sees clearly the fulfillment of his being and is thus capable of making the envisioned self a reality.*

[56]Kwame Ture and Charles V. Hamilton, *Black Power: The Politics of Liberation* (Vintage, 1992), 164–77.

[57]Cone, *Black Theology and Black Power* (Orbis Books, 2008), 62–63, 157n1.

This is 'Black Power!' " He explains further, "As long as man is a slave to another power, he is not free to serve God with mature responsibility. He is not free to become what he is—human."[58] For Cone, Black power is neither arbitrary willfulness nor brute force but a conscious process of self-realization and humanization whereby Black persons free themselves from the evil forces of a racist society in order to serve God as they ought. Although not all who seek this sort of empowerment are Christian, Cone argues that Black power is "consistent with the gospel of Jesus Christ," because it carries forward Christ's liberative work in history. Moreover, he contends that proponents of Black power are in a unique position to keep Christianity from completely losing its way, just as Athanasius did during the fourth-century Arian controversy. Cone identifies racism as the great heresy of our age and sees Black power as a necessary means of resisting it.[59]

To be sure, Cone does not attempt to rid his theology of anger. He recalls, "It was the challenging and angry voice of Malcolm X that shook me out of my theological complacency," and he describes himself as an "angry black man, disgusted with the oppression of black people." Nor does he commit himself to nonviolence as an exclusive method. Rather, like other Black power leaders, he keeps open the possibility of armed self-defense and even rebellion, as needed.[60] In this respect, he differs significantly from Abba Moses and Thurman. However, he evokes other aspects of Christian asceticism through his readiness for spiritual combat against demonic powers, his demand for costly acts of repentance on the part of White Christians who have profited from anti-Black racism, and his urging of Black Christians to exercise responsible agency over their lives in a way that benefits their communities.[61] Whatever its limitations, the much-derided racial separatism of Cone's sources is analogous to monastic withdrawal: both are efforts to break free from the moral corruption of the broader culture. Nonetheless, Cone always maintained that Black power

[58]Cone, *Black Theology and Black Power*, 39.
[59]Cone, *Black Theology and Black Power*, 48, 73.
[60]Cone, *Black Theology and Black Power*, viii, 2, 138–43.
[61]Cone, *Black Theology and Black Power*, 150–53.

was meant to liberate White people too, precisely by releasing them from being "enslaved to their own egos."[62] Both victims and agents of oppression need to renounce the false consciousness it creates in them, all the lies about inferiority and superiority. Black power signifies this universally obligatory act of renunciation.

Eros

Black feminist and womanist thinkers draw on the traditions of nonviolence and power just discussed but also critique their patriarchal, masculinist ethos and their marginalizing of Black women's distinctive contributions. More specifically, many protest the sexual objectifications of Black women's bodies that have occurred in culture and imagination as well as in overt acts of assault and rape. To resist such evil, these thinkers employ multiple strategies that could initially seem anti-ascetical. Although the monastic fight against sexual sin (*porneia*) may provide a useful basis of comparison, monastic literature heaps blame on (Black) women and thereby both badly misidentifies the source of real sexual evil and exacerbates its effects. At the same time, the Black feminist and womanist affirmation of eros subverts the timeworn ascetical practice of deriding Blackness, bodies, women, and sexuality. Nevertheless, common ground can be reached through a recasting of *porneia* as a symbol of the sexual violence that Black women more typically suffer, not commit, and through a recognition that eros, like anger, is a natural gift from God that serves a good purpose when well ordered.

As I noted earlier, Brakke cites the story of a monk who was first tempted by the apparition of an Ethiopian woman, then repulsed by her odor. Brakke provides several other examples that repeat the same pattern of associating dark female flesh with evil erotic power. For instance, he mentions the case of Daniel of Scetis accosting a fellow monk who was frequenting the public baths. The monk insisted he was perfectly chaste, but Daniel saw demons surrounding him: "an Ethiopian woman seated on his shoulders

[62]Cone, *Black Theology and Black Power*, 41.

. . . was embracing him tenderly, while another Ethiopian woman, in front of him, dealt with him roughly and was teaching him an indecent act." Brakke also recounts the tale of Arsenius, a monk who traveled to Alexandria but decided to return to his desert cell after encountering "an Ethiopian slave-girl"—this time a real person, not an apparition—who "approached and touched his sheep-skin" and, after being rebuffed, said, "If you are a monk, go to the desert."[63] Whether demonic or human, Black women appear in such stories as dangerous temptresses. They anticipate the modern stereotype of the Jezebel, which has been discussed in detail by womanist theologians such as Emilie Townes and Kelly Brown Douglas. Through such consistently negative portrayals of Black women's sexuality, these stories contribute to what Townes calls "the cultural production of evil."[64]

The *Life of St. Mary of Egypt* offers an intriguing counterexample by telling the story of a darkly hued woman who left her licentious past behind in order to become what Benedicta Ward calls an "icon of repentance." According to this sixth-century monastic narrative, a twelve-year-old Alexandrian girl named Mary ran away from her family in an effort to satisfy her insatiable sexual desires. For seventeen years, she had as many partners as she could find, often accepting no money in return. The implication is that she lived as a prostitute but was so enflamed by lust that she hardly cared about financial remuneration. One day, she followed a crowd of men onto a ship that was destined for Jerusalem. When she attempted to enter the church there, she was repelled by a supernatural force. This experience initiated a process of conversion. After shedding tears and praying to the Virgin Mary, she fled into the desert, where she lived a solitary life for forty-seven years, until the monk Zossima finally chanced upon her. When he approached, he realized that "she was naked, her body black as if scorched by the fierce heat of the sun." However,

---

[63]Brakke, *Demons and the Making of the Monk*, 157, 171.

[64]Emilie M. Townes, *Womanist Ethics and the Cultural Production of Evil* (Palgrave Macmillan, 2006), 39, 171, and Kelly Brown Douglas, *Sexuality and the Black Church* (Orbis Books, 1999), 36–40.

she was not there to tempt him. Instead, he learned from her how to be less perfectionistic in his ascetical quest and trust more in the extravagant mercy of God.[65]

The same principles that we used to interpret Abba Moses are pertinent here as well: first, we should be skeptical of this text's depiction of Mary's sinfulness, because it reflects cultural prejudices; second, we should endeavor to see her as a person. Even if some details in this account are fictional (which is likely), Mary represents the reality that many women in the ancient world, whether enslaved or not, were engaged in sexual labor. *Porneia*, which is usually translated as "fornication," typically implied liaisons with prostitutes and other men's slaves. Jennifer Glancy demonstrates that a man's sex with his own slaves was permitted by the Jewish and Christian texts that we know prior to the third century and, therefore, not categorized as *porneia*. This term referred exclusively to an impermissible expansion of sexuality beyond the home.[66] In monastic contexts from the fourth century onward, *porneia* gained a wider range of meanings related to the danger of sexual desire in general, even while one was sleeping, becoming synonymous with lust.[67] As we have seen, Evagrius included it in his list of "evil thoughts." Still, the cautionary image of the "harlot" remained paradigmatic.

The fact that the *Life of St. Mary of Egypt* attributes a high degree of agency to the titular character is both important and problematic. It is important because the recognition that she and other similarly employed women, past and present, have desires they seek to fulfill and make choices toward those ends honors the subjectivity of such persons. Perhaps some of the real human beings from sixth-century Egypt who lie behind the central figure of this text did not have sex merely because of economic need, social pressure, or patriarchal violence but because they wanted

[65]Benedicta Ward, SLG, *Harlots in the Desert: A Study of Repentance in Early Monastic Sources* (Cistercian, 1987), 41, 44–49.

[66]Jennifer A. Glancy, "The Sexual Use of Slaves: A Response to Kyle Harper on Jewish and Christian *Porneia*," *Journal of Biblical Literature* 134, no. 1 (2015): 215–29.

[67]Harmless, *Desert Christians*, 232–35.

to. Perhaps too, as the story emphasizes, some felt differently at a later date and received a divine calling to become celibate. In our effort to liberate women like Mary from representing erotic evil, we should not exclude the possibility that a person with her life experiences could freely interpret them in line with the categories of sin and grace that this monastic narrative utilizes. The ascetical refusal of sexuality, including marital sexuality, has been an empowering decision for some women, such as Macrina, for example, and the Black Catholic founder of the Sisters of the Holy Family, Henriette Delille.[68] Any assumption that Mary of Egypt's decision to flee to the desert was necessarily a form of false consciousness would be depersonalizing of her.

Yet the story's attribution of agency is also problematic because it reinforces the idea that Mary and other women who exchange sex for survival are fully consenting to this activity, a perspective that disregards the complex webs of coercion and nonautonomy that are often involved. The line between prostitution and slavery is alarmingly thin in many cases, and this was certainly true in the Roman Empire.[69] Moreover, some women are just literally enslaved; their bodies are used without their consent for pleasure or procreation. As Glancy clarifies, early Christian writers did not consider it to be a case of *porneia* when such exploitation was limited to women who were a man's own property, even if he was married. Abraham's treatment of Hagar as a sexual surrogate, analyzed so powerfully by Delores Williams as a model of Black women's experience,[70] was normal by the standards of Jewish and Christian antiquity. The disreputable hypersexuality that monastic literature demonized and identified with Black women was a strangely inverted sign of actual women's contextual pow-

---

[68] Gregory of Nyssa, *The Life of Macrina*, in *Lives of Roman Christian Women*, trans. and ed. Carolinne White (Penguin, 2010), 22–48, at 25 (para. 5), and M. Shawn Copeland, *The Subversive Power of Love: The Vision of Henriette Delille* (Paulist Press, 2009).

[69] Thomas A. J. McGinn, *The Economy of Prostitution in the Roman World: A Study of Social History and the Brothel* (University of Michigan Press, 2004), 55.

[70] Delores S. Williams, *Sisters in the Wilderness: The Challenge of Womanist God-Talk* (Orbis Books, 2003), 21–26, 55–63.

erlessness. Seeing Mary of Egypt as a person means seeing that many in her situation were there not by choice but because they had few, if any, other options. To demean such persons further by making them the very faces of evil betrays a profound lack of empathy and understanding.

To salvage a positive relationship between Black life and Christian asceticism, it is necessary to redefine *porneia* as sexual violence and to hold those who perpetrate such violence responsible for it, sparing its victims any stigma or judgment, since this only causes additional harm. On this account, *porneia* would include the sexual abuse of enslaved or free women, men, and children. It would include any "pornotroping" representations that mark them as available for sexual consumption—to borrow a term that Hortense Spillers uses to describe an aspect of the slave trade's conversion of Black women's bodies into "flesh."[71] These are the demonic violations of personhood against which we should do battle. This is the often-racialized sexual sin that a new, Black-life-affirming Christian asceticism must confront.

Traci West points out another serious problem: in addition to being blamed, Black women survivors of sexual violence are often not believed in the first place. Their ability to perceive reality is denied, and this revictimization can be severely damaging at a spiritual and psychological level. West describes the experience of a Black woman named Yvonne who was sexually violated as a young girl. Neither the police nor her family accepted her account of what happened. Reflecting back as an adult, she explained, "Where I lived in the South, any time a black woman said she was raped she was never believed." West argues that "Yvonne's story indicates a need to be recognized as a bearer of truth."[72]

[71]Hortense J. Spillers, *Black, White, and in Color: Essays on American Literature and Culture* (University of Chicago Press, 2003), 206. See also Biko Mandela Gray, *Black Life Matter: Blackness, Religion, and the Subject* (Duke University Press, 2022), 102–105, and Alexander G. Weheliye, *Habeas Viscus: Racializing Assemblages, Biopolitics, and Black Feminist Theories of the Human* (Duke University Press, 2014), 89–112.

[72]Traci C. West, *Disruptive Christian Ethics: When Racism and Women's Lives Matter* (Westminster John Knox Press, 2006), 57–58, 62.

The monastic goal of defeating *porneia* cannot be achieved until women are presumed to be, not sirens or deceivers, but credible witnesses whose voices must be taken seriously.

West clarifies that Yvonne's "yearning for this kind of recognition represents one element in a communal longing for supportive connections with others and reflects a spiritual aspect of our humanity."[73] This deeply felt desire to be seen, heard, and trusted is a form of spiritual eros that points beyond carnal pleasure toward the goal of building loving relationships with others and with God. Like the angering part of the soul, the desiring part can be channeled toward such higher ends. Eros can be distinguished from *porneia* and, in fact, harnessed as a powerful means of resisting it. Audre Lorde makes this argument in her classic essay, "Uses of the Erotic: The Erotic as Power," and many Black feminist and womanist thinkers, including West, have followed her lead.[74]

Keri Day draws on Lorde's argument in her womanist theological critique of neoliberalism. She strikes an ascetical chord by challenging her readers to renounce the "acquiring mode," a contemporary term for the evil thought that Evagrius calls "love of money" (*philarguria*). Day shows that the neoliberal obsession with individual material gain leads us to view ourselves and others as "salable" commodities whose value is determined by quantitative measures of success or failure.[75] Like *porneia*, the acquiring mode degrades the human person into a consumable object. The two vices are closely related, and Day suggests that they demand the same response: a communal practice of love in which agape and eros are inseparable.

Like Lorde, Day is adamant that "the erotic *is not* the pornographic." True eros does not abuse or objectify other persons. Rather, it "seeks to unify and connect all of creation." It moves us to desire and work creatively for a better world and "more fully awaken to the divine spark planted within us." When we get in

---

[73]West, *Disruptive Christian Ethics*, 62.

[74]Audre Lorde, *Sister Outsider: Essays and Speeches* (Crossing, 2007), 53–59.

[75]Keri Day, *Religious Resistance to Neoliberalism: Womanist and Black Feminist Perspectives* (Palgrave Macmillan, 2016), 48–54.

touch with such natural, God-given eros, we "refuse to settle for the status quo" and "start to expect joy and justice from our life pursuits." Repudiating the Platonic dualism that shaped much early Christian ascetical suspicion of the body, Day contends that eros connects bodily feelings with transcendent spiritual desires. She clarifies that eros gets corrupted into *porneia*, not when it is incarnated through sexual activity that is healthy and good but only when it is perverted into an instrument of "power-over" others, which contradicts its unitive nature.[76] Understood in this Black feminist and womanist way, eros is not an enemy of asceticism. Rather, it propels ascetical striving for a different way of life beyond the death-dealing forces of neoliberalism, patriarchy, and anti-Blackness.

Conclusion

In this chapter, I have argued that one of the major streams of Christian spirituality, namely asceticism, need not be situated in opposition to Black life, as often happens. Instead, the two can come together in a theory and practice I am calling "Black asceticism." If Moses the Black is the founding inspiration of this possibility, the concepts of fugitivity, nonviolence, power, and eros—understood in the preceding ways—are some of its constitutive elements. Far from being a vehicle of diabolical evil, Black life is perpetually in flight from it and in battle against it. While the means of this struggle vary, the dream of a holistic freedom uniting body, soul, and community remains fairly consistent. To defend the Black capacity for asceticism is to uphold the human dignity and moral agency of Black persons in defiance of all those who would see us as unholy phantoms of appetite and aggression. While renouncing the vices of White supremacy, we ask others to do likewise and join us in the desert of our rebellion.

[76]Day, *Religious Resistance to Neoliberalism*, 81–85.

8

Training the Soul

A Black Catholic Journey Through the Spiritual Exercises

It is now common to think of racism, not merely as a prejudiced mind-set of a hateful individual but as a set of cultural and structural forces that violently govern bodies, and so it is. Racism—indeed, the very idea of race—marks bodies with words that supposedly signify pigment, geography, and genealogy but that were invented for the purpose of assigning particular kinds of labor, social advantage, and fully recognized humanity to some and not others. These words, as if from a box of Crayola crayons, call bodies black, white, brown, yellow, and red. They color-code the distribution of pleasures, privileges, and rights, on the one hand, and exploitations, traumas, and premature deaths, on the other. To perceive this injustice, it suffices to study what has happened to bodies that are so "marked," to borrow M. Shawn Copeland's apt phrase.[1]

This chapter first appeared in *Praying for Freedom: Racism and Ignatian Spirituality in America*, ed. Laurie Cassidy (Liturgical Press, 2024), 23–38. It has been lightly edited.

[1]M. Shawn Copeland, *Knowing Christ Crucified: The Witness of African American Religious Experience* (Orbis Books, 2018), 61–80. See also Bryan N. Massingale, *Racial Justice and the Catholic Church* (Orbis Books, 2010), 13–15, 74–78.

However, to understand and resist the full magnitude of this injustice, it is necessary to recognize its effects on the *souls* of Black folk, White folk, and everyone in between.[2] Our souls—those mysterious centers of thought, emotion, and decision that our bodies sustain—are not spared the harms of a racist system of social control. Our capacities to understand, feel, and choose are each compromised in their own ways. This sinful system affects our cognition by filling our minds with falsehoods about others and ourselves and by weakening our ability to think creatively beyond the racial scripts in which we have been formed. It affects our emotional sensitivity by triggering painful feelings, such as anxiety, shame, and anger, and by hardening our hearts to the sufferings of others who differ racially from us. It affects our wills by encouraging choices that violate the common good and by making us behave like pawns in a sadistic game. Racialization distorts the soul's basic capacities for knowledge, affect, and volition, and it does this across the racial spectrum.

Although such soul damage spreads widely, leaving hardly anyone unscathed, Bryan Massingale and Laurie Cassidy argue that its effects vary significantly by race.[3] For example, a White person who unconsciously accepted the racist cultural message that Black people are worthless would be morally corrupted by this falsehood, and this would be a real loss, but a Black person who succumbed to this lie would be inwardly crushed by it. Their sense of self would be torn asunder. The anxiety, shame, and anger that a White person may feel in an honest conversation about

---

[2]W. E. B. Du Bois, *The Souls of Black Folk* (Simon & Schuster, 2005); Michele Elam, *The Souls of Mixed Folk: Race, Politics, and Aesthetics in the New Millennium* (Stanford University Press, 2011); Frantz Fanon, *Black Skin, White Masks*, trans. Richard Philcox (Grove, 2008), 89–119; Phillis Isabella Sheppard, *Self, Culture, and Others in Womanist Practical Theology* (Palgrave Macmillan, 2011), 23–39; and Andrew Prevot, "Sources of a Black Self? Ethics of Authenticity in an Era of Anti-Blackness," in *Anti-Blackness and Christian Ethics*, ed. Vincent W. Lloyd and Andrew Prevot (Orbis Books, 2017), 77–95.

[3]Massingale, *Racial Justice and the Catholic Church*, 19–24, and Laurie Cassidy, "Contemplative Prayer and the Impasse of White Supremacy," in *Desire, Darkness, and Hope: Theology in a Time of Impasse*, ed. Laurie Cassidy and M. Shawn Copeland (Liturgical Press, 2021), 103–29.

White supremacy may be difficult to bear, but it is not the same as the anxiety, shame, and anger that a Black person endures when their humanity is denied by virtually the whole political, cultural, and religious establishment. Acquiring the inner freedom to act boldly for the sake of a better world can help a White person live into the truest version of themselves, as it can for everybody. However, for a Black person to be free in this sense means something especially poignant when set against the background of their community's bitter history of unfreedom.

However, I do not want to draw the lines too sharply in my analysis. Although our souls are not raceless transparencies, but rather sponges that soak up the messy stuff of our racial worlds, many things are true of our souls insofar as they are human and not only insofar as they are racially divided. Moreover, the struggle against racism must be a shared struggle if it has any hope of victory. For these reasons, although I offer a Black perspective on Saint Ignatius of Loyola's Spiritual Exercises, I emphasize their contribution to the common human challenge to understand, feel, and choose rightly, which no one can evade. I am also mindful that each person's experience of the Spiritual Exercises is singular. God's movements are tailored to the inner and outer circumstances of each person. A racially conscious reception of Ignatian spirituality must not overlook these *universal* and *individual* dimensions, even as it acknowledges that Black and White souls often carry different burdens.

As other chapters in this book indicate, I do not insist that the Spiritual Exercises should be the only spiritual means of combatting racism. Nor do I assume that they will necessarily be the most effective means for everyone. However, I do argue that those who participate (however formally or informally) in the spirituality they represent can use it to strengthen their souls for the fight against racism that we all must wage. This particular way to receive Ignatian spirituality ought to be incorporated into the ways it is generally taught and practiced, so that its socially transformative effects are not limited to a narrow few. In making this claim, I echo the arguments of other Black Catholic interpreters of the Spiritual Exercises such as Massingale, LaReine-Marie

Mosely, and Patrick Saint-Jean.[4] In what follows, I share some of my own distinctive wrestling with this spiritual training program. Like feminist commentators Katherine Dyckman, Mary Garvin, and Elizabeth Liebert, I highlight its mixture of "problems and possibilities."[5]

My Experience of the Nineteenth Annotation

If you ask a Jesuit about the Spiritual Exercises, the first thing you will likely hear is that they are not a text to be read but something to be experienced. And rightly so. Ignatius's volume called *The Spiritual Exercises* is a handbook for leaders of retreats. It offers a structure and set of best practices to help spiritual directors guide participants through a month-long, or in some cases year-long, series of activities that are meant to strengthen their souls, deepen their intimacy with God, and help them make important decisions about their lives. A few years ago, as a faculty member at Boston College, which is a Jesuit Catholic university, I had the opportunity to participate in such a retreat—to have "the experience," so to speak. I did the year-long version, outlined in a section of the text called the Nineteenth Annotation, which allows Ignatius's prescribed spiritual practices to be integrated into the rhythms of one's daily life.[6] I carved out pockets of time each week throughout the academic year to do the necessary prayers, meditations, contemplations, and examens and to meet with my spiritual director and a small faith-sharing group who

[4]LaReine-Marie Mosely, "Negative Contrast Experience: An Ignatian Appraisal," *Horizons* 41 (2014): 74–95; Massingale, "Racism Is a Sickness of the Soul: Can Jesuit Spirituality Help Us Heal?" *America* (November 20, 2017); and Patrick Saint-Jean, SJ, *The Spiritual Work of Racial Justice: A Month of Meditations with Ignatius of Loyola* (Anamchara, 2021).

[5]Katherine Dyckman, Mary Garvin, and Elizabeth Liebert, *The Spiritual Exercises Reclaimed: Uncovering Liberating Possibilities for Women* (Paulist Press, 2001), 3–24. Although I focus more on race than gender here, I recognize with womanist scholars that these are interlocking realities. See Stacey M. Floyd-Thomas, ed., *Deeper Shades of Purple: Womanism in Religion and Society* (NYU Press, 2006).

[6]Ignatius of Loyola, *The Spiritual Exercises of Saint Ignatius*, trans. George E. Ganss, SJ (Loyola, 1992), secs. 19, 27.

were members of my campus community doing the same retreat.

The best way I can describe this experience is to embrace Ignatius's analogical use of the word "exercise." Just as we train our bodies to function well by doing things such as walking and running, so, too, we must train our souls to be ready to discover and enact the will of God, in whatever circumstances we find ourselves.[7] My spiritual director tried to get me to stop intellectualizing the process, which was my tendency as an academic. He wanted me to "let my imagination run wild," as he put it, and to spend more time with the emotions—the movements in the heart—that these exercises were generating for me.

Although this was very good advice for my personal spiritual journey, I continued then—and I continue now—to find value not only in experiencing the Spiritual Exercises but also in thinking critically about them and how they have been used and received. My goal as a theologian is to maintain an interactive unity of prayer and thought. In my scholarship, I have studied the influence of Ignatian spirituality on theologians working in Europe (e.g., Erich Przywara, Karl Rahner, Hans Urs von Balthasar, Henri de Lubac, and Michel de Certeau) and Latin America (e.g., Ignacio Ellacuría, Jon Sobrino, Segundo Galilea, and Dean Brackley). I have discussed contested questions such as the meaning of the "consolation without preceding cause" and the sociopolitical stakes of the Ignatian model of spiritual discernment.[8]

In my teaching, I regularly introduce undergraduate students to Ignatius through a combination of traditional and experiential pedagogy. After going over some key points in his life story,[9] I

---

[7]Ignatius, *Spiritual Exercises*, sec. 1.3, 21.

[8]Andrew Prevot, *Thinking Prayer: Theology and Spirituality amid the Crises of Modernity* (University of Notre Dame Press, 2015), 70–110 and 218–79; Prevot, *The Mysticism of Ordinary Life* (Oxford University Press, 2023), 31–138; Prevot, "Henri de Lubac (1896–1991) and Contemporary Mystical Theology," in *A Companion to Jesuit Mysticism*, ed. Robert A. Maryks (Brill, 2017), 279–309; and Prevot, "Ignatian Spirituality, Political Effectiveness, and Spiritual Discernment: Dean Brackley's Account of Liberation Theology," *Political Theology* 18, no. 4 (2017): 309–24.

[9]Ignatius, *A Pilgrim's Journey: The Autobiography of Ignatius of Loyola*, trans. Joseph N. Tylenda, SJ (Ignatius, 2001).

ask the students to journal about a difficult decision that is facing them. I explain some of his Rules for the Discernment of Spirits and then lead the class in a meditation (often the Meditation on the Two Standards).[10] Finally, I facilitate a conversation about how this sort of exercise may or may not help them decide what to do.

When I participated in the Nineteenth Annotation, the Movement for Black Lives was in its early stages.[11] Trayvon Martin was dead, but Michael Brown was still alive. Although the violence facing the Black community and the activism rising up from it occupied my mind nearly every day, my daily experience of the Spiritual Exercises seemed to occur at a remove from such pressing realities. At the time, I was doing research on the prayerful roots of Black theology—thinking especially about how James Cone drew on the songs that enslaved Black people composed, sung, and danced together in the wilderness.[12] While Ignatius's exercises certainly strengthened me, I was not in the habit of applying them directly to the fight for racial justice. Instead, when seeking resources that could help me and others resist a resurgent White supremacy, I looked to the Black spirituals that Cone wrote about so movingly.

In subsequent years, I have started to ask what these two traditions of Christian spirituality have to do with one another. As a Black Catholic, this question was almost inevitable for me. But such a connection should not be sought only by Black Catholics. The pursuit of racial justice should form part of the common practice of the Spiritual Exercises for everyone, regardless of each person's race. Promoters of Ignatian spirituality and those who stand to benefit from it live in contexts (such as the United States) that are shaped by White supremacy and anti-Black racism. However, the racial injustice of the larger social context is not the only problem. There are also specific histories of Jesuit involve-

---

[10] Ignatius, *Spiritual Exercises*, secs. 136–48, 65–67; secs. 313–36, 121–28.

[11] Olga M. Segura, *Birth of a Movement: Black Lives Matter and the Catholic Church* (Orbis Books, 2021), 1–22.

[12] James H. Cone, *The Spirituals and the Blues: An Interpretation* (Orbis Books, 2008), and Prevot, *Thinking Prayer*, 280–325.

ment in the owning and selling of slaves and other violent actions toward persons of color, which raise challenging questions.[13] Why did the Spiritual Exercises fail to prevent such behavior? If these techniques succeed in preparing one to glorify God with one's life, why have their followers so often been unwilling or unable to fight racism or even to recognize it as an evil that is hateful to God? Although I do not have answers to all of these questions, I hope that my reflections as a Black Catholic journeying through the Spiritual Exercises will help reveal why they could and should strengthen our racially wounded souls for a shared struggle against racial injustice.

The Principle and Foundation

The text of *The Spiritual Exercises* begins with a single-page section meant to give one a basic orientation. At the start of this section, which is called The Principle and Foundation, Ignatius writes that "human beings are created to praise, reverence, and serve God our Lord."[14] *Human beings*. From the first line, I have to ask if I am included. Does my body make it less likely for some retreatants who hear this word "human" to picture a person like me? Already, though, I am speculating about what others think about me, and this is not the purpose for which I, a human being, was made. I agree with Ignatius that I am meant to praise, reverence, and serve God our Lord. Although this list of self-surrendering activities gives me pause, its divine focal point reassures me. That my created purpose should be to serve and glorify another pokes at old wounds. That I owe such deference exclusively to God applies a healing balm. I am meant to be no human being's slave.

Ignatius goes on to explain, "The other things on the face of the earth are created for the human beings, to help them in the pursuit

[13]Cyprian Davis, OSB, *The History of Black Catholics in the United States* (Crossroad, 1990), 35–37, and Laura E. Masur, "Plantation as Mission: American Indians, Enslaved Africans, and Jesuit Missionaries in Maryland," *Journal of Jesuit Studies* 8 (2021): 385–407.

[14]Ignatius, *Spiritual Exercises*, sec. 23.2, 32.

of the end for which they are created."[15] Again, a doubt creeps into my mind: Am I a person or a thing that is meant to be used? Drawing such a sharp ontological dividing line between humans and other instrumentalized creatures seems dangerous to me. As a Black person, it seems far too easy to slip from one side of this line to the other, depending on who is doing the sorting, and to end up with my dignity denied. Moreover, when I see, hear, and touch the things around me, they do not seem to be mere tools of human self-actualization. Like Daniel Castillo, I am concerned that the Principle and Foundation may inadvertently suggest an anthropocentric perspective that reduces the meaning of animals, plants, seas, and skies to their utility for human ends. One front in the battle against racism is the struggle for environmental justice. This struggle requires care for our common home and all its inhabitants, along with resistance to what Pope Francis calls the "technocratic paradigm." It means treating things not as disposable objects but as fellow creatures.[16]

Let me turn now to Ignatius's famous doctrine of *indiferençia*. To attain the end for which we were created, he says that "it is necessary to make ourselves indifferent to all created things," adding that "we ought not to seek health rather than sickness, wealth rather than poverty, honor rather than dishonor, a long life rather than a short one, and so on."[17] What he means is that we should not put our individual cares ahead of the primary work of doing God's will. I agree with Ignatius on this point.

Yet I confess that I am not indifferent to the wretched conditions of inaccessible health care, widespread impoverishment,

---

[15]Ignatius, *Spiritual Exercises*, sec. 23.3, 32.

[16]Daniel P. Castillo, "'To Praise, Reverence, and Serve': The Theological Anthropology of Pope Francis," in *The Theological and Ecological Vision of Laudato Si': Everything Is Connected*, ed. Vincent J. Miller (Bloomsbury, 2017), 95–108, at 96; Pope Francis, *Laudato Si'*, On Care for Our Common Home (Libreria Editrice Vaticana, 2015), nos. 101–14; Melanie L. Harris, *Ecowomanism: African American Women and Earth-Honoring Faiths* (Orbis Books, 2017); and Cone, "Whose Earth Is It, Anyway?" in *Risks of Faith: The Emergence of a Black Theology of Liberation, 1968–1998* (Beacon Press, 2000), 138–45.

[17]Ignatius, *Spiritual Exercises*, secs. 23.5–23.6, 32.

and social stigmatization that plague poor Black neighborhoods. It would be callous and absurd to ask a community not to care about such hardships when they have been specifically allotted to them because of their race. In solidarity with other Black people, I demand a spirituality that talks positively (thus not indifferently) about their search for life-sustaining material goods and that regards the equitable distribution of such goods as a moral, political, and religious imperative. At this early point in the Spiritual Exercises, it is not yet clear whether they are equipped to satisfy this demand.

Even so, I believe Ignatius is correct to insist that these sorts of goods are incapable of completely satisfying any human being, regardless of racial background. The human soul needs more than material supports. It needs to give itself into God's hands. Though not affiliated with Ignatius, my heroes in the Black Christian freedom struggle abandoned themselves to lives of reverent service, just as he would have advised them to do. I am thinking, for example, of the Black women, men, and children who braved fire hoses, police dogs, and overcrowded jail cells in Birmingham, Alabama, in the demonstrations that led to the 1964 Civil Rights Act.[18] They understood that if the situation required it, as it surely did, it would be right for them to risk their possessions, social standing, and even health for the sake of doing what God willed. Their transformative social impact depended on their actively acquired strength of soul—which is to say, their *indiferençia*. Brackley calls this virtue a freedom to love.[19]

The First Week

The First Week of the Spiritual Exercises is a period of honest self-examination. It is a time to take stock of one's personal faults and failings, while viewing oneself in the larger context of fallen

[18]David Aretha, *The Story of the Birmingham Civil Rights Movement in Photographs* (Enslow, 2014).

[19]Dean Brackley, *The Call to Discernment in Troubled Times: New Perspectives on the Transformative Wisdom of Ignatius of Loyola* (Crossroad, 2004), 10–13.

humanity. It is an opportunity to ask questions that might spark conversion, such as, "What have I done for Christ? What am I doing for Christ? What ought I to do for Christ?"[20] Contemporary interpretations of this week sometimes deemphasize the threat of punishment for sin and focus more positively on God's mercy.[21] In the original text, however, Ignatius does not mince words.

I have wrestled in particular with the fifth exercise of the First Week, which is the Meditation on Hell. It asks the retreatant to imagine this place of damnation in vivid detail, applying all five senses: looking at the burning bodies, hearing the screams, smelling the smoke and the rotting flesh, tasting one's tears and sadness, and feeling the flames on one's skin. The desire that is supposed to guide this horrifying exercise has to do with increasing one's motivation to do the right thing. Ignatius says, "If through my faults I should forget the love of the Eternal Lord, at least the fear of those pains will keep me from falling into sin."[22] This multisensory anticipation of hell is supposed to function as a deterrent.

I find this exercise useful for a different reason. It reveals our unsettling human capacity to visualize torture. It shows that the unthinkable is not unthinkable for us. The fact that we are capable of doing such a mental exercise is itself a sign of the evils that we may dream up for others and ourselves, and that some human beings have put into practice. As Ignatius intended, I do experience this exercise as a confrontation with sin but not mainly through a consideration of its eschatological consequences. Instead, this exercise primarily makes me confront the relative ease with which we are able to conjure up the cruelest possible scenarios. We should be troubled by how susceptible our minds are to such destructive ideations.

More concretely, this exercise makes me think of the hell of the slave ship: persons abducted, chained, beaten, raped, starved, crammed together in filth, some dead, some dying, some wanting

---

[20]Ignatius, *Spiritual Exercises*, sec. 53.2, 42.

[21]Kevin O'Brien, SJ, *The Ignatian Adventure: Experiencing the Spiritual Exercises of Saint Ignatius in Everyday Life* (Loyola, 2011), 79.

[22]Ignatius, *Spiritual Exercises*, sec. 65.5, 46.

to die, transported to a foreign territory in which they would be forced to work under the lash, in which they would be torn from their loved ones and children, in which they would be classified as objects meant only for others' gratification.[23] My mind wanders to the hell of the master's quarters, the hell of the cotton field, the hell of the lynch mob, the hell of gang violence, the hell of the prison cell, the hell of being treated each day like a worthless nothing.[24] These hells are real and historical. They have been made by human minds and human hands. This truly is a world dominated by sin, and we are all living in it, and no one is innocent.

The Second Week

In the Second Week, Ignatius instructs one to begin contemplating biblical mysteries such as the incarnation of the Word, the infancy of Jesus, and his earthly ministry. This week includes meditations that urge one to follow Christ as one's king and to live under his holy banner and not that of the devil, which is characterized by sinful attachments to wealth, honor, and pride. The point of this week is to begin moving out of a condition of sin toward a practice of discipleship. It involves a period of preparation for a choice about the particular state of life in which one will follow Jesus. Ignatius calls this "the Election."[25] He is specifically envisioning vocational choices for either married or celibate life, but one can use the exercises of this week as tools to help one make any number of decisions that may shape one's personal path.

It would be worthwhile for those experiencing the Second Week to use it as an occasion to decide what they are going to

[23]Christina Sharpe, *In the Wake: On Blackness and Being* (Duke University Press, 2016); Édouard Glissant, *Poetics of Relation*, trans. Betsy Wing (University of Michigan Press, 1995), 5–7; and Willie James Jennings, *The Christian Imagination: Theology and the Origins of Race* (Yale University Press, 2010), 176.

[24]These hells, as I am calling them, have been represented in a soul-shaking, multisensory fashion by the Equal Justice Initiative in Montgomery, Alabama. For more information, see https://museumandmemorial.eji.org/.

[25]Ignatius, *Spiritual Exercises*, sec. 135, 64; secs. 169–89, 74–80.

do concretely to become agents of change in the fight for racial justice. There are many ways to join the struggle, and one does not need to do them all, but there must be some way to use one's gifts to resist the overwhelming maelstrom of sin that is racism. If one hopes to make the right kinds of practical choices, even when it is costly to do so, one must develop a strong soul. For Ignatius, as we have seen, this means being "indifferent," in a particular sense. But more than that, it means knowing how to think rationally and imaginatively, how to interpret one's deepest emotions productively, and how to detect signs of the interior presence of God when they occur. These points correspond roughly to what Ignatius calls the "Three Times . . . for Making a Sound and Good Election."[26]

Ignatius advises the use of reason specifically when one has no immediate experience of God's intentions for one's life and when the practice of sorting through one's feelings has not yielded sufficient clarity. He calls this a "time of tranquility" and suggests that in such moments one should think carefully about the action one is weighing and about the goals that one has for it, and then "see to which side reason more inclines." He also recommends using one's imaginative capacities to view the possible course of action from various angles that may be illuminating, asking questions such as how it relates to the love of God, what a righteous person would do in the same situation, and what one would like to have done when looking back at this moment from one's deathbed or from judgment day.

Perhaps more common than the time of tranquility is a time in which one's emotions are trying to tell one something important about the right thing to do. Ignatius's treatment of this time of election encourages us to increase our emotional intelligence. Generally speaking, he thinks we ought to do the things that bring us deep spiritual joy, make us feel more alive and at peace in ourselves, and strengthen our capacity for faith, hope, and love. He calls these inner feelings "consolations." But he warns that such consolations can be deceptive and sometimes involve evil desires

[26]Ignatius, *Spiritual Exercises*, secs. 175–77, 76.

and impulses. Therefore, it is important to study them "with great vigilance and attention," noticing if there is any sign of demonic misdirection in them such as a mixed motive or a concession to sin. Conversely, experiences of "desolation" around a sinful action can be contrastive signs sent by God that are meant to turn one around and lead one in a positive direction. Discerning the movements in our souls requires introspective practice and the loving attention of others such as trusted friends and spiritual directors.[27]

Finally, in rare cases, Ignatius thinks God may move the soul so immediately, indubitably, and completely that it has little need for rational deliberation or prolonged emotional discernment. As one example of this time of election, Ignatius cites Saul's experience of Christ on the road to Damascus, which changes his heart and converts him into the Apostle Paul (Acts 9:1–19).[28] Ignatius also describes a particular type of consolation that is not connected with any concrete object but is like a river of divine joy washing over the soul and inundating it entirely. In his words, "It is the prerogative of the Creator alone to enter the soul, depart from it, and cause a motion in it which draws the whole person into love of His Divine Majesty." This is the "consolation without preceding cause."[29] One should not count on such mystical experiences, but one should not rule them out either. They can and do happen. In the Black Christian tradition, the female preacher Jarena Lee has an experience of sanctification that seems similar to what Ignatius means by a consolation without preceding cause. She describes a moment of ecstasy that felt "like an ocean of light and bliss." This extraordinary event fortified Jarena Lee's resolve to preach the gospel and serve God and neighbor through her ministry.[30]

Although the fact that God opposes racism should be clear with or without the Spiritual Exercises, the cognitive and affective tools employed during the Election period of the Second Week

---

[27]Ignatius, *Spiritual Exercises*, sec. 176, 76; secs. 313–36, 121–28.

[28]Ignatius, *Spiritual Exercises*, sec. 175, 76.

[29]Ignatius, *Spiritual Exercises*, sec. 330, 126.

[30]Jarena Lee, *The Life and Religious Experience of Jarena Lee*, in *Sisters of the Spirit: Three Black Women's Autobiographies of the Nineteenth Century*, ed. William L. Andrews (Indiana University Press, 1986), 25–48, at 34.

can help one decipher the individual choices that one is called to make in the divinely willed fight against racism. They can help one break through the false consciousness, emotional barriers, and spiritual inertia of one's racially damaged soul and arrive at personally tailored, antiracist action plans for one's renewed life in Christ. The question is not whether to resist racism but *how* to do so. Our minds and hearts have work to do to answer this question well.

The Third and Fourth Weeks

The Third and Fourth Weeks of the Spiritual Exercises ask the spiritual trainee to plunge into the saving mysteries of Jesus's death and resurrection. These weeks bring one into contact with his suffering human flesh, which he shares with all the crucified and lynched peoples of the world, and with his glorified body, which gives hope that the violence of history will not have the final word. In the meditations of the Third Week, Ignatius wants us to feel the suffering of Jesus. To this end, he offers the following guidance: "I will try to foster an attitude of sorrow, suffering, and heartbreak, by calling often to memory the labors, fatigue, and sufferings which Christ our Lord suffered, from his birth up to whatever mystery of his Passion I am contemplating at the time."[31] The goal is to be with Jesus in his mortal anguish, to place oneself imaginatively and affectively in the scene.

Christopher Pramuk notes that Billie Holiday's 1939 recording of Abel Meeropol's "Strange Fruit" acts in a similar way. Like Ignatian meditations on the crucified Jesus, the lyrics and somber tones of Holiday's protest song draw those who listen to it into a scene of intense physical and psychological torment and invite them to connect emotionally.[32] Inspired by Holiday and other Black musicians, artists, and poets, Cone argues that the

[31] Ignatius, *Spiritual Exercises*, sec. 206.4, 84.

[32] Christopher Pramuk, "Beauty Limned in Violence: Experimenting with Protest Music in the Ignatian Classroom," in *Transforming Ourselves, Transforming the World: Justice in Jesuit Higher Education*, ed. Mary Beth Combs and Patricia Ruggiano Schmidt (Fordham University Press, 2013), 15–29, at 20.

relationship between Christ on the cross and the Black body on the lynching tree is no mere analogy. Christ is present in and with the thousands of African Americans and other racially marginalized people who have been mutilated and murdered by White supremacists. Cone concludes, "*Every time a white mob lynched a black person, they lynched Jesus.*"[33]

While the sorrowful meditations of the Third Week are designed to make us feel regret for our sins and gratitude for the awesome love that Christ shows by dying for us, reflecting on them in connection with the horrors of lynching puts me in touch with other emotions such as righteous anger at the cruelty of such actions and fear of having my Black male body treated so violently. Although the Third Week ought to increase solidarity with the victims of history by forging deep emotional bonds with them, the word "solidarity" is perhaps too anemic to capture all that could and should take place in this part of the Spiritual Exercises. These meditations cultivate a flesh-and-spirit unity between the incarnate God, the lynched person, and me for which no words are fully adequate.

Yet Ignatius is adamant that this violence is not the ultimate truth of things. The Fourth Week invites one to experience the joy of the resurrection. In addition to meditating on biblical verses related to this mystery and responding joyfully to them, Ignatius encourages retreatants to find happiness in their natural environments: "I will avail myself of light or the pleasant features of the seasons, such as the refreshing coolness in summer or the sun or heat in winter, as far as I think or conjecture that this will help me to rejoice in Christ my Creator and Redeemer."[34] Ignatius believes that God wants human beings to flourish and be glad.

Although the Third and Fourth Weeks highlight dramatic tensions between death and resurrection, they may also help participants sustain hope amid the seemingly mundane difficulties of everyday life. These difficulties may have to do with employment, relationships, families, or mental and physical well-being.

---

[33]James H. Cone, *The Cross and the Lynching Tree* (Orbis Books, 2011), 158.

[34]Ignatius, *Spiritual Exercises*, sec. 228.4, 93.

Donelda Cook, an African American psychotherapist, explains how Ignatian spiritual practices helped one of her Black female clients navigate hardships and blockages in her life and reconnect with a feeling of joy in God's presence.[35] Ignatius affirms that the small crosses and triumphs of quotidian life may be opportunities to strengthen the soul and participate in a larger salvific process.

The Contemplation to Attain Love

The retreat concludes with a final exercise called the Contemplation to Attain Love. I would like to bring my own reflections to a close by commenting on this highly cherished feature of Ignatian spirituality. The first point of this contemplation instructs one to recall the many gifts one has received from God. Its goal is not merely to inspire gratitude but to motivate an extravagant return gift of one's whole existence. Ignatius here offers his famous *Suscipe* prayer: "Take, Lord, and receive, all my liberty, my memory, my understanding, and my will—all that I have and possess. You, Lord, have given all that to me. I now give it back to You, O Lord. All of it is yours. Dispose of it according to your will."[36] This experience of divine-and-human mutuality presupposes freedom and strength on both sides. It presupposes that my soul has been nourished and enriched and that I have the agential capacity necessary to surrender it fully to God's will. To the extent that racism damages and weakens our souls, it prevents us from enjoying this deeply consoling mystery, at least to the level we should.

The remaining parts of the exercise seek to raise our awareness about the active presence of God in all things. The world around us is no longer framed as a set of instruments for human use. It is described as a place teeming with divine life and initiative. God is "working in the heavens, elements, plants, fruits, cattle,

---

[35]Donelda A. Cook, "Crossing Traditions: Ignatian Prayer with a Protestant African American Counseling Dyad," in *Casebook for a Spiritual Strategy in Counseling and Psychotherapy*, ed. P. S. Richards and A. E. Bergin (American Psychological Association, 2004), 173–86.

[36]Ignatius, *Spiritual Exercises*, sec. 234.4, 95.

and all the rest." God "dwells also in myself, giving me existence, life, sensation, and intelligence." My power, "justice, goodness, piety, mercy, and so forth" come from this divine source within me and within the whole of creation.[37] Looking around at the dismal state of human affairs and the pessimism that characterizes much public discourse, particularly about race, it may seem that we simply lack the virtues and gifts that we need to make a better world that would be more in keeping with God's loving designs. But Ignatius helps us recognize that this is not the case. Everything we need has already been given. The created order is radiant with divine blessings, both material and spiritual, external and internal. Everything we would require in order to live the right way is already ready at hand, including God's own personal nearness.

We have to take responsibility for receiving and activating the gifts that are being lavishly poured out upon us. We need to do this together and without delay. A racism-defeating abundance of love is within reach, if we but train ourselves to attain it and put this training into practice. Because some will refuse to do this work, there will undoubtedly be incidents of violence and even calamity, but all I can say, to echo Saint Paul, is that where sin abounds, grace abounds all the more (see Romans 5:20). Such is the hope that I have gained from praying according to the principles outlined by Ignatius.

---

[37]Ignatius, *Spiritual Exercises*, secs. 235–37, 95.

9

People of Action

African American Catholics on the Path to Sainthood

At the time of this writing, the Catholic Church has not recognized any African American saints. There are many early Christian saints from North Africa, such as Augustine of Hippo and his mother Monica, the martyrs Perpetua and Felicitas, and Antony of Egypt. As chapter 7 indicated, being from Roman North Africa would not necessarily have made one Black by the standards of the time. Yet some, such as Saint Moses the Black, were described in ways that emphasized their darker complexion and Black African (or Ethiopian) lineage. There are saints of African descent from the modern period such as Benedict the African, the Franciscan friar from sixteenth-century Sicily whose father was likely a slave from the African kingdom of Borno, and Martín de Porres, the mixed-race barber and lay Dominican from seventeenth-century Peru whose mother was an emancipated slave from Panama. More recently, we have the witness of Saint Josephine Bakhita, a Sudanese woman from Darfur who was kidnapped and enslaved as a child and who eventually became a Canossian sister in Italy. She passed away in 1947 and was canonized in 2000.[1] African

I presented an earlier version of this chapter as a keynote talk at the Mystical Theology Network conference at St. John's College, Oxford University

American Catholics turn to these African and diasporic saints for inspiration and intercession, while awaiting the day that one or more of their own may be so elevated.

Hope is growing that this day may not be too far in the future. Formal processes are underway for seven African American Catholics, who are affectionately dubbed "The Saintly Seven." Pierre Toussaint (1766–1853), Mother Mary Elizabeth Lange (c. 1789–1882), Mother Henriette Delille (1813–1862), and Father Augustus Tolton (1854–1897) have been declared "Venerable," which means that the Roman Dicastery for the Causes of Saints has determined that they are models of extraordinary virtue. Julia Greeley (c. 1840–1918), Father Martin de Porres Maria Ward (1918–1999), and Sister Thea Bowman (1937–1990) have been given the title "Servant of God," which means that the church has opened an official inquiry into their sanctity. Although beatification and full canonization will require verified miracles, it is not necessary to wait for such processes to conclude in order to pray to such potential saints and seek to follow their shining example.[2]

This period of waiting is also an opportune time to reflect on them theologically. Beyond noting that they are all devout African American Catholics, can we discern other more specific similarities between them? Do they share a charism, that is, a distinct emphasis in their approach to Christian life? Moreover, in what ways are they different, and what do these differences teach us about the diversity of both Catholic and Black experience in the United States? How does each one interweave particular strands of apostolic, sacramental, mystical, and ascetical spirituality from the Christian tradition? What do their lives reveal about the Black

---

(March 20, 2024), and as the annual Sheffer Lecture at the Colorado College (April 8, 2024).

[1]Lori De Lucia, "The Exceptional History of a Black Saint in Sixteenth-Century Palermo. And Why It Matters," *Transition: An International Review* 132 (April 2022): 54–67; Celia Cussen, *Black Saint of the Americas: The Life and Afterlife of Martín de Porres* (Cambridge University Press, 2014); and Enrico Ille, "Bakhita, Josephine," *Oxford African American Studies Center* (September 30, 2012).

[2]Michael R. Heinlein, ed., *Black Catholics on the Road to Sainthood* (Our Sunday Visitor, 2021), 22.

community's ongoing struggle for freedom and the possibilities for interracial understanding and even love? What do they have to say to a church and a country that are still struggling to face these realities in an honest, healthy, and hopeful manner?

Similarities and Differences in Social Location

Some of these questions can be addressed by comparing and contrasting their social locations. Although their genealogies include probable and, in some cases, clear racial mixture, all seven are at least partly of African descent. In an idiosyncratic U.S. way of speaking, this means they are Black. More specifically, all have ancestors who were victims of the trans-Atlantic slave trade. All have direct family ties to African persons who were forcibly abducted, crowded onto ships, transported like cattle, and sold to the highest bidder. Three of the seven began their lives as slaves: Toussaint in Haiti and later New York, where slavery remained legal until 1827; Tolton and Greeley in Missouri, not far from the childhood home of Samuel Clemens, who later adopted the pen name, Mark Twain. Two others lived as racially mixed, free women of color in Southern, slaveholding states, namely Lange in Maryland and Delille in Louisiana, though, like Toussaint, Lange was originally from the Caribbean. Two grew up during the Jim Crow era. As a Black girl in Canton, Mississippi, Bowman had direct experience of the segregated South. Ward encountered analogous forms of racial discrimination as a biracial child in the Northern and mid-Atlantic cities of Boston and Washington, D.C., and later as a priest serving in the Brazilian region of Andrelândia.[3] While

[3]Ellen Tarry, *The Other Toussaint: A Modern Biography of Pierre Toussaint, A Post-Revolutionary Black* (St. Paul Editions, 1981), 8–100; Caroline Hemesath, OSF, *From Slave to Priest: A Biography of the Reverend Augustine Tolton (1854–1897): First Afro-American Priest of the United States* (Franciscan Herald Press, 1973), 8; Blaine Burkey, OFM, Cap., *In Secret Service of the Sacred Heart: The Life and Virtues of Julia Greeley* (Julia Greeley Guild, 2012), 14; Diane Batts Morrow, *Persons of Color and Religious at the Same Time: The Oblate Sisters of Providence, 1828–1860* (University of North Carolina Press, 2002), 17; Cyprian Davis, OSB, *Henri-*

their hues ranged from light to dark, all experienced anti-Black racism firsthand.

The most harrowing story may come from Tolton's biography. When the Civil War broke out, and young Augustus was only six years old, his enslaved father, Peter Paul Tolton, ran away from the plantation where he worked from sunup to sundown harvesting grain for a whiskey factory. He left his wife and three children to enlist in the Union army and fight for the freedom of his family and his race. He died in the war. Meanwhile, conditions worsened for the slaves who remained. Augustus's mother, Martha Jane, grieved bitterly at the sight of her two sons being whipped by the slavedriver. Risking death, she decided to flee with her boys and her baby girl who was not yet two years old. They narrowly escaped capture before being assisted by Union soldiers who helped them find a rowboat that they used to cross the Mississippi River into Illinois and relative freedom.[4]

The young Julia Greeley would have been living in the same geographical area at the same time. It was there that she too endured the scourge of a master's whip, but in her case, it gouged out one of her eyes. For the rest of her life, the hole that remained shed constant tears. We do not know much about her childhood, but her face bore the marks of her trauma.[5] As a house slave in the French Caribbean colony of Saint Domingue, Toussaint had a different experience. He was a young man torn between the French Catholic settler world of his uncommonly benevolent masters, who encouraged him to read and treated him with kindness, and the Black world of the enslaved fieldworkers who gathered secretly in the woods, worshipped traditional African gods, and prepared for armed revolution. Toussaint was relieved that he

---

ette Delille: Servant of Slaves, Witness to the Poor (Archives of the Archdiocese of New Orleans/Sisters of the Holy Family, 2004), 2; Maurice J. Nutt, *Thea Bowman: Faithful and Free* (Liturgical Press, 2019), 19; and Carlos Junior de Magalhães, "I Believe Fr. Martin Maria de Porres Ward, OFM Conv. Should Be a Saint. Here's Why," *Black Catholic Messenger*, January 14, 2023.

[4]Hemesath, *From Slave to Priest*, 9–11.

[5]Burkey, *In Secret Service*, 37, 41.

and the bulk of his household relocated to New York before the coming insurrection would have compelled him to betray one or both of these parties.[6] Though always demeaning, slavery was not a homogenous reality.

These seven holy persons of African descent varied by class, gender, and vocation. Like many former slaves, Tolton and Greeley were among the Black working poor who had to find whatever odd jobs they could to make ends meet. After moving to Denver, Colorado, Greeley labored as a maid in various homes and for a short time as a cook in a brothel when she could find no other work. Greeley remained mostly illiterate throughout her life. Before becoming a priest, Tolton worked on the line at a cigar factory and as a janitor at a saloon.[7]

Though not wealthy, Lange and Delille were French-speaking people of some means who were neither at the top nor the bottom of French colonial hierarchies. In fact, Delille and her family owned slaves. This was a common practice among free persons of color in antebellum New Orleans, done for morally variable reasons ranging from the pursuit of wealth to the protection of the vulnerable. In the lead-up to the Civil War, local laws greatly restricted the possibilities for emancipation. If freed slaves were not seized and forced back into bondage, they were often expelled from the state and even the country, in some cases by being shipped to Liberia. Keeping someone, including even one's own family members, enslaved while giving them a relatively comfortable living situation was sometimes the most protective thing one could do in this oppressive context—which is not to say that this was always the motivation.[8]

Toussaint's skill at producing the finest French hairstyles brought him into close contact with the upper echelons of the Francophone expatriate society in New York following the French and Haitian Revolutions. Through his work, he became a confi-

[6]Tarry, *Other Toussaint*, 8–100.

[7]Burkey, *In Secret Service*, 79, and Hemesath, *From Slave to Priest*, 15, 47.

[8]Morrow, *Persons of Color*, 18, and Davis, *Servant of Slaves*, 7, 15.

dant of the political and economic elite, including the Schuyler sisters who make a memorable appearance in Lin-Manuel Miranda's *Hamilton*. Even while he remained a slave, Toussaint earned enough money to fund the household of his widowed mistress, Mrs. Berard, who liberated him on her deathbed, and to purchase the freedom of his sister Rosalie and his future wife, Juliette, all the while raising money for charitable causes and the construction of Catholic churches.[9] While Toussaint was the greatest earner of these seven potential saints, as figures of the twentieth century Bowman and Ward lived in a more economically auspicious time period for Black people. As the child of a medical doctor and a teacher, Bowman belonged to a growing population of African Americans who were making their way into the middle class. Although the segregated conditions of her hometown limited her opportunities, she did not live in poverty.[10] While Ward resided in D.C., his father worked as a butler, and he attended Dunbar, a prestigious public high school for African Americans, the very first of its kind. These are signs both of his family's modest social standing and its upward mobility.[11]

At first, the gender differences between these seven seem obvious: four are women, and three are men. However, a closer look reveals that gender identity was a complicated feature in many of their stories. Though a man, Toussaint spent much of his life in feminized domestic spaces. As a slave in Haiti, he worked in the house with his mother and grandmother, not the fields with his father and brother. As an adult in New York, his profession was to be a hairdresser for women. He won a following of devoted clients by interacting courteously with them and staying up to date on the latest trends.[12] Conversely, by founding religious

[9]Tarry, *Other Toussaint*, 133, 140, 162, 171, 194.

[10]Nutt, *Thea Bowman*, 14.

[11]"Cause Fr. Martin de Porres Maria Ward," Our Lady of the Angels Province, Franciscan Friars Conventual, https://www.olaprovince.org/locations/the-cause-for-fr-martin-de-porres-maria-ward-ofm-conv-2/; and NPR Staff, "In Nation's First Black Public High School, A Blueprint for Reform," *National Public Radio*, July 29, 2013.

[12]Tarry, *Other Toussaint*, 16, 159.

orders, Lange and Delille resisted the belittling expectations that were placed on them as Black women. Lange and her community, the Oblate Sisters of Providence, refused to be treated as mere domestic servants for the Sulpician seminary, even though this request was made of them.[13] Delille and her community, the Sisters of the Holy Family, opted out of the system of concubinage, known as *plaçage*, that shaped the lives of many free women of color in New Orleans.[14] Neither Mammys nor Jezebels, these Black women religious rejected the stereotypes.[15]

Lange, Delille, Ward, and Bowman were teachers who used this profession to empower themselves and others. Lange and Delille educated young girls of color in the basics of religion and literacy and in practical skills such as sewing, which would help them survive and advance in their social contexts.[16] Offering language and religious formation classes was a vital part of Ward's missionary work in Brazil. As a teacher, he was known for his sense of humor.[17] Bowman taught at high school, college, and graduate levels. She earned a master's and PhD in English literature from the Catholic University of America, where she wrote a dissertation on the literary style of Saint Thomas More, one of her favorite models of moral courage. In the classroom, she introduced students to the great works of the English canon, along with important books by African American authors such as Alice Walker and Toni Morrison. She also taught more practical classes in homiletics. Although she was not permitted to preach in church, she helped ordained and lay ministers of different genders

[13] Cyprian Davis, OSB, and Jamie Phelps, OP, eds., *"Stamped with the Image of God": African Americans as God's Image in Black* (Orbis Books, 2003), 49–51.

[14] M. Shawn Copeland, *The Subversive Power of Love: The Vision of Henriette Delille* (Paulist Press, 2009), 4–6.

[15] Diane Batts Morrow, "The Difficulty of Our Situation: The Oblate Sisters of Providence in Antebellum Society," in *Uncommon Faithfulness: The Black Catholic Experience*, ed. M. Shawn Copeland, with LaReine-Marie Mosely, SND, and Albert J. Raboteau (Orbis Books, 2009), 26–46, at 29.

[16] Cyprian Davis, OSB, *The History of Black Catholics in the United States* (Crossroad, 2004), 101, and Davis, *Servant of Slaves*, 37, 46, 76.

[17] Brian O'Neel, "Meet the Most Recent American Black Catholic on the Road to Sainthood," *National Catholic Register*, November 18, 2024.

and races learn this art through her summer courses at the Institute of Black Catholic Studies at Xavier University in New Orleans.[18]

Through their activities as vowed women religious, Lange, Delille, and Bowman exercised distinctive forms of religious authority. Near the end of her life, Bowman was invited to address a gathering of the United States Conference of Catholic Bishops. She spoke, and they listened. She gave them instructions to link their arms and join together in song, and they complied, belting out the lyrics to the civil rights anthem "We Shall Overcome." With prophetic courage, Bowman advocated for greater cultural inclusion in the church. As mother superiors, Lange and Delille acted as strong leaders of their religious congregations, overcame institutional hurdles, and worked to retain the support of the White male clerical establishment.[19]

African American priests were not a reality in Lange and Delille's time. Racist attitudes in the church foreclosed vocational opportunities for Black Catholic men. When Tolton was ordained in 1886, he became the first African American priest who was open about his racial identity.[20] For many years it had seemed unlikely that he would ever reach this goal, because no U.S.

---

[18] Shannen Dee Williams, *Subversive Habits: Black Catholic Nuns in the Long African American Freedom Struggle* (Duke University Press, 2022), 246, and Nutt, *Thea Bowman*, 60, 63, 77.

[19] Nutt, *Thea Bowman*, 112, and Morrow, "Difficulty of Our Situation," 34–42.

[20] Before Tolton, three brothers—James, Patrick, and Alexander Healy—became priests. They had some African ancestry on the side of their mother, who was a lightly colored slave on their father's plantation. Although technically slaves according to the laws of Georgia, they were raised by their father as sons. He sent them to the North to be educated, and it was there that they became Catholic, received calls to the priesthood, and started illustrious careers. James became the bishop of Portland, Maine. Patrick became a Jesuit and a highly transformative president of Georgetown University. And Alexander became a renowned canon lawyer and theologian present at the First Vatican Council. By the one-drop rule, these Healy brothers were Black, and some of their contemporaries discerned this in their appearance. Nevertheless, they did not associate with the Black community and often passed as White. Their morally dubious decision not to claim their African ancestry certainly smoothed the road to their success. Regardless of how one views this choice, it was not an option for the darker and unmistakably Black Tolton. See Davis, *History of Black Catholics*, 146–55.

seminary would admit him, but he finally found acceptance at the missionary college of the *Propaganda Fide* in Rome.

More than sixty years later, when Ward discerned a call to the priesthood, he worried that he might face similar racial barriers. Writing to the vocation director of the Conventual Franciscans, he asked cautiously whether they would admit him, since "perhaps, it might be your policy not to accept colored just now." The response he received was welcoming, though seemingly conditional on the kind of service they imagined him doing: "we have been working in fields that might promise an open door to colored applicants." The question of how best to navigate the racial politics surrounding vocations to the priesthood was evidently on the minds of both parties. Yet they reached a happy outcome: Ward became the first African American to join this religious community and thrived in his role as a missionary to South America.[21]

Only two of our seven potential Black Catholic saints were laypeople: Toussaint and Greeley. And Greeley's lay status requires some qualification. She was a third-order lay Franciscan. She practiced a celibate, mendicant lifestyle in service of the poor, not unlike the first-order friars and second-order nuns of the same religious family.[22] As a solitary person who was active in building loving community, she could be revered today as an icon of a vocation to singleness. Toussaint was the only married one. He loved his wife Juliette dearly and was brokenhearted when she died. Letters between them indicate their deep mutual affection.[23] Taken together, these seven Black Catholics represent diverse but equally valid ways to receive God's "universal call to holiness."[24]

Spiritualities of Action

These graced individuals were united by a shared emphasis on action. They were busy people, always doing things, always find-

[21] "Cause Fr. Martin."

[22] Burkey, *In Secret Service*, 31.

[23] Davis and Phelps, "*Stamped with the Image of God*," 27.

[24] *Lumen Gentium* (November 21, 1964), chap. 5.

ing ways to pour themselves out for others. They did not wait for anyone to tell them what they could do. They took initiative. They did not despair in the face of seemingly insurmountable obstacles. They set plans into motion. They were not mere racialized bodies pushed around by the material forces of White supremacy—which is sometimes the impression given by well-meaning scholarly efforts to describe the awesome power of such a violent system. Rather, they were human agents striving to do God's will. More specifically, they were modern inheritors and adapters of the *vita apostolica*, the active way of life of the first apostles, which was recovered in the Middle Ages by Franciscans, Dominicans, Beguines, and other missionary and reformist movements that pushed beyond the spirituality of monastic enclosure.[25] They were ascetics, but their asceticism was oriented toward transformative action in the world.

It is no mere coincidence that Greeley was a lay Franciscan, that Tolton was mentored at a young age by Franciscan priests,[26] that Ward was a Conventual Franciscan, and that Bowman was a Franciscan Sister of Perpetual Adoration. The active spirituality of *Il Poverello* was evident in their lives, just as it was in Angela of Foligno's (see chapter 5). No one embodied Saint Francis of Assisi's Christlike humility and generosity more radically than Greeley. Though poor, she did not cling to her meager possessions but gave them away freely. She pulled a red wagon behind her as she walked the streets of Denver, filling it with donations that she then quickly dispersed, always insisting that someone else needed them more than she did. She begged for groceries, coal for heat, clothes, and baby carriages, and delivered them in secret, often under the cover of night, helping anyone in need, regardless of color. She visited the sick and imprisoned. She even gave away her own burial plot to a Black man who died and was headed for the potter's field. She lived the corporal works of mercy.[27]

---

[25]Bernard McGinn, *The Flowering of Mysticism: Men and Women in the New Mysticism, 1200–1350*, vol. 3, *The Presence of God: A History of Western Christian Mysticism* (Crossroad, 1998), 5.

[26]Hemesath, *From Slave to Priest*, 50.

[27]Burkey, *In Secret Service*, 11, 27, 28, 32.

Tolton did not wait for his priestly career to begin before serving the poor. Even while seminaries across the United States rejected him because of his race, he used his gifts to start a Sunday school for poor Black children in Quincy, Illinois. Later, as pastor of St. Monica's in Chicago, he not only ministered to the spiritual needs of Black Catholics in the city; he also raised funds for their material welfare, begging for food, clothes, and hospital beds, working himself to the point of exhaustion.[28] Those promoting Ward's canonization emphasize that "he was always generous towards the poor, with whom he often shared what little he had."[29] After completing her religious formation in Wisconsin, Bowman returned to Canton to teach the impoverished Black children there an important lesson: They can change things. It was the early 1960s, and the Civil Rights movement was in full swing. Churches, homes, and activist headquarters in Canton were bombed by White supremacists. In the midst of such violence, Bowman sought to empower the young with a message of hope. She taught the children to sing Negro spirituals, and they recorded an album to raise funds for their school. She gave them the promise of a brighter future.[30]

Other traditions beyond the Franciscan shaped the apostolic activities of these seven virtuous Catholics. Greeley attended a church administered by priests in the Society of Jesus, a religious order that has since its founding emphasized the unity of contemplation and action. In Rome, Tolton was influenced by the missionary zeal of seminarians from across the globe. Bowman was inspired by the independent Black churches that led the Civil Rights movement, which she knew from her Southern upbringing, and by the pan-Africanist Black power discourse that affirmed cultural difference and self-determination, which she encountered while pursuing her doctorate in Washington, D.C., in the late 1960s and early 1970s.[31] The teenage Ward had become Catholic

28 Hemesath, *From Slave to Priest*, 58–60, 138–45.

29 "Cause Fr. Martin."

30 Nutt, *Thea Bowman*, 43–49.

31 Burkey, *In Secret Service*, 32; Hemesath, *From Slave to Priest*, 90; and Nutt, *Thea Bowman*, 53–56.

in the same city three decades earlier. He was moved by the liturgy at St. Augustine's Catholic Church, which is the mother church of Black Catholics in the nation's capital (and my current home parish).[32] Both Bowman and Ward were raised as Methodists before joining the Catholic Church, and it is plausible that their Wesleyan background—like Zilpha Elaw's (see chapter 6)—also influenced their active spiritualities.

The small library of Delille's Sisters of the Holy Family included action-oriented spiritual classics such as Saint Francis de Sales's *Introduction to the Devout Life*, Saint Ignatius of Loyola's *Spiritual Exercises* (discussed in the previous chapter), and a biography of Saint Elizabeth Ann Seton.[33] Seton had founded the Sisters of Charity of St. Joseph's, the first American congregation of women religious. Their mission to serve the poor provided a model for Delille and her community. Focusing on impoverished Black people in New Orleans, the Sisters of the Holy Family cared for elderly and infirm slaves who had been abandoned by their masters; they educated young women of color, whether enslaved or free; and they did these things in explicit "imitation of the first Christians."[34]

All of these potential saints were devoted to the Eucharist. While following the example of other saintly Christians, they also directly took Jesus's self-sacrificial love as their guide. Celebrating and receiving his love during Mass prepared them to embody it in the world. Bowman belonged to a community of religious women dedicated to perpetual Eucharistic adoration. The sixteen-year-old Tolton felt called to the priesthood on the Feast of Corpus Christi on the very day he had received his first communion. Greeley and Toussaint were daily communicants. Ward's passion for the Eucharist was so unrelenting that he continued to say Mass even

[32] O'Neel, "Meet the Most Recent."

[33] Davis, *Servant of Slaves*, 105–106.

[34] Davis, *Servant of Slaves*, 37. This quote comes from a document outlining the "Rules and Regulations for the Congregation of Sisters of the Presentation." This was a lay association of women, organized by Delille, that gradually evolved into the religious order called the Sisters of the Holy Family.

after experiencing symptoms of a heart attack. Delille wrote an inscription in a book of Eucharistic devotions: "I believe in God. I hope in God. I love. I wish to live and to die for God." Lange and the Oblate Sisters of Providence suffered when their patron Fr. Joubert died and the other priests of his order stopped attending to their sacramental needs. Undeterred, they walked more than a half-hour from their convent to attend Mass each Sunday. In all of these cases, the Eucharist was not an alternative to an active life of Christian service but a sustaining source of it.[35]

An analogous point can be made about certain popular Catholic devotions. Greeley was a member of the League of the Sacred Heart, also known as the Apostleship of Prayer, an international community of persons who consecrate their daily works of charity to the Sacred Heart of Jesus (a spiritual tradition promoted by Pope Francis's encyclical *Dilexit Nos*). As Greeley walked the streets, tending to the needs of the poor, she also handed out literature from this devotional society, dropping off pamphlets at fire stations around the city. Her constant prayer to be one with the Sacred Heart of Jesus motivated her compassionate action.[36] Lange's membership in the Association of Holy Slavery of the Mother of God might be seen in a similarly positive light. Although the name of this devotional society could appear to sacralize the idea of slavery, the goal of its adherents was to imitate Mary's absolute and—we should note—freely chosen obedience to the will of God. Lange's desire to surrender herself entirely to God gave her strength to persist in her apostolic efforts despite fierce opposition.[37]

One might ask, Are these seven Black Catholics mystics? This is a difficult question with no clear-cut answer.[38] On the one hand, the details of their interior lives largely remain hidden to us. We

---

[35]Hemesath, *From Slave to Priest*, 27; Burkey, *In Secret Service*, 11; Tarry, *Other Toussaint*, 112; "Cause Fr. Martin"; Nutt, *Thea Bowman*, 100; Davis, *Servant of Slaves*, 35; and Morrow, "Difficulty of Our Situation," 36.

[36]Burkey, *In Secret Service*, 20–22.

[37]Davis, *History of Black Catholics*, 100.

[38]See chapter 6 for further discussion of the meaning of Christian mysticism and the ways in which it may extend beyond Eurocentric parameters.

do not have autobiographical or hagiographical reports of visions, locutions, raptures, or experiences of sublime unknowing. As a modern construct describing an individual with a radically altered state of consciousness, the category of "the mystic" may not be perfectly apt. On the other hand, we do know that they prayed both liturgically and privately and that they responded to others with a love that was so energetic and indiscriminate as to suggest an immanent divine source. Is it possible to love as they did, in the fearsome circumstances that they faced, without God's animating presence? Is it possible to give so completely of self without having the mind of Christ, without being another him? Theirs are the kinds of active lives that encourage what I might call a conjectural attribution of mystical grace.

To be clear, some conjecture is required even in cases of canonically recognized mystical texts, such as, for example, Teresa of Avila's *Interior Castle*—which is another volume that Delille's religious community had in their small collection.[39] It is always possible that a person who identifies a divine movement in their soul has been deceived. To affirm that true mysticism is at work, one must take the evidence available with a degree of faith or trust. This evidence need not be a book. It could be an embodied life. And, in fact, Teresa herself has more confidence in the true union with God revealed through neighbor love than in any dazzling ecstasies, which she thinks, in some instances, could be works of the imagination or the devil.[40] How these saintly seven acted shows us something about what they felt, thought, and desired. It opens a small window into their interior relationships with God.

Lessons for Today

What do these holy men and women have to say to a society and a church still marred by anti-Black racism? Do their practices

[39]Davis, *Servant of Slaves*, 105.

[40]Teresa of Avila, "The Sixth Dwelling Places," in *The Interior Castle*, study ed., trans. Kieran Kavanaugh, OCD and Otilio Rodriguez, OCD (ICS Publications, 2020) chap. 6, 268–75.

of sanctity make a specifically Catholic contribution to the struggle for Black liberation and interracial healing? No doubt, each of them suffered from a White supremacist social order. It is a sad but true fact of history that many American Catholic leaders were emotionally and economically aligned with this structure of sin. Although papal statements such as Pope Gregory XVI's 1839 *In Supremo Apostolatus* condemned the slave trade, the Vatican's track record on the issue was mixed at best, and, as chapter 2 noted, the U.S. bishops generally did not favor abolition. In fact, some bishops openly defended the institution of slavery using dubious biblical, moral, and philosophical arguments. It was common to reference the "curse of Ham," Pauline exhortations to "obey your masters," the separation of religious and secular authority, and the supreme heavenly reward that God held in store for dutiful slaves and benevolent masters alike.[41]

The American Catholic mistreatment of Black people, including Black Catholics, was not limited to supporting slavery. Some parishioners objected to Greeley sitting in a pew near the front of the church because she was Black. Tolton was blocked from becoming a priest for many years, and when he finally did, he was bullied so aggressively by a fellow priest in his diocese that he was forced to relocate to another city. Toussaint was turned away from the cathedral his fundraising helped to build. A slave-owning priest denied pastoral care to the Oblate Sisters of Providence, called them a failure, and hoped they would disband.[42] All seven of these holy men and women experienced injustices at interpersonal and structural levels. The choices they made to support the spiritual and material well-being of themselves and others defied such racism and revealed its absurdity. They were subjects, not objects, and this fact alone is revolutionary given their circumstances.

Yet in certain respects they did not fit the mold of freedom

---

[41] Davis and Phelps, *"Stamped with the Image of God,"* 35–43.

[42] Burkey, *In Secret Service*, 50; Hemesath, *From Slave to Priest*, 36, 123; Tarry, *Other Toussaint*, 171, 323; and Morrow, "Difficulty of Our Situation," 35.

fighters. Whatever their private viewpoints were, those who were adults during the time of slavery—namely, Toussaint, Lange, and Delille—did not speak out publicly against the institution. This reticence can be explained by the precarity of their situations and the high costs they would have paid for any open abolitionism, but it remains true that their modes of liberative action were often less confrontational than progressive commentators today might want.[43] In what may be the clearest case, Toussaint did not flee his master's plantation to join the guerilla army in the woods. The option to participate in a collective uprising against slavery was presented to him, and he refused it. I do not mean to critique this choice, which was understandable given the scale of the looming violence and his emotional ties to his master's family and his sister, Rosalie, who was being taken to New York. However, this choice raises complex questions about how best to interpret the social significance of his life.[44]

On their speaking tours, Tolton and Bowman challenged their audiences to recognize the God-given dignity of Black people. In one speech, Tolton described his experience meeting Catholics from "Africa, China, Japan, and other parts of the world" while studying in Rome. He argued, "The Church which knows and makes no distinction in race and color had called them all. When the Church does all of this, is she not a true liberator of the race?"[45] While affirming the goal of Black liberation, Tolton offered an idealized image of a racially inclusive universal church that did not match the contemporary ecclesial realities in his nineteenth-century U.S. context. Perhaps he was trying to speak a better and truer church into existence. Or perhaps he was simply unwilling to let such local distortions override his vision of the church's authentic nature as a diverse communion grounded in love.

---

[43]Davis, *Servant of Slaves*, 52.

[44]Deborah Sontag, "Canonizing a Slave: Saint or Uncle Tom?" *New York Times*, February 23, 1992. See also Malcolm X, "Message to the Grassroots," in *Malcolm X Speaks: Selected Speeches and Statements*, ed. George Breitman (Pathfinder, 1989), 8–22, at 14–19.

[45]Quoted in Tarry, *From Slave to Priest*, 126.

Among these seven potential saints, Bowman seems to have been the most vocal proponent of Black empowerment. Although she spoke often of the Black community's history of oppression and continuing experiences of discrimination, her message was mainly a positive one about the beauty of Black culture and spirituality. While addressing the U.S. bishops, she said,

> What does it mean to be black and Catholic? It means that I come to my church fully functioning. That doesn't frighten you, does it? I come to my church fully functioning. I bring myself, my black self, all that I am, all that I have, all that I hope to become, I bring my whole history, my traditions, my experience, my culture, my African-American song and dance and gesture and movement and teaching and preaching and healing and responsibility as gift to the church.[46]

By pressing for greater diversity and inclusion at all levels, Bowman contributed to a major cultural shift in postconciliar U.S. Catholicism. Yet her rhetoric stopped short of holding the church morally and financially accountable for owning and selling slaves and cooperating with segregationist regimes. Is a Black style of worship enough to bring about liberation and repair?

While Lange, Delille, Tolton, and Bowman labored primarily for the well-being of their Black communities, Toussaint and Greeley are noteworthy for the comparable service they rendered to vulnerable White people. Toussaint took in Black orphan boys from the streets of New York; housed, clothed, and fed them; and apprenticed them to himself or others so that they could learn a trade. At the same time, he raised funds for an orphanage for White children and brought them food and toys. When the city suffered periods of deadly disease, he risked his life ministering to the sick, regardless of their race. In what is perhaps his most scandalous activity, he used his earnings to finance his mistress's

---

[46]Thea Bowman, "Being a Black Catholic," in *Sister Thea Bowman, Shooting Star: Selected Writings and Speeches*, ed. Celestine Cepress, FSPA (Franciscan Sisters of Perpetual Adoration, 1999), 29–37, at 32.

household after his master died, caring for her as a dear friend.[47]

Greeley's works of love similarly knew no barriers of color. Many of the poor to whom she dispersed goods were White people; such were the demographics of Denver at the time. She rendered this service secretly to spare her beneficiaries any racial embarrassment. The one photograph we have of her shows her holding one of the White children whom she cared for as a maid. As an adult, this person—Marjorie Ann Urquhart Simpson—reflected back on her close bond with Greeley, saying, "When she would come to take care of me in the morning, my Mother [*sic*] said I would kiss her cheeks, eyes, ears, mouth and hug her to let her know how I loved her." Although Greeley wore simple clothes herself, usually a plain black dress and black hat, one of her acts of charity was to solicit donations of fine dresses from wealthier girls who did not need them, so that poorer girls would have something nice to wear to their school dances and social events.[48]

None of these morally courageous men and women would have dedicated their lives to the Catholic faith in the dramatic ways they did if not for the care and support they received from at least some White Catholics. Toussaint had the Berard family who spoke with him as a person and gave him educational opportunities. Lange had Fr. Joubert as a clerical backer of her religious congregation. Delille relied on Fr. Rousselon for a similar purpose. Tolton became a priest thanks to the encouragement and advocacy of Fr. McGirr. Greeley had Fr. Koch, who received her as a laywoman into the Franciscan order. Ward had Fr. Celestine, his encouraging vocations director. Bowman had her fellow Franciscan Sisters of Perpetual Adoration, including Sr. Dorothy Kundinger, affectionately called "Dort," who moved into the Bowman household to take care of Thea and her aging parents during Thea's battle with cancer.[49] This is not a complete list. All of these stories reveal the good fruits that come from interracial

[47]Tarry, *Other Toussaint*, 132, 175, 191, 205, 242.

[48]Burkey, *In Secret Service*, 11, 23, 28–29, 41.

[49]Tarry, *Other Toussaint*, 165; Davis, *History of Black Catholics*, 99; Davis, *Servant of Slaves*, 47–49; Hemesath, *From Slave to Priest*, 80; Burkey, *In Secret Service*, 31; "Cause Fr. Martin"; and Nutt, *Thea Bowman*, 85.

solidarity and even intimacy. These potential saints were not separatists, except for occasional reasons of practical necessity. They desired and embodied a true universalism, a life-affirming catholicity that regarded each person—whether dark or light, young or old, healthy or afflicted—as a precious child of God deserving of extravagant love. This borderless relationality is something to celebrate.

However, there is a danger that some will think the holiness they displayed favors a politics of reconciliation *as opposed* to liberation or that it has nothing to do with racial politics at all, since in certain respects it was colorblind.[50] There is a risk that, by extolling the virtues of these seven specifically chosen Black Catholics, the church will (even if inadvertently) insinuate that other Black persons, especially those with higher levels of righteous indignation, are spiritually or morally inferior, when this is far from the truth. Acknowledging a few "good" or "token" members of a marginalized group unfortunately often functions to stigmatize others and to delay more meaningful progress. If interpreted in the wrong ways, canonization could lead some Catholics to congratulate themselves prematurely on their racial inclusiveness and moral purity, even while refusing the hard work of further reparative action. This would be a shameful outcome. In the case of these saintly seven, therefore, distinguishing canonization from tokenism is crucially important.

What, then, is the right lesson to draw from their examples of holiness? In my view, the key is that they were *people of action*. They were moral subjects in their own histories. They were divinely empowered agents who did not settle for the lot that was given them but worked tirelessly to make a difference in the lives of the people they encountered. It would be rather absurd to look to them for guidance on how to quash social movements or how to feel satisfied with the status quo. These saints-in-the-making had a sacred desire for a better world and a better church. Put

[50]For an account of why seeking reconciliation without liberation is problematic, see James H. Cone, *God of the Oppressed* (Orbis Books, 1997), 207–26.

simply, their lives do not say, "Stop." They say, "Go." They say, be the transformative divine energy that all the suffering need. Be it in word and deed, song and truth, peace and resistance. Let no one stifle the Spirit within you. Do more. Go forth and be the healing and freedom that God's will demands.

Index